CREATING A VIRTUAL LIBRARY

A How-To-Do-It Manual for Librarians

Edited by
Frederick Stielow

HOW-TO-DO-IT MANUALS FOR LIBRARIANS

NUMBER 91

NEAL-SCHUMAN PUBLISHERS, INC.
New York, London

Additional Contributors

Thomas Bialek
Joshua Cohen
Linda Crow
Denise A. Garofalo
Susan Hauserman
Mary Keelan
Edward J. Rubeo
Marie Smith
Mohamed Toufali

Designed by Deborah Begley
with the assistance of Kate Merry and Peggy Winn

The editor is donating his royalties to the Foundation for Hudson Valley Libraries.

Published by Neal-Schuman Publishers, Inc.
100 Varick Street
New York, NY 10013

Printed and bound in the United States of America.

Library of Congress Cataloging-in-Publication Data

Creating a virtual library : a how-to-do-it manual /
edited by Frederick Stielow.
p. cm. — (How-to-do-it manuals for librarians : no. 91)
ISBN 1-55570-346-1
1. Library information networks. 2. Web sites—Design.
3. Libraries—Special collections—Web sites. 4. Digital libraries—Design. I. Stielow, Frederick, 1946– . II. Series : How-to-do-it manuals for libraries ; no. 91.
Z674.75.W67C73 1999
025'.00285'5276—dc21 98-54786
CIP

CONTENTS

LIST OF FIGURES

PREFACE

Although most libraries and archives have at least one staff member with an understanding of basic Web design and remote service concepts, most do not yet have a staff member who can work with intermediate and advanced Web concepts. Once these libraries decide to move beyond their "starter" Web sites, they must outsource the design and maintenance of their virtual library to experts in Web design and construction who usually do not understand the principles and perspectives of library service. The end result is often a very expensive virtual presence that doesn't meet user needs

PURPOSE

After building their own virtual library, the staff of the Mid-Hudson Library System (Poughkeepsie, New York) wrote *Creating a Virtual Library: A How-To-Do-It Manual* to enable other libraries and archives to take control of their own Web site expansion. This how-to manual provides clear instructions for mounting a relatively advanced virtual library within a short period of time, for low costs, and even with an initially under-trained staff.

The term virtual library simply means that all services are provided through the Internet, rather then in a building. Virtual libraries—like traditional libraries—vary greatly in size, appearance, and purpose.

AUDIENCE

Although *Creating a Virtual Library* will help anyone interested in providing information services using the Internet, Intranets, or Extranets, it is primarily aimed at library and archival managers. Examples are taken from the library and archival worlds not simply because everyone likes a book that speaks specifically to his or her needs, but because libraries can and should play a pivotal role in providing Internet services. Libraries and archives are in a unique position to offer nonthreatening, noncommercial sites that deliver effective services to *all* people.

SCOPE

Creating a Virtual Library assumes that readers have some familiarity with Web site development. In addition to covering the nuts-and-bolts of building a virtual library, the manual stresses the administration, content, and policymaking components required to develop virtual libraries. The authors discuss the four most common (and somewhat overlapping) formats or ingredients needed to build a virtual library:

- *Electronic resources connections* provide the switching needed to facilitate one-stop information retrieval. These "collectives" can link to the Web, online catalogs, as well as to digital resources or databases built or subscribed to by the library (e.g., CD-ROMs, electronic pathfinders, digitized collections, and services like those provided by UMI, EBSCO, SIRS, etc.).
- *General Web libraries* organize selected Web sites so that library users find information retrieval more manageable (and useful) than that available from search engines. The manual uses these ambitious undertakings primarily to demonstrate technical skills or generalizeable models.
- *Special resource collections* are electronic versions of what librarians have long called "special collections." They include links to related topical sites on the Web and may feature value-added resources from the library.
- *Digital archives* hold collections of materials that have been rekeyed or scanned for inclusion in the virtual library.

STRUCTURE

Creating a Virtual Library is designed so as to describe a technical concept or service principle and then illustrate its application. Thus, most chapters begin with a general discussion, then offer broadly applicable guidelines or technical suggestions, and end with capsule descriptions of the Mid-Hudson Library System's experiences involving this aspect of its virtual library development.

The main text is divided into nine chapters that parallel the steps involved in creating a virtual library.

Chapter 1, "Designing Virtual Libraries for Human Beings," provides mission-driven guidelines for conceiving, planning, and designing virtual libraries and helpful hints that are drawn both from experience and from studies of human-computer interfaces.

Chapter 2, "Managing Virtual Library Projects," discusses project management and presents a matrix for planning virtual library projects.

Chapter 3, "Developing Policies for the Virtual Library," addresses the policies needed for creating, maintaining, and supporting patron use of the virtual library.

Chapter 4, "Visualizing the Virtual Library," uses the physical library and its staff organization as a top-down organizational model for a virtual library.

Chapter 5, "Building Virtual Library Suites," helps readers begin the actual process of creating the first "rooms" in their virtual libraries.

Chapter 6, "Selecting Virtual Resources," provides a process and tips for managing in-house electronic resources.

Chapter 7, "Mounting the Virtual Library on the Web," illustrates how to build virtual libraries using currently available, inexpensive Web-editor software.

Chapter 8, "Maintaining the Virtual Library," provides the nitty-gritty technical details for site management, ranging from checking links to blocking hackers.

Chapter 9, "Enhancing the Virtual Library," explores the developing Web standards and options for building an even better, more technically exciting site.

Building a virtual library requires more than computers, skills, and a familiarity with library service principles; it also requires flexibility, humor, and a sense of comfort with the ambiguity of cyberspace. The manual presents both the principles and one library's experience with the process of conceiving, building, and maintaining its own virtual library. Applying these principles with a sense of adventure as well as a mastery of the technology can not only be more professionally rewarding but should result in a more usable product.

INTRODUCTION: LESSONS FROM THE PAST

Fred Stielow

> *There were . . . doors . . . a third, which led to a new room, no different from the others except for the scroll which said "Obscuratus est sol et aer," announcing the growing darkness of sun and air. From here you went into a new room, whose scroll said, "Facta est grando et ignis," threatening turmoil and fire. . . . I cannot explain clearly what happened, but as we left the tower room, the order of the rooms became more confused. . . . We tried to orient ourselves by the scrolls . . . , [but] sometimes the scrolls repeated the same words in different rooms. . . . It was not at all clear why they were painted on the walls or what logic was behind their arrangement.*
>
> —Umberto Eco, *The Name of the Rose*

Many regard the Web with the same awe that 13th-century visitors to Umberto Eco's mystical library labyrinth felt. One enters a virtual lair—a twisted and disorienting landscape of constantly changing and overlapping strands—without a map. One faces new magical languages (such as HTML and Java) and lesser realms of jargon and acronyms without a translator in sight. Graphical gargoyles and annoying commercials pop up unannounced with secret passwords and hidden traps or dead ends. Important sites appear, only to be lost from view. Even the most straightforward query leads to a maze with thousands of "hits" from innumerable locations—but with no assurance of a proper answer.

Such problems and frustrations are basic to the communications revolution enveloping the world. Over the past 50 years, computers and related electronic media have filtered down from military, industrial, and academic realms into the day-to-day lives of ordinary people. Beginning with ENIAC (the first computer) in World War II and Univac's prediction of the 1952 presidential election results, the movement has been unstoppable. The microchip of the 1970s speeded up developments and set the stage for the rise of personal computers in the 1980s.

In the 1990s the Internet was suddenly plucked from quiet academic backwaters. E-mail surfaced as a threat to the postal service, which dates back to Benjamin Franklin, and to Alexander Graham Bell's newfangled telephones from the last century. Where the word "web" once conjured up spiders or a children's story, a different meaning emerged with unprecedented speed. A proper noun almost unknown in 1993 is capitalized by 1996. The word is now international shorthand for a seemingly omnipresent World Wide Web (WWW, or W3). This Web may prove the single most powerful agent for change in the modern era.

COMPARISONS TO THE PRINT REVOLUTION

Just like the Web has in the mid-1990s, 500 years ago an innovation turned the world upside down—providing useful grist for the modern manager's mill. Following the downfall of Rome, Western civilization retreated into a desert of illiteracy. The landscape was broken by occasional monkish oases, which housed the knowledge of the ancients. These institutions gained their fame and purpose by copying and preserving handwritten codices. In 1455, however, the invention of a goldsmith from Mainz appeared on the scene. By the turn of the next century, Gutenberg's printing press had eliminated the scribal librarians' long monopoly over the provision of reading matter. Secular printers supplanted Catholic monks in the dissemination of knowledge. Publishers, who were arguably the world's first industrialists and the fathers of capitalism, emerged as the defining profession for a true information revolution.

As Elizabeth Eisenstein describes in *The Printing Press as an Agent of Change,* the effects cascaded down throughout society, and often in unpredictable ways. Poetry separated from music. Christendom was fractured by the Protestant Reformation. Capitalism appeared, an age of discovery dawned, and human thought processes were altered by the scientific method. At a more prosaic level, published literature came to be more respected than handwritten or oral transmissions. Libraries separated from their local archival and copying functions to concentrate on national and internationally produced works.

Print itself expanded to an unimaginable extent. Over the centuries, the press spewed out an almost inconceivable array of atlases, broadsides, dictionaries, encyclopedias, hornbooks, novels, and sheet music. People were exposed to newspapers, magazines, pulp fiction, textbooks, vernacular bibles, and eventually computer manuals. In the process, humanity gained such now ubiquitous elements as checks, paper money, and greeting and business cards. These innovations are now commonplace objects, which we easily take for granted.

Equally important for our considerations is the fact that each of the new resources demanded different reading skills and conventions. To begin to project the implications for our era, ponder the skills required in Gutenberg's time compared to your own skills in reading from a computer view of his Bible [www.osl.state.or.us/csimages/bible/page4bw.GIF].

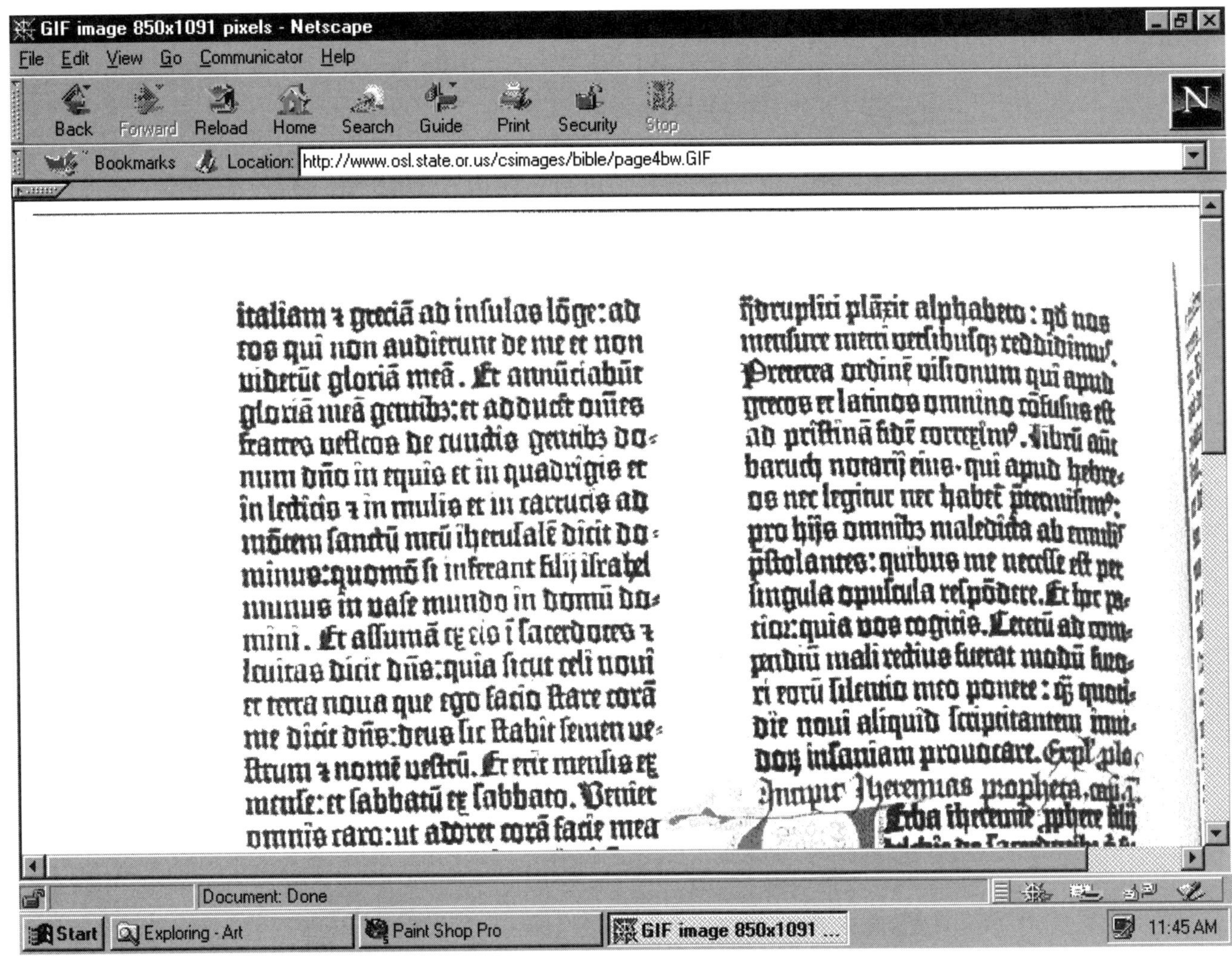

italiam ꝛ greciā ad insulas lōge: ad
eos qui non audierunt de me et non
viderūt gloriā meā. Et annūciabūt
gloriā meā gentibꝫ: et adducēt oēs
fratres vestros de cunctis gentibꝫ do-
num dn̄o in equis et in quadrigis et
in lecticis ꝛ in mulis et in carrucis ad
mōtem sanctū meū iherusalē dicit do-
minus: quomō si inferant filii israhel
munus in vase mundo in domū do-
mini. Et assumā ex eis i sacerdotes ꝛ
leuitas dicit dn̄s: quia sicut celi noui
et terra noua que ego facio stare corā
me dicit dn̄s: sic stabit semen ve-
strum ꝛ nomē vestrū. Et erit mensis ex
mense: et sabbatū ex sabbato. Veniet
omnis caro: ut adoret corā facie mea

sidrupliū plāxit alphabeto: qđ nos
mensure metri versibusqꝫ reddidimus.
Preterea ordinē visionum qui apud
grecos et latinos omnino confusus est
ad pristinā fidē correximus. Librū aūt
baruch notarii eius qui apud hebre-
os nec legitur nec habet pretermisimus:
pro hiis omnibꝫ maledicta ab emulis
pstolantes: quibus me necesse est per
singula opuscula respōdere. Et hec pa-
tior: quia nos cogitis. Ceterū ad com-
pendiū mali redius fuerat modū fue-
ri eorū silentio meo ponere: qđ quoti-
die noui aliquid scriptitantem inui-
dorū insaniam prouocare. Explicit plo
Incipit Jheremias propheta. ca. i.
Verba iheremie filii

Figure I-1: ***Gutenberg Bible, Sample Page, Oregon State Library***

RISE OF MASS LITERATURE AND MODERN LIBRARY APPROACHES

Printed formats first reached their zenith in the 19th century, as part of another peaceful revolution—the rise of the masses. The advent of cheap wood-pulp paper and advances like the Linotype and photographic engraving produced a quantum leap in production and enhanced graphical content. Such innovations alone could not account for the first mass culture. It demanded legions of newly educated from the burgeoning public school movement of the period. With such a union, the volume of reading materials exploded. For the first time in history, the ability to read became the norm. Illiteracy would no longer be tolerated in the West.

The eruption of print also brought perceived threats to the moral order, which rivaled the Catholic Church's fears of the original press and the edicts of Martin Luther. Interestingly, sex, rather than subversion or religion, now emerged as the major object of concern. Much to the chagrin of some arbiters of good taste, casual reading expanded. "Popular" genres rapidly emerged to capture a growing new market. Illustrated magazines, dime novels, consumer catalogs, and above all the modern newspaper with its comic strips and gossip columns began their rise to prominence. Their appearance was critical for the dissemination and creation of the shared climate of opinion, fads, and tastes that define a mass culture. The new output also brought different reading styles and conventions (reading murder mysteries takes different skills from reading a classic), along with the development of sophisticated propaganda techniques, the advent of the essentially new field of journalism, the birth of professional advertising—and professional librarianship.

Librarians would help calm the perceived perils. These specialists developed their own mildly revolutionary techniques. Dedicated reading spaces appeared along with spaces set aside for reference, serials, reserves, and the like. Librarians even solved part of the literary danger problem by creating children's rooms to serve as protective zones. Most important, the field brought order to the tidal wave of new literature with the use of classification systems. At the turn of the century, the Dewey Decimal and soon the new Library of Congress schema were beginning to provide an unprecedented ability to control the equally unprecedented expansion of knowledge. With newly designed and scientifically ordered stacks, the public and scholars alike gained the power of browsing. One could all but absorb recorded knowledge by simply walking down the aisles, or, after the turn of the century, by thumbing through the latest in descriptive innovations—the card catalog.

CYBER-INCUNABULUM

There is much to be learned from these history lessons and the role of our institutions in the past. Since Mosaic and especially since the arrival of its big browser brother Netscape in 1994, the Web has wreaked changes that may equal the print revolution and rise of popular literature in scope. The comforting knowledge and retrieval structures brought forth in the last century are certainly being challenged by the even greater explosion of resources. Distinctions between libraries and archives are vanishing. With the Web, those fields are even regaining some of the publishing power lost in the Renaissance and entering a new cycle of institutional reinvention. At a broader level, the previous permanence of "it is written in stone or in the book" gives way to the mutability of word processing. The lines between authors and technology are again blurring, while sound and moving images intrude on previously fixed printed texts. Even the academic standby of footnoting is bedeviled by constantly changing home pages.

The rush to the new does not deny continuity with the past—or the lessons from print. Ironically, the Web rests on a Hypertext Markup Language (HTML) standard, which is but a subset of the Structured Generalized Markup Language (SGML) designed to automate the print outputs from publishers. Just as new typefaces were sculpted for better legibility of print, Verdana and other fonts are appearing to ease reading on computer screens—browsing and navigating among the vast accumulations of information remain major concerns. We can even begin to personalize some of the current changes. Thus, Tim Berners-Lee of MIT serves as father of the Web and a potential heir to Gutenberg. Marc Andreessen of Mosaic and Netscape fame can compare to Aldus Manutius—Erasmus's collaborator and the creator of portable reading with the "Aldine" pocketbook editions. Bill Gates of Microsoft may hark back to Peter Shoeffer and Herr Furst, who knew how to turn the profit from the bankrupt Gutenberg's invention.

Shoeffer was Gutenberg's son-in-law and Furst was the publisher/entrepreneur who underwrote the press.

Still, the rapidity of current change gives pause and contributes to an added sense of urgency. The speed of developments will far outstrip that of the incunabulum—the first fifty years of printing. We cannot even pretend to divine what will happen. At the moment, too few people are trained in the reading, let alone the writing of hypermedia. Most cannot intuitively use the Web in the way that they do a table of contents, a magazine, comic book, or training manual. As artificial intelligence studies demonstrate, the mental processes for Web use are complex and learned behavior. Reading for print is constantly reinforced over a long period of time—from initial schooling to nighttime novel reading and scanning a newspaper on the train. But equivalents are not fully in place for the new medium. People will need time to alter print-bound habits; new generations will need to absorb these changes as their birthright. We are very likely immersed in an inescapable "Cyber-Incunabulum"—a period of at least a full generation in which conventions are inculcated and the new formats, like virtual libraries, are put on trial.

This revolution will likely prove as interesting and unpredictable as its print predecessor:

- Will interactive MUD (multiuser domains) rooms, chat or palace rooms, push technologies, Webcasts, or even virtual libraries pass the test of time?
- What will be the fate of the novel, magazine, or other print forms?
- Will written poetry and music come together again, perhaps with the addition of multimedia as a new art form?
- Do we currently have the graphical genius equivalent of typographers Bodoni, Baskerville, and Garamond?
- When will adequate new citation controls emerge to match Pierre Bayle's late 17th-century creation of the footnote?
- What genres may evolve to equate to Henry Fielding's novels, Diderot's encyclopedia, Franklin's almanac, Ben Johnson's dictionary, the Sears catalog, Pulitzer and Hearst's modern newspapers, or even Stan Lee's comic books?

ISLANDS IN THE STORM: LIBRARIES AS COMFORT ZONES

Libraries are stepping forward to take their place within the newest communication revolution. The Public Library Server page [sjcpl.lib.in.us/homepage/PublicLibraries/PublicLibraryServers.html] and Libweb [www.lib.washington.edu/^tdowling/libweb.html] amply demonstrate a pioneering role. The question is the future nature of that role. In a September 22, 1997, *Time* article, for example, AOL President Steven Case's redesigned services are described with a familiar analogy:

> In Case's marketing terms, simplicity is what puts the fingers on the mice. A new generation of the AOL software . . . has been relentlessly tested by potential users—self-confessed computer idiots all. . . . Who, after all, has time to pore over 10,000 pages in search of just the right nuggets of data? So AOL's new interface offers a

> nearly seamless link between the Web and AOL. Everything is as neatly organized as a small-town library.

The irony of the model and situation should not be lost. The library and archival challenge is fairly straightforward. Our institutions are the logical candidates to bring stability and to ensure intellectual freedom and "commercial-free" coordination to the Web. Regardless of their size, these comfort zones—our libraries—must not hide from their professional duty or avoid these opportunities. History may even repeat itself. Just like the scriptorium of old with its specialized holdings, today's libraries and archives will increasingly find that their Web strengths lie in their specialized and local holdings.

1 DESIGNING VIRTUAL LIBRARIES FOR HUMAN BEINGS

Fred Stielow and Edward J. Rubeo

How many times do you encounter a Web logo that is aesthetic and welcoming but that takes an inordinate amount of time to load? How often do you encounter a window with no exits, or one that leads to dead links—to nowhere? How frequently do you have to scroll through screens of materials before encountering the key links or information that you are looking for? Do you confront type sizes too small for normal readers, or screens too cluttered to decipher readily? Why does it feel so awkward and time-consuming to navigate through some of the most attractive sites? Why do you see printed examples of Web designs laid out to fit normal sheets of paper, rather than the size of a typical Web browser screen? Why are so few sites built with an awareness of international communications standards or indications of metatagging and related structures for enhanced retrieval?

Given the current revolutionary and evolutionary state of affairs, such frustrating scenarios will likely occur for some time. Unlike print media, the Web is too new. Instead of rushing to develop a technically dazzling site, this manual encourages you to step back for a commonsense look at Web design from a managerial perspective.

WEB DESIGN DILEMMA

With a complex mix of never-before-available graphical and interactive features, the Web all but screams for stylistic sophistication. Designers face the artistic trial of the ages: bringing order to this revolutionary idiom. Although Web style manuals and experts pop up with uncommon regularity, even a cursory analysis reveals that form does not necessarily follow function—current or future. Many and perhaps most sites are rooted in the printed page, or to a lesser degree slowed by technical tricks, which are less than satisfying to hurried users. Few sites address the combination of physical and psychological traits of people who are seeking information. Direct obser-

Scroll Note: One should expect the eventual emergence of conventions for graphical structures, colors, and even sound marks to assist in scrolling (i.e., something to parallel the tag lines used at the top of phone book pages). Until then, scrolling will remain inefficient—never approaching the power of skimming through a book.

vation suggests that we are only scratching the surface of this new click-and-scroll medium.

However, some fairly effective models are making their entrance and taking hold as styles. You may also note that many of the most technologically loaded sites have retreated from their initial dazzle to more modest options. The inescapable dilemma, however, is timing. It simply may be too early for clear conventions or definitive design standards. Since no one can have all the answers at this moment, logic calls for an "emperor's new clothes" warning: When dealing with Web design, rely on common sense and critical analysis. Instead of dazzle, start from the institutional mission and keep things simple enough to understand. We hasten to add the need for a good sense of humor—along with flexibility and the understanding that there are no final answers. This is a pioneering and exploratory era.

INITIAL DESIGN GUIDELINES

Despite the daunting challenges of what we called a Cyber-Incunabulum in the introduction, the task of creating a virtual library is feasible. No technological blocks stand in the way—only organizational and design questions. You can step forward without great electronic sophistication and produce a first-rate virtual library. Even the smallest public or school library can participate and make a difference. Given the dearth of effective guidelines and the likelihood of limited staff or resources, you may need a guinea pig, however. The following guidelines present the thinking behind one set of experiences and some related findings from HCI (human-computer interface) studies.

WEB PROJECT DESIGN GUIDELINES

A. Management

- KISS (Keep It Short and Simple)—simplicity is the overriding rule. Solutions should be flexible and rooted in common sense. If you don't understand what you want, how can you manage or contribute to the project?
- Avoid "reinventing the wheel." Look to build upon the work of others and rely on tried-and-true mechanisms.
- Beware of proprietary applications. Rely instead on standards (e.g., this manual relies on HTTP 1.1, as well as HTML 3.2 and 4.0 protocols).
- Let your information or output be driven by the context and

needs of the institution—not by technology or what you can find on the Web.

- Integrate Web projects into the general work flow (e.g., if a newsletter is started in a word processor, consider it an electronic document that is ripe for systematic HTML dumps into an appropriate spot on your site.
- Remember this process will not be perfect; it is a process for ongoing education and improvement.

B. Physical Design

- Research other Web sites for appealing looks, feel, and functionality (e.g., see how Amazon.com works to satisfy its customers and really makes it hard for users to leave without buying something).
- Notice that Web-site design is a hierarchical or top-down discipline, leading from the overall motif, or entrance, through multiple levels to specific content.
- Be sure that your site immediately identifies and promotes your library or archives.
- Build from book conventions and think about how icons or graphics may help users identify the site and navigate.
- Avoid the temptation to design for an 8½-by-11-inch sheet of paper—this view does not exist in the virtual world.
- Design with an eye to the size and orientation of the typical Web browser. Depending on the number of tool bars or features engaged, this is an enlarged postcard view that ranges from 8 inches by 4 inches to 8 inches by 6 inches.
- Don't clutter the screen—a clean, crisp, graphical layout is your goal. (Note: you may have pull-down menus or other interactive features to satisfy the need to pack in information links.)

C. Navigation

- Design for immediate and ongoing activity with internal and external links—direct navigation through the point-and-click mouse interface is the distinguishing characteristic of the Web.
- Try to have the operative portions of your site no more than three levels or clicks away from the entry points.
- Avoid navigation that relies too heavily on scrolling or cursoring through ever-unfolding screens. Serial access is useful, but currently underdeveloped and with its own physical limitations.
- Consider multiple traffic patterns and understand that your viewers gain unprecedented navigational powers that take them easily beyond your controls.

- Strive for transparent or intuitive interfaces, but keep in mind that users will still need help to use your site.
- Be consistent and try to use the same navigational techniques throughout your site.
- As you become more technically advanced, become aware of HTML titles and metatags that can be used to enhance searchability.

D. Use

- Always design with human (versus computer) information seeking and language foremost in mind, but remember to provide help and training.
- Consider your intended primary (and perhaps secondary) audience—rather than a general visitor.
- Design not only for one-time users, but for repeat patrons—include structures to teach how to maximize use.
- Present crisp text with clear visual signals (like bullets and indents)—Web denizens tend to scan more than read. (See the hypertext hints on page 14 for additional information.)
- Avoid long lists of choices in favor of language hierarchies with limited options (Bear in mind the Miller number of seven, plus or minus two.)
- Be consistent in your design, and pick one side of the screen for navigational buttons. It is not clear yet, however, which side is preferable. Most people are right-handed and mouses are generally hung along the right side. Yet, left-side navigation seems to be winning out—our reading conventions are from left to right and the right side of the screen already holds the scroll bar.
- Make sure the type is large enough to be readable and that it does not blend into any background color or pattern.

The Miller Number is the result of a series of psychological tests that revealed that humans dealt with information clustered in groups of no more than seven, plus or minus two.

E. Maintenance

- Remember that, because of the short half-life of the typical Web site, the inclusion of external links demands ongoing monitoring and updating.
- Web sites can hold fixed information blocks, similar to a printed book, that are designed for only occasional updating. Take the time to make certain that these areas are especially well written and grammatically correct.
- Sites also can have very current data—some demanding daily updates. Be aware of staffing and user implications when committing to such areas, and frame your design to facilitate repeated entry. (Refer to the discussion of dynamic HTML options in Chapter 9.)

F. Automation

- Given staffing demands and the capital investments required in a rapidly changing environment, think about outsourcing as many of the technological services as possible—work with your Internet service provider (ISP).
- Do not design for the "cutting-edge" of technology. You will take too much time learning and likely lose many users who have less-sophisticated browsers.
- Tackle the easiest elements first. The difficult problems may be solved along the way.
- Consider enabling text-only "links," or "non-frames" and other simplified alternatives to ensure the widest audience.
- Don't be discouraged when technological factors, such as loading speed, browser types, and color pallets, force compromises with design ideals.
- Start now, but don't try for too much at once. When staging project development, keep in mind your physical resources and the likelihood of growing staff expertise and better software tools.

WRITING IN HYPERTEXT AND PRINT COMPARISONS

The primary model in this manual is a navigation or traffic control center. The bulk of design discussion thus concentrates on graphical interfaces. Still, virtual libraries do contain written material, and you can expect an increasing demand for internally developed content. But writing for the Web calls for different skills and concerns from those for dealing with print. On one hand, readers lose much of the comfort that comes from immersion in a single text. The joys of nighttime reading with a truly portable random-access medium, like the book, and soothing reflected light give way to a harsher technology. Users face bedtime bruising with a laptop, and eyestrain from taxing background light sources. The spatial clues and span of vision that allow one to scan two pages of text at a glance vanish before the limits of 24 lines of computer type—or an 18-line Internet browser. Though dating to early Christianity, the book still remains an exceptional technological advance capable of holding its own even on the Starship Enterprise.

Hypertext allows for major stylistic advances well beyond the limits of ink on paper. You can link automatically to references and text elsewhere. **Hypermedia** enables the introduction of images, sound, and video.

On the other hand, we are not engaged in an either-or debate. The new media have their own place and peculiar advantages—especially for referencing and quick searches. Hypertext is not frozen, as ink on paper. Instead of footnoting and defining words directly on the page or at the end of the document, hypertext has interactive links to glossaries or other documents for use only when needed. Readers can bring up descriptive images, sound, and moving visuals that are impossible in a bound volume. Indeed, readers can literally reformulate what is on the screen into their own unique books, or travel around the world to resolve reference questions in the blink of an eye. Such unprecedented reader empowerment suggests a need for the following hints for writing in hypertext.

TEN HYPERTEXT WRITING HINTS

These hints are far from exhaustive, but they should start to prepare you for a daunting task—establishing understandable conventions for your library or archival site. The manager should also strongly consider consulting someone with artistic skills (see Chapter 2). Aesthetics and good management are not necessarily linked. If you provide the reading and library conventions, a designer can help blend the classic "rules" of composition with considerations such as the following.

1. Include visual components (e.g., bullets, indentations, and outlining formats) to assist scanning.
2. Use short paragraphs (generally not exceeding one browser screen, or roughly 18 lines in length).
3. Consider a fairly terse style (perhaps 50 percent of the verbiage that you would put forth in a printed commentary).
4. Aim for an interactive text, with embedded connections to related materials or explanations.
5. Empower readers so they can move freely about the site and create their own reading patterns.
6. Never exceed two screens without including a hyperlink. Be certain at least to have links from major elements to the top of the document or the "home" area.
7. People are used to reading in "longitudinal" rectangles (e.g. most books are taller than they are wide), as opposed to the "horizontal" space of the browser.
8. The eye tends to travel from the foreground to the background and moves from light to dark areas.
9. In most Western cultures, readers gravitate from the left to the right and from the upper left corner of the page to the lower right.
10. It is wise to consider the painter's "rule of thirds"—the tactic of dividing a canvas for horizontal or vertical balance in one-third and two thirds of the total space—it will enhance your sense of graphical proportion.

Catalog Cards as Hypertext: The 20th-century innovation of catalog cards uniquely foreshadows hypermedia. Such elements as tracings (the supplemental subject and name reference seen on the bottom of cards) and syndetic references (See; See also) are natively interactive. Tracings and references send the user to other cards; a simple click in hypertext retrieves the references for the user.

Knowing natural preferences, the designer can somewhat control where the user's eye will initially fall, making intelligent decisions about how to lead the eye among choices and even deal with the computer screen's horizontal layout. Some direct applications should be apparent below, but basic cautions remain. Planners face a number of questions presently as unsolvable as koans. These questions call for common sense, alternatives, and predictable improvements, yet remain open to debate. Over time any checklist or evaluation tools will need to be reviewed or replaced—eventually to fade away as more conventions, consensus, and true experts emerge.

HOME PAGE ANALYSIS AND DESIGN

With such pointers in hand, let us turn to a critical application. The home page is the entrance into your site. The home page for a library or an archives may double as its virtual library or merely provide a link to that facility. Whatever the case, your home page should establish the navigational and design trends for the rest of the site. Design should start from two principles. First, you cannot escape established reading conventions and must consider the trappings traditionally used to help readers navigate a book or magazine. Second, the Web is not print—it is a different medium and design should be based on its interactive nature.

Now, consider a very specific visual question: what will people see when they open a site? The answer is a postcard image and a basic screen of roughly 8 inches by 5 inches—half the size of a sheet of regular paper. What does this basic screen do? Based on a very informal survey by the MHLS staff, we can project that most home pages combine three functions:

- **Identification:** Like a magazine cover and a title page, an opening line or a graphic image identifies the location and may publicize its owner and services.
- **Narrative Introduction:** Many sites include a written description that works something like a book preface. The text tends to introduce the institution, its practices, and the purpose of the site. Information about the designer is often included. The material frequently has embedded links and may open to blocks of bulleted lists.
- **Navigation:** In addition to embedded or bulleted features in the narrative, the screen can have a distinct set of navigational buttons, that is, links to other pages on the site. This region is analogous to an interactive table of contents.

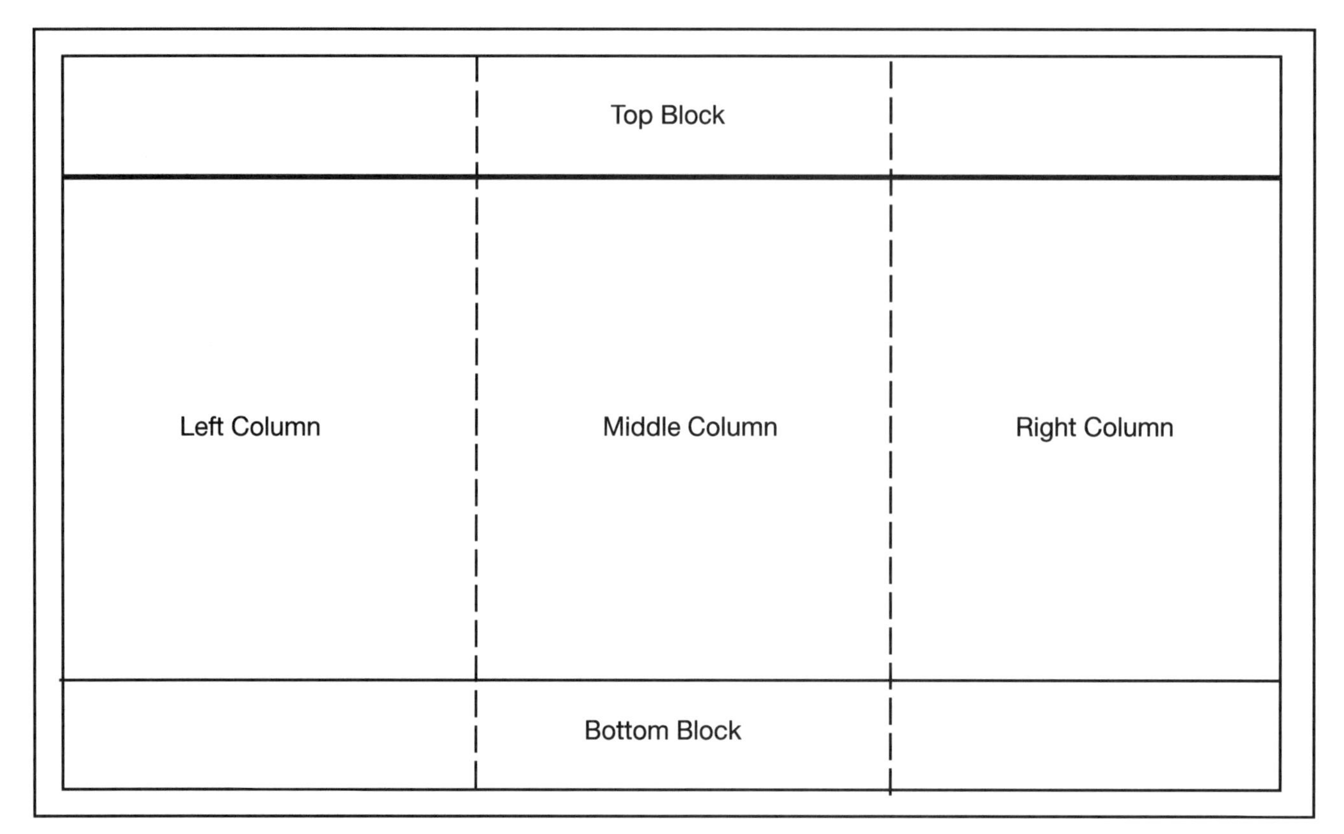

Figure 1–1: Layout for Home Page Grid

The informal survey also brought out other trends. With some probing, we found that designers—even professional designers—tend to rely on a limited set of styles. We were able to break these models down into grids. Over 90 percent of the sample could be reduced to a few simple geometric patterns that can be viewed as a series of blocks and columns as shown in Figure 1–1.

Instead of a middle column, the home page may use a split-screen model with an enlarged left or right column. Columns themselves can be subdivided into tables or cells.

The analysis also disclosed some obvious problems and ongoing developments. Many of the earliest sites can be reduced to two blocks stacked on top of each other. Typically, a centered or left-justified logo or title at the top acts as the identifier and the major design feature. The identifier can get so large that it takes over the entire opening screen. Even when sufficient space is allowed for a lower block with narrative information, the reader generally must scroll down to links. Navigation concerns were obviously given short shrift and any initial

SAMPLE SITE

LOGO

This Sample Site Digital Startup (SSDS) is a project of the Non Such School of Advanced Heuristics. The Non Such School does not exist, but if it did it would have an outstanding faculty and be in a lovely setting. This site was designed on a cold and dreary morning by an advanced team of Mary Smith, e-mail smith@nonsuch.org, Harry Spencer, e-mail spencer@nonsuch.org, and Miles Hacker, e-mail anonymous@nonsuch.org. The team graciously acknowledges the leadership of Computer Science Chair Miriam Zoner, e-mail zoner@nonsuch.org and School President Ivory Tower.

* Computer Center Resources
* Non Such Memorial Library OPAC
* Web Search Engines
* Zoner Engineering School Tetrahydrate Project

Figure 1–2: Simple Stacked Model

screen design discipline was absent. Still, this model, shown in Figure 1–2, produces the first and easiest method for a home page or virtual library.

Subsequent designs put more of a premium on navigation. One approach has been to place a string of navigation buttons below the identifier. Since a large identifier or greeting can easily push such buttons off the visible page, an even better design alternative has arisen that places buttons across the top block, as seen in Figure 1–3.

administration computer center library catalog web search engines

SAMPLE SITE

LOGO

This Sample Site Digital Startup (SSDS) is a project of the Non Such School of Advanced Heuristics. The Non Such School does not exist, but if it did it would have an outstanding faculty and be in a lovely setting. This site was designed on a cold and dreary morning by an advanced team of Mary Smith, e-mail smith@nonsuch.org, Harry Spencer, e-mail spencer@nonsuch.org, and Miles Hacker, e-mail anonymous@nonsuch.org. The team graciously acknowledges the leadership of Computer Science Chair Miriam Zoner, e-mail zoner@nonsuch.org and School President Ivory Tower.

_ Computer Center Resources
_ Non Such Memorial Library OPAC
_ Web Search Engines
_ Zoner Engineering School Tetrahydrate Project

Figure 1–3: Top Block with Navigation Buttons

The number of possible variations even within our reduced geometric set is substantial. You may see several columns, or columns divided into a grid or table. Some designs combine several approaches—for example, top and bottom buttons, or a split screen with the addition of top navigational buttons. We also noted a trend toward a simple two-column, split-screen model. Here, identifiers appear in the top block or head of either column. Typically, the left-hand column is narrower and holds a bank of navigational buttons. The middle and right become a single right-hand column. That enlarged block can hold the narrative and include its own set of hyperlinks. This simple motif is increasingly used by some of the most technologically advanced institutions—such as Sun Microsystems [www.Sun.COM/styleguide/] as shown in Figure 1–4.

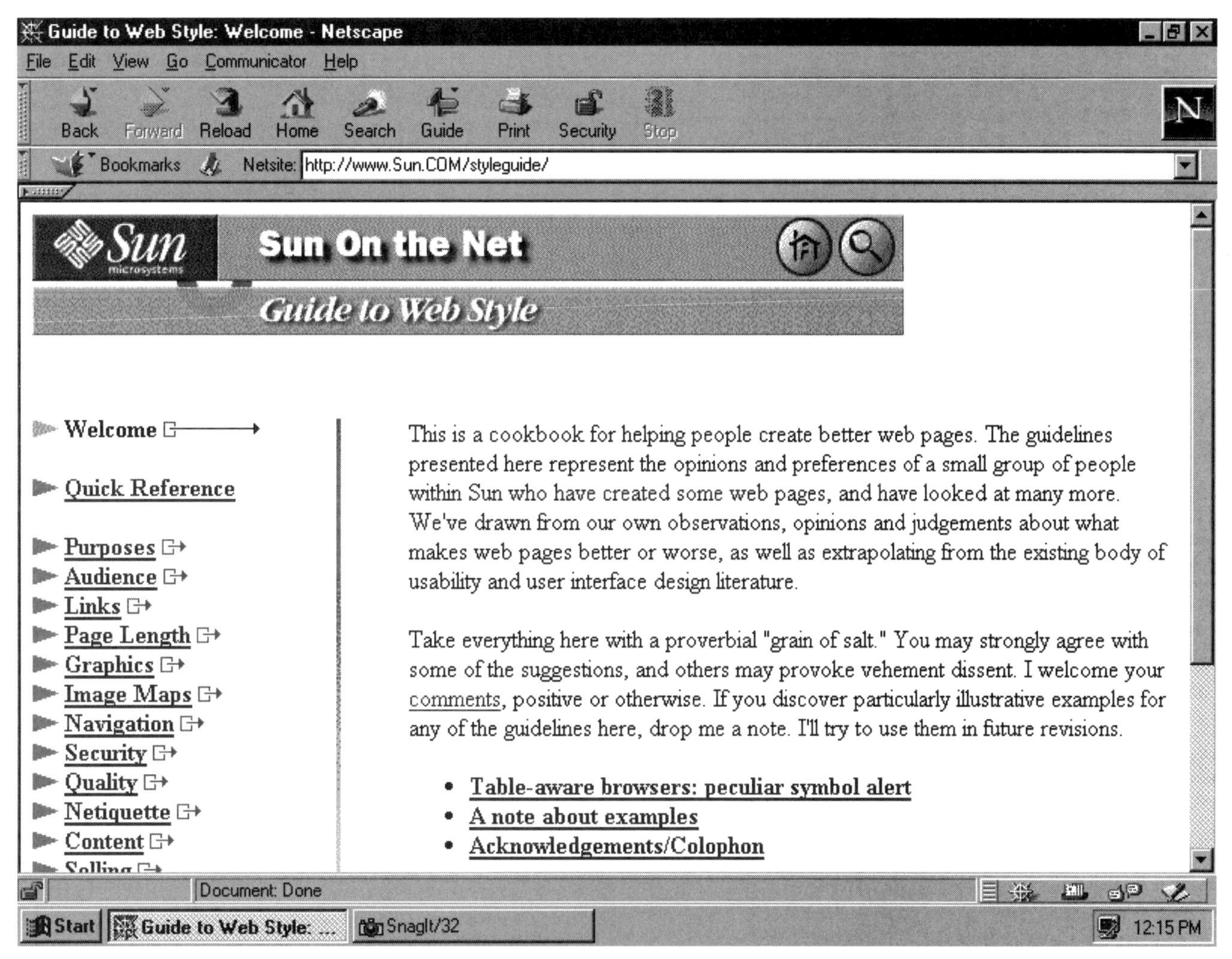

Figure 1–4: Top Identifier and Split-Screen Model

END NOTES FROM MID-HUDSON

With this analysis in mind, Mid-Hudson turned to its home page design. The staff had never built a Web page, so we knew things had to be kept simple. We also wanted to ensure a dignified image with a quick and clear identification for anyone "surfing" into the site, and we were determined to make it easy for such users to navigate to their area of need.

MHLS primarily dispenses a variety of services to member libraries. The nature of that largely repeat audience of professional librarians precluded the need for a prominent opening narrative and also informed the rest of the site development.

Our initial design proved similar to the front cover of an academic journal. The opening image was a split-screen model. The left side held the title or identifier with address information and an established logo. The right column disclosed the table of contents—an interactive navigation table with buttons to our site's seven major categories. With this division, repeat visitors could immediately address their information needs—often without waiting for the logo to load. A brief introductory narrative was then relegated to a text block below, available by scrolling down or using a navigation button.

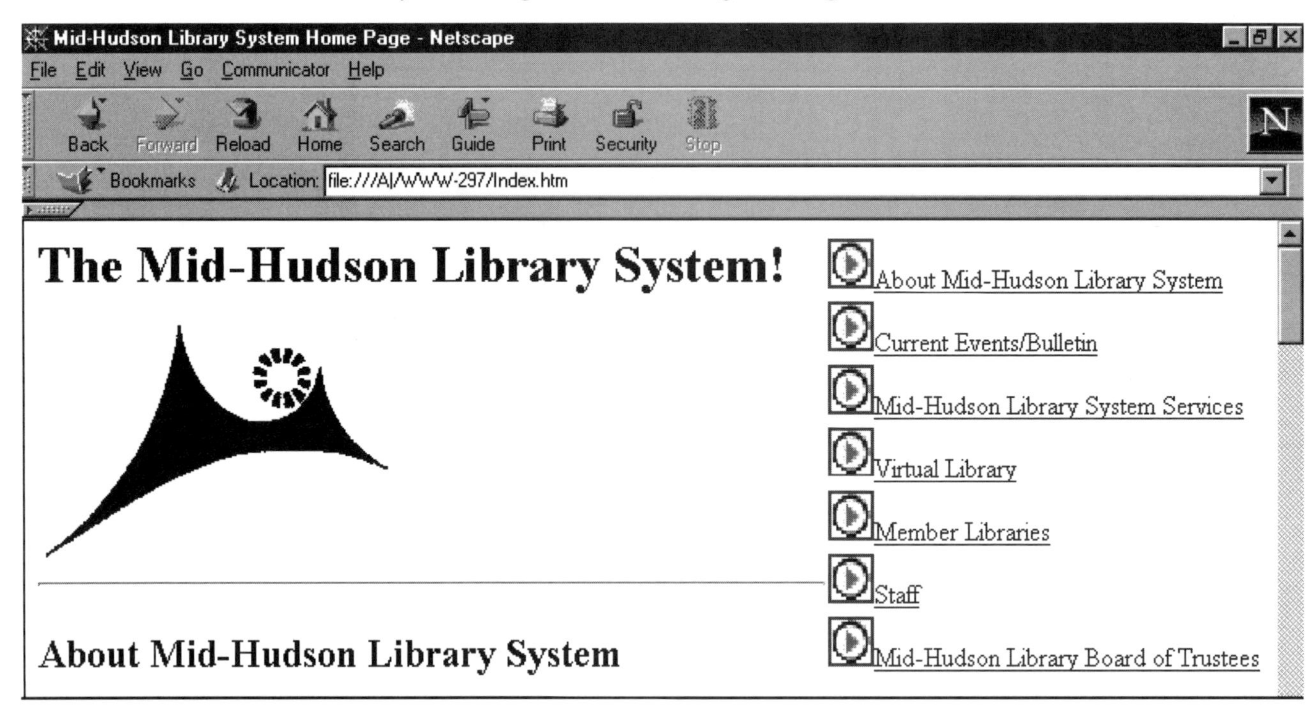

Figure 1–5: Original Model, Mid-Hudson Library System Home Page

The descriptions to this point reflect a learning process and effective compromises—but they are drawn from a bit of common sense and analysis. The efforts were deliberately introductory because the staff needed training. Instead of presenting minute detail or painting with watercolors (so to speak), we only needed a sketch to help our users quickly find what they needed. Such design concerns as color, texture, and typeface, along with multimedia applications were ignored in favor of the default modes of our Web editor software. Although our aesthetics remained weak, we were able to improve the initial design with some minor changes to the color and background texture. As seen in Chapters 8 and 9, the development of additional artistic factors or features (such as frames and pull-down menus) were left for a later phase.

FINAL THOUGHTS

Just as Erasmus in the early days of printing had to work closely with his printer Manutius, planners in our time require technical and design knowledge that will lead to future familiarity, conventions, and technological improvements. Although a great deal of critical analysis may be demanded at the moment, the learning curve for hypertext and Web design will inevitably flatten. The amount of technical information needed for implementations remains in flux, but new and constantly improving software is easing the way for ever-more transparent applications. However, many seemingly logical design options are precluded by technical factors. For the moment, Web design is a constantly evolving art form that remains dependent on the interplay of standards, editors, and browsers

RESOURCE NOTE

The list of people willing to provide information or sell services is quite long and growing. We are still in a very experimental arena without synthesis between technical and aesthetic factors. Even the best sources frequently display designs conforming to nonexistent sheets of paper, and the implications of click-and-scroll or organizational levels are still not fully plumbed. Still the state of the art is not that bad and is constantly improving. The following sources are only indicative of the kinds of resources available:

- Alertbox: Current Issues in Web Useability [www.useit.com/alertbox]
- Apple Web Design [applenet.apple.com/hi/web/intro.html]

- Human and Computer Interface VL [usableweb.com/hcivl]
- Kirsanov's Top Ten Tips [www.design.ru/ttt/]
- Yale Style Manual [info.med.yale.edu/caim/StyleManual_Top.html]
- Sun Style Guide [www.Sun.COM/styleguide/]
- Web Developers Virtual Library [www.stars.com]
- Web Design for Librarians [scc01.rutgers.edu/SCCHome/web.htm#/WebDesignResources]
- Web Page Design [ds.dial.pipex.com/pixelp/wpdesign/wpdintro.htm]
- Web Pages That Suck [www.webpagesthatsuck.com]
- Webmaster T's World of Design [www.globalserve.net/~iwb/world]

2 MANAGING VIRTUAL LIBRARY PROJECTS

Fred Stielow

Building from the design discussions in Chapter 1, this chapter looks to the administrative factors to guide the construction of an institutional Web site. The new presence is seen as an inescapable part of the administrative overhead—part of a growing communications chain that includes mailing addresses, telephone listings, fax numbers, and e-mail addresses. Ubiquity does not deny that the technological onslaught can be disconcerting to even the most forward-looking manager.

THE RISE OF CHANGE MANAGEMENT: A NOTE ON PLAY

How do you deal with a Web project as a manager? Of course, any activity should be mission-driven and integrated with ongoing functions. Certain traditional, common-sense management aphorisms (keep it simple, avoid reinventing the wheel, do not design for the cutting edge, and rely on standards) continue to apply. But automation is having an effect on some previous management standbys. Some modern administrative models and practices are being altered. The Information Age and changing nature of the workforce are leading to a breakdown of 19th-century bureaucratic hierarchies.

Supervisors in cyberspace simply cannot be overly rigid. They must recognize that it is a moving target and an exponentially expanding resource within an era of almost unpredictable change. There must be room for mistakes and redesign. This flexibility is especially important during the introductory stage of any automation venture, when the learning curve is at its greatest. Rather than rigid order, play and the leisure time for reflection become essential elements for the production of good sites. Hence, your staff should be empowered with the fun of "surfing," the opportunity to "romp" with new technological "toys," and the facility for "creative borrowing" from other locations. The new times presuppose the following humbling changes from an industrial mindset in which the boss supposedly had all the answers.

- Junior staff members will likely have or gain more technological knowledge on specific applications than their managers.
- Few effective products will appear exactly as first planned, and you will gain sophistication as the project progresses.
- Implementation will become progressively easier and less expensive over time.
- Unexpected software and hardware advances may radically alter your approaches.
- Web sites are not truly perfectible or fixed products with final completion dates, but instead are constantly evolving and imperfect creations.

Approximation-based management is a new buzz phrase that refers to concentrating projections to the present or reasonably foreseeable future.

Team management and enhanced communication are now at the fore. Within such a fluid environment, rigid administrative frameworks are only partially suitable. The new key is flexibility and the ability to respond to unforeseen developments—especially from the technology realm. You are led to embrace the underpinnings of "approximation-based" or "change" management. The four principal aspects of change management are:

- Fixed, long-range, five- or ten-year strategic planning gives way to factors and a time period that the manager can actually project (that is, cycles of no more than three years).
- Instead of having a rigid design, each plateau or stage within a planning process can engender a review of the whole or a massive redesign.
- Bureaucratic hierarchies and middle management abdicate in favor of teams and a meritocracy with a tailored array of talents to meet specific tasks.
- Effective team deployment empowers the members—even to challenge prior assumptions and the sanctity of the original plan or its creator.

WEB PROJECT OUTLINE: A SYSTEMS ANALYSIS APPROACH

Web projects lend themselves not only to certain management styles, but also to particular planning processes. The complexities and possibilities that underlie a successful Web effort are perhaps best controlled with systems analysis. This established planning process helps break complex problems into manageable subsets. Following lines similar to the creation of a computer program, systems analysis follows a regular set of planned stages or linear problem-solving steps: definition, data gathering, analysis, projected solution, piloting, debugging, and evaluation.

Experience suggests that you will find some trained programmers who overlook any or all of the first three steps of systems analysis when dealing with broad implementations. Everyone wants to leap into projected solutions. In addition, you will likely discover a natural tendency to focus on the technical side and overlook such equally important factors as organizational design and content selection. Thus, ongoing managerial vigilance is required. In particular, you are advised to lay out a logical progression and calendar of steps to guide your project (to take you through a preliminary or planning stage, through prototyping and piloting, and into ongoing maintenance), but with the flexibility to reorder plans as exigencies arise.

STEPS IN PROJECT PLANNING USING A SYSTEMS ANALYSIS APPROACH

The following process is one of many possible scenarios. It may be more detailed than your actual applications require, so be prepared to cull and reorder the elements to fit your particular situation.

A. INITIATION PHASE

1. Project Definition

The Web is such a "sexy" and exciting prospect that managers today are often blindly eager to join in the fun. Yet the ramifications of an institution's site are far too important to allow for only faddish development. Keeping this in mind, your most significant step is to formulate a clear idea of the desired output—what the site is intended to do. This goal should be balanced with an understanding of how the site relates to the institutional mission, and how the project can be integrated with ongoing functions. When defining the project consider the following three questions:

- Is the purpose to have an electronic sign proclaiming or marketing the institution?
- Is the project a new work product or supplemental resource—such as a virtual library?
- Is the purpose to provide staff with alternative sources of information for their jobs?

All of these are valid reasons, but the site design should reflect and further the purpose of the institution. You might want to resort to the tried-and-true, standard questions—and communicate the answers to the Web team. For example:

Five Project Definition Questions

- Who is the intended audience—a specific local group, or a more general/national audience?
- What is the scope of the project—what elements are included, what resources are in place, what do you want to present?
- Where will the operations and machinery be located—in-house or contract services?
- When will it be launched—a rough timetable?
- Why do you need to undertake such an effort?

2. Authorization

Before authorizing action, top management must understand the answers to the above questions. Analysis should include some perception of staffing, cost-benefit implications, and potential impact not only on extant operations, but also on those that are likely for the future. If commitment is forthcoming, it should go beyond mere lip service—it must include active support and the promise of resources over time. Management should ensure that its participants have proper lines of communication and produce consistent documentation.

Bureaucracy Warning: The lessons of management theorist Max Weber and others still hold. Bureaucratic infighting is a normal response to innovation and its call on resources. However good and obvious your Web project appears on the surface, some resistance is likely to emerge. Depending on the locus of opposition, top management may need to ensure a modicum of protection and establish proper reward structures for the team members.

3. Web Policies—Legal/Ethical Concerns

The manager must be proactive at the start of a project to ensure that it does not inadvertently put the institution at risk. While the Web slides over political boundaries, anyone doing business across such lines may be subject to another group's regulations. In October 1998, the European Union implemented advertising guidelines for the Web, which must be followed by institutions interested in conducting e-commerce in its countries or face penalties. Anyone working in finance, law, or medicine must be careful and refrain from giving formal advice without carefully considering the risks. Thus too, the for-profit sector is especially encouraged to keep abreast of legal and ethical issues, using sites such as Harvard's Cyberlaw [cyber.law.harvard.edu/spaces.html], the Electronic Privacy Information Center [www.epic.org], or Cyberspace Laws [www.cyberspacelaws.com].

Today's legal climate also demands that nonprofit libraries and archives establish reasonable Web information policies. As Chapter 3 discusses, copyright and privacy rights are of primary concern and influence policies and rules for site development and operations. Other legal questions involve external contracting and use policies for in-house patrons.

Note on Children: If your site or facility serves children, you should be attuned to the legal implications of Web access.

4. Initial Staffing Analysis and Team Selection

The selection of the Web team is at the heart of a Web project. This high-level process takes into account communication, and political, strategic, and technical factors. Since many institutions may outsource the technology, a computer department is obviously not a requirement—but some in-house understanding of automation is. Even for those with a strong technical staff, political realities decree the incorporation of as many of the potential stakeholders as possible. No single individual possesses all the skills to make a good site—let alone a virtual library. However, among the skills that must be represented, on a Web team, six are particularly important.

Six Skills Needed on a Web Team

1. managerial competence
2. information and user handling expertise
3. content specializations
4. design skills (graphics, layout, typeface)
5. implementation capabilities
6. maintenance responsibilities

Double check current and potential in-house abilities against the project's design. If holes exist, management will need to consider training and hiring options or subcontracting some or all of the development. If there are extant team structures, the selection of cocaptains for content, design, implementation, and maintenance may be quite simple. More traditional hierarchies will need to take extra steps to balance needed skills and the demands of ongoing duties. Upper management may need to be sensitive to the potential for internal upset such a project can cause and be prepared for departmental clashes over resource allocation.

5. Project Timetable and Documentation

Certain milestones evolve naturally in the planning process, but what is really needed is an outline of expected accomplishments and their timing.

Communications and Paper Trail Note: Coordinating electronically in the form of shared directories and e-mail groups is highly recommended. The by-products are also a useful paper trail of decisions and the various permutations that the team will take. Management should, however, establish procedures to ensure that such data are retained and not inadvertently eliminated.

Given the learning curves involved and the impossibility of a fully perfected product, one should not expect final answers. A prototype can be placed online in a fairly short period of time—albeit with the follow-up of piloting and debugging to allow for improvements before making a marketing release. Whatever the case, the team should set up a realistic set of projections based on their goals, functional analysis, and the expertise and staffing time in hand.

Stages or development plateaus should be scheduled for completion and evaluation as a normal part of the planning process. The actual timetable should be clear to participants and submitted for management review. The type of projects suggested in this workbook are rather straightforward and may only call for a simple Gantt chart, bar graph, or timeline to set the milestones and mark progress.

B. PROTOTYPE PHASE

Smaller institutions, especially those where the director is actively involved in the project development, will likely fold the initiation and prototype phases into one. For larger enterprises, the team will now take over actual implementation and assume responsibility for fulfilling the general mandate and priorities of management. It is crucial that the team understand prior thinking, negotiate any needed changes, and coordinate its directions and timing with management and the institutional mission. Thus, we begin by retracing and filling out some of the steps from the first phase.

1. Project Definition, Policies, and Timetable

Implementers should grasp and embrace the type of site and outputs that management saw as justification for the project. In addition, established policies and the timetable must be laid out—or delegated to the team for administrative review. Prior directions should not deny the possibility of changing any of the areas. The team should be free to engage in questions and negotiations as part of its buy-in and shared vision with management.

2. Three Elements of Background Research

All team members should become involved in the "play" of looking for good ideas and concepts. Data gathering initially concentrates on a top-down view of three elements:

- **Organizational Factors:** Start at home. What services or elements do you have and intend to present through the Web? How can you best lay out the site to organize and display them for your intended audience. (See Chapter 4.)
- **Audience:** For whom are you designing the site? For this type of Web project, it is important to settle on a primary target audience and then to try to understand its particular methods of information retrieval. Do you also have a secondary user group in mind? (See Chapter 6.)
- **Content:** What specific information needs to be in place to encompass the services or elements that you intend to present? What is available from other sites? What will you need to develop in-house? What policies are applicable? (See Chapter 7.)

3. Analysis

The team is brought together to evaluate the findings in the context of the project definition and functional needs. This step provides another important opportunity to communicate with upper management. Are things pretty much following the initial outline? Do any of the concepts or definitional structures need changing?

Maintenance Reminder: Frequent updating is a bane for management. Your planning should consider the differences between relatively static or rarely updated information versus that which frequently changes.

4. Design Solution

With analysis and consensus in place, the process flows into an initial concrete and functional design. Remember the importance of flexibility. Your site will change and improve as the technology and your expertise evolve.

5. Offline Mounting

Before launching your site on the Web, it should be mounted for inhouse viewing, analysis, and debugging. Your implementation will combine the skills of the staff and the possibilities framed by the software editor and current standards.

C. PILOT PHASE

With an experienced staff, you may not require much double-checking and oversight. In such environments, piloting can be folded into the prototype phase.

1. Technical Implementation

With a workable presence, it is time to open your site on the Internet. This phase should include the definition of performance benchmarks (such as the addition of new specialty areas or a scheduled annual review) and the installation of counters or other measuring devices to monitor services. (See Chapter 9.) Two easily overlooked topics that should be addressed are online help and security.

- **Online Help and Training:** Make sure that your implementation and design include appropriate training and online help, as well as the navigational structures to help people find their way.
- **Security:** For some, this area is a subset of the larger automation context with firewalls and virus detection in place. For most, it is best handled as part of contract negotiations that outsource the physical site to an Internet Service Provider (ISP). Outside of a well-tuned firewall, your primary protection rests in maintenance concerns through regular back-ups and perhaps a mirror site. (See Chapters 3 and 8.)

Firewall: A combination of hardware and software that regulates the flow of information packets and can protect a local area network from security break-ins from external connections.

2. Content, Technology, and Design Evaluation

The team will need to examine its handiwork, continue research and grant activities, and come together for periodic reviews of the basic elements of the site, which are as follows.

- **Design/Organization:** The evaluation of the pilot should include a critical review of the design motif and organizational structures. With luck and proper planning, one will not need a radical redesign, but some minor tinkering may be in order. The major activity will likely be improving the graphics, and other visual design features.
- **Content:** Even with quantitative and feedback measures, user panels may prove significant for qualitative evaluation. However, the biggest changes are likely to be confined to information suites in response to collection development needs or grant opportunities.
- **Technology:** Usage data from the Web server, counters, or other survey techniques provide the basic quantitative data for discussion. The team's ongoing research should include new developments coming on the scene. (See Chapter 8.)

3. Enhancement Plans and Implementation

Based on the preceding analysis, the addition of special resource areas, and software improvements, sites will have to undergo periodic upgrades. Such improvements need to be planned. They should include benchmarking along with the regular stages for team decision making and schedules for uploading. The danger is that piecemeal "improvements" can easily get out of hand and wreak havoc with the overall integrity of the site, as well as place an undo burden on staff.

Metatags Metatags are data encoding structures used to decide the contents of the sites. The use of judiciously chosen metatags as special descriptors can enhance access by the commercial search engines.

Use Improvement Hint: The managerial ideal is to secure formal links or buttons to your site on the home pages of desired users. Even better is to have users default to your site as their opening or "home" site.

4. Marketing and Training

The unveiling of a site is often the time for a well-earned celebration. Those interested in general use should be aware of how to list with the appropriate commercial search engines and how to use *metatags*. Building more localized patron activity typically devolves to other forms of publicity and networking with groups or individual users. Although the site should be as easy to use as possible and have built-in help features, some supplemental training or printed handouts are still in order. Such efforts should be considered and planned as part of the site's marketing.

D. MAINTENANCE CYCLE

Eventually you will enter the ongoing process of tweaking, fixing possible errors, working on security and backups, and making sure that the site remains in operation. Maintenance can extend to the simple addition of new links, which do not affect the overall design of the site. The addition of other sites should be an ongoing process in keeping with basic selection criteria, which are discussed in Chapter 6. The site itself should provide electronic feedback mechanisms in the form of e-mail reply forms or CGI scripts for user comments and recommendations. The content specialists should have the ultimate say on any inclusion or deletion, but the maintenance specialist should be empowered to set up a reasonable schedule for such additions. You will also want to ensure that the appropriate software or human monitors are in place for electronic site evaluation (for example, to guarantee currency and reduce the number of "dead links").

CGI: Common Gateway Interface: Internet programs that can be used to extend interactivity on the Web.

Maintenance largely adheres to the same functional outline as the piloting phase, with the possible exception of a marketing stage. We do suggest that the maintenance cycle be linked to an annual calendar of events. Assuming that priority time is set aside for any new grant project, existing elements should be systematically reviewed and enhanced as needed in a regularly scheduled sequence. Unless there are new projects, this may also be the time to dissolve the team and return control to the appropriate departments.

CONTRACTUAL OPTIONS

Rather than having an in-house concentration, management may consider hiring out all or part of the project. Determining fair pricing for such services remains one of the more interesting enigmas of the moment—a topic that will be left to your marketplace. The broader policy and implementation questions with contracting, however, do need to be touched on.

A. DESIGN AND INSTALLATION

Much of the previous development and stages for an in-house project remain applicable. Contracting does not change the fact that Web projects demand a unique blend of aesthetics and an understanding of internal communications. The latter requires an intimate knowledge of the corporate culture to ensure the site's functional integration with other institutional functions. Hence, much of the initiation phase should be duplicated. Only team selection needs to be changed to add a contracting option. With that, the administration should run a normal check of credentials and prior work samples (to review skills, as enumerated on page 27 for team members). The administration should also be willing to engage with its contractor in a fairly active manner in keeping with the initial factors outlined for prototyping:

1. Project Definition, Policies, and Timetable

This stage is exactly what it says. Unless agreement is reached at this stage, the project will falter.

2. Background Research

- Organizational Factors/Design
- Audience
- Content

The contract should establish performance penalties and an appropriate timetable for the transmission of the end product, but should also provide for the interim delivery of a conceptual model or prototype for discussion and finalization. One of the major dangers for a product developer is management's tendency to request additional changes and during the review process to dither with what was agreed upon earlier. If this occurs, management should understand it may incur added financial costs. More important, such endeavors are defined as works for hire that include a creative component. Since U.S. law relegates the copyright to the original artist in these instances, management must specify the transfer of rights as part of the contract.

B. OFFSITE OPERATIONS AND ISPs

Until recently, virtual library building has been concentrated in operations with substantial computer and Internet resources, but most enterprises may be better off today contracting for such services. Such contracting may prove more cost effective than hiring your own staff and capitalizing equipment. Your contract should stipulate size limitations, downloading times, and techniques and intervals for updating the site; it should also provide security guarantees—including at least a three-day power backup.

END NOTES FROM MID-HUDSON: THE PRELIMINARY PHASE

PROJECT DEFINITION

The "what" of a virtual library at Mid-Hudson flowed rather directly from a base set of questions and broader imperatives to get ready for the revolution.

Why?

The rationale behind a virtual library project was readily apparent for Mid-Hudson. The Web is not going to leave the picture. The Internet, GUI interfaces, and Z39.50 compliance were destined to be a part of future delivery mechanisms. MHLS was already contracting with a library automation company, who declared its future enhancements lay with HTML. MHLS also had engaged and negotiated with magazine vendors, who issued similar announcements and product delivery lines. Staff needed appropriate training and experiences in the medium to ensure future effectiveness. Ultimately, we accepted an inescapable destiny—Web-based services were a must for the coming professional identity of librarians and archivists.

GUI: (pronounced gooey) stands for Graphical User Interface. It is an interface that uses graphics and a mouse in addition to characters and keystrokes. Windows is a GUI interface and DOS is a text-based interface.

Z39.50 is a database standard for Internet communications. It allows a library to group other libraries' databases together for a single search, in effect, creating a local union catalog.

Mid-Hudson faced the practical realities of a widely disbursed, poorly funded, and often technologically challenged set of member libraries. Web implementations could address several heretofore unsolvable information delivery problems along with the chimera of electronic coordination for interlibrary loans. A virtual library also provided the opportunity for a proactive intellectual freedom response—along with the intriguing prospect of providing national leadership from the boondocks. Finally, a virtual library could demonstrate the benefits of cooperative collection development that married the information skills of its members to the technological knowledge of the MHLS staff. The results could be a marketing tool for library advocacy and grantsmanship, as well as a positive identity for all involved.

Who?

Although we factored in the patrons and organizations in our five-county area, the primary audience was the 66 MHLS member libraries. This focus led directly to the organizational pattern and contours of the content to be presented.

Where?

In keeping with our extant facilities, staff training needs, and future activities, the work would be initially conducted within MHLS headquarters.

When?

The "when" for the virtual library was actually part of a broader and ongoing Web and managerial initiative. As previously indicated, Mid-Hudson defined two stages over a single year for its initial Web development. The first stage was the building of its home page, which was a "crash" effort designed for a two-month period. The second stage, virtual library construction, was to be less rushed, but still rapid, with a fully presentable offering within a ten-month window.

AUTHORIZATION?

The question of authorization and administration commitment was effectively a given. The MHLS board of trustees was eager to meet the challenges of the Information Age. The director determined that a Web presence and virtual library services were inherently consistent with the MHLS institutional mission and an inescapable conclusion for its services.

TEAM SELECTION

The Web project was also part of a wider managerial shift. In addition to preparations for a new automation system, the project was the first step in an overall push toward team management and new evaluation techniques. Staff were interviewed, files reviewed, and a notice posted for those with an interest in the Web. Analysis revealed a lack of HTML and Web experience. Any initial reliance on outside contractors was deferred, however, to the longer-range importance of having trained, graphical-interface expertise on staff. The subsequent commitment to trial-and-error methodologies was obviously fraught with potential complications and demanded flexibility.

Fortunately, MHLS did have a solid talent pool with an eagerness to learn. Because of the managerial implications and need for prior experience, the project coordinator slot fell by default to the director. With the member libraries, including a physically adjacent central library in Poughkeepsie, N.Y., we also assumed we would have few worries over content specialists. System headquarters itself sported a number of computer-literate library consultants. Mid-Hudson also had a printing department with a graphic artist to help with the design. The resident artist was somewhat familiar with computer graphics and received extra enticements in the form of a new Macintosh computer and a color laser printer during the course of events. The primary resort was to the MHLS technology department, which offered solid computer skills, but still needed proper software and staff training for the Web. In addition, a small pool of after-hours computer operators presented a ready reservoir of talent for ongoing maintenance and updating. Finally, the team-building exercise also uncovered a part-time employee with an abiding interest in the project, who emerged as our primary technologist and Web guru.

INITIAL PROJECT REVIEW

The rosy hypothetical picture did have its thorns. As with many similar projects, technological concerns and implementation dominated the first two phases. Content development remained largely in the hands of the director and did not initially benefit from the working librarians. We also neglected to get counters in place early on. The eager embrace of the new technology delayed the transfer of maintenance activities to the off-hours personnel. In addition, those designing specialized sites did not always ensure that their locations were integrated with the rest of the site and its database structure.

Even the attempt to introduce team management disciplines proved problematic. The direct involvement of the director skewed the power relations and negotiations faced by a more typical team. While this structure may have eased the introduction of team management, pre-existing offices did not disappear and staff time was limited. Finally too, we may have been better off giving up some of our toys. Instead of investing in file servers and allied software, we are coming to realize that outsourcing the physical site to an ISP might have been wise.

Still, the desired outcomes were largely achieved, and with some pleasant surprises. In addition to the book offer from Neal-Schuman, our efforts were good enough to bring the exceptional—yet too frequently overlooked—skills of public libraries to the attention of other public agencies and nonprofit organizations. The level of Mid-Hudson's Web development had sufficient appeal for the United Way, school systems, and other local agencies to seek community partnerships with us. In the process, too, our staff expertise developed beyond what could have been predicted. The new skills and products also facilitated unexpected successes with grants and national recognition from MCI.

3 DEVELOPING POLICIES FOR THE VIRTUAL LIBRARY

Fred Stielow

The manual now turns to the administrative aspects for the preliminary phase of the project. These aspects include formal policies, an organizational model, and selection/development procedures, along with an emphasis on special resources centers. Such elements are as crucial to success as the physical implementations, which are detailed in Chapters 7–9.

Policy making lies at the heart of managment, but the Web escalates its importance for libraries and archives. Building from the legal concerns introduced in Chapter 2, this chapter advises you to take precautions before mounting any Web presence. Managers must understand the ramifications and ensure that appropriate steps are taken to meet legal, ethical, and professional considerations. This chapter addresses the related policy responses for the creation, maintenance, and in-house use of your virtual library.

PRIVACY POLICIES

Privacy is the issue of the moment. Internationally, the European Union is leading the way. Its October 1998 advertising guidelines demonstrate a strong interest in the privacy rights of consumers and in blocking institutions from reselling or otherwise abusing sales data. Somewhat less stridently but with equal resolve, the U.S. Federal Trade Commission (FTC) has joined the fray. In 1997 the FTC went on record to demand that Web sites provide notice on the collection and use of personally identifiable information on their users. The commission singled out four core principles—notice, choice, access, and security—as necessary for any policy response. As its June 1998 *Privacy Online: A Report to Congress* outlined:

> These core principles require that consumers be given notice of an entity's information practices; that consumers be given choice with respect to the use and dissemination of information . . . that consumers be given access to information about them . . . and that the

> data collector take appropriate steps to ensure the security and integrity of any information gathered.

As one might suspect, sites aimed at children require extra precautions. Readers should be aware, for example, that the Consumer Federation of America, the Center for Media Education, and other groups are incensed by the appearance of new Web cartoon barkers. Similar to characters that were outlawed from television in the 1950s, these creations are seen as unfairly enticing kids to their sponsors' products. The FTC itself is specifically reacting against inducements for children to provide information on themselves or their families. This same June 1998 report recommended that

> Congress develop legislation placing parents in control of the online collection and use of personally identifiable information from their children. Such legislation would require Web sites that collect . . . to provide actual notice to parents and obtain parental consent.

A note of caution is thus in order even for innocuous nonprofit organizations. Anyone with a Web presence will need to stay abreast of changes through sites like Cyberspace Laws [www.cyberspacelaws.com]. Yet, appropriate responses are quite clear:

- For the moment, most sites should avoid the collection or use of personally identifiable information. Aggregate statistics can provide sufficient information to help improve the site's performance.
- As Chapter 9 demonstrates, personally identifiable information will become increasingly important for the interactive learning centers of the future. A program can reside in the background and monitor a user's patterns, create a profile, and apply that information to automatically offer related materials. Libraries or archives collecting for such purposes will need to make the provision of such information a patron option.
- Those collecting personally identifiable information for other purposes have a very simple solution provided by the FTC. They can supply their visitors with notice of the practices on the site:

> **PRIVACY NOTICE:** THIS SITE COLLECTS INFORMATION ON ITS VISITORS FOR MANAGEMENT PURPOSES, BUT DOES NOT RESELL OR OTHERWISE USE THESE DATA. FOR FURTHER INFORMATION, CONTACT WEBMASTER . . .

COPYRIGHT AND FAIR USE ALERT

Copyright is in even greater flux and will require ongoing observation. (See Stanford's Fair Use [fairuse.stanford.edu], Texas's Intellectual Property [www.utsystem.edu/ogc/IntellectualProperty/cprtindx.htm], and US Copyright Office [lcweb.loc.gov/copyright/].) The Digital Millennium Copyright Act of late 1998 (with Congress's pledge of two additional years of monitoring), only reaffirms the uncertainties. For the moment, the same principles of disclosure and openness used for privacy are the best defense.

THREE AREAS OF WEB BUILDING AFFECTED BY COPYRIGHT

1. **Site Building:** Consider copyright when borrowing design or code from another site. This may involve some attempt to notify that site (which may, in turn, request recognition or even payment). Note, too, the importance of complying with licensing and overlapping copyright as part of the contracting for an electronic resources library.
2. **Digital Archives:** The institution must be especially diligent when placing digitized materials on its site. In keeping with the 1976 U.S. Copyright Act (Title 17: U.S. Code), a document is vested with two forms of property rights. Physical ownership of the item does not automatically convey intellectual or creative title. Unless you have clear intellectual ownership, we recommend against a complete scanning and downloading to the site. Instead, you may want to include some excerpts—ticklers to invite further inquiries. This limited approach also helps protect your institution's copyright.
3. **Free Web Listings:** Although serious threats have arisen, American libraries and archives remain free to provide unfettered access to most Web resources under the Fair Use Clause of the Copyright Act. Congress has also granted a liability exemption for the unknowing transmittal of illegally used copyrighted information. Nevertheless it is wise to observe the following "netiquette":
   - When listing a site, extend the courtesy of notifying the source—especially if it is a local agency.
   - Many materials on the Web may be in violation of someone's copyright. Obviously, no library or archives has the right to break the law and post or link to such material. Yet it may be impossible to make more than a well-intended attempt to exclude such material. However, your policy and guidelines to selectors should demonstrate sys-

Staff and Consultant Rights: While copyrights for interpretive discussions and presentation design for digital archives transfer automatically to the institution when regular staff are involved, be sure to guarantee similar transfer as part of your contract with any external agent. (See related discussions in Chapter 2.)

Trademark Warning: Commercial enterprises should take care not to include the trademarked names of their competitors within metatag fields or other devices used to attract visitors to their sites.

tematically applied *good faith efforts* to exclude offending sites. In addition to proper practice, such adoption also provides practical legal defenses for your institution.

COPYRIGHT WARNING SIGN

Consider informing users, in addition to your technical staff and collection development specialists, of potential limitations on the reuse of information gleaned from the Web. The proactive electronic or physical posting of a Web copyright notice sign similar to the one required for photocopiers is not a bad idea:

> **Web Copyright Notice:** Information is provided in keeping with the Fair Use clause of the U.S. Copyright Statute (Title 17: U.S. Code). The institution cannot guarantee the accuracy of any information found by linking to external sites and access does not confer copyright. Those who choose to look at such data should be aware that some items may be posted in violation of copyright. You must always take appropriate precautions before any use to ensure copyright compliance.

EIGHT ADDITIONAL ETHICAL AND LEGAL CONSIDERATIONS

Although the preceding precautions will handle the key initial areas, policy issues will inevitably arise for your virtual library—especially from a potential blurring of lines with commerce:

1. In addition to taking precautions for children, commercial and even nonprofit sites must be doubly careful when giving out advice on financial, legal, and medical topics. If you engage in such arenas, be sure to spell out your disclaimers carefully.
2. Although libraries have long engaged in commercial relationships with vendors, the virtual library brings forward other considerations. Does the listing of a travel or other for-profit service on a Web site imply product approval by the library?
3. Should your institution accept funds or Web services from sponsors—in the same way that it accepts support for fundraising events? Should you then provide sponsor recognition on your site? What are the implications of accepting support,

for example, from the Gates Library Foundation with its integral promotion of Microsoft products?

4. Will you offer space in your virtual library selections for solicitations and shared sales profits with sites like Amazon.com, or will you actually charge for their inclusion as advertisements?
5. Will you accept advertisements and charge for such listings in your virtual library?
6. Will the library preclude links to chat rooms or to certain types of information? On what basis?
7. Do you need to establish collection development policies that *actively* consider "alternative sources" for the Web? Will certain sites (which are described in Chapter 9) receive lower selection priorities, for example, because they do not bring advanced searching features or are not tuned to the major search engines?
8. Should you avoid potential product liability issues by keeping to only positive selections—for example, disallow such selections as "The Ten Worst Sites"?

USE POLICIES

Institutions incur responsibilities when they provide in-house access to the Internet. If their users include children under 18 years of age, the onus is especially great and demands formal policies.

ADULT RIGHTS AND THE CHILDREN'S QUESTION

Note for Higher Education: Most colleges and universities enroll students under the age of 18 and they may well need to pay attention to the following discussions concerning minors.

Libraries are in a very difficult position. On one hand, the Supreme Court's decision in the challenge to the Communications Decency Act (CDA) reaffirmed the public library's mandate to provide adult clientele with unfettered access to constitutionally protected information—including that found on the Web. This mandate is unequivocal; public institutions must guarantee the rights of their adult clientele. On the other hand, repositories cannot ignore the actions of legislators and the courts responding to perceived threats for children. The child is in a specially protected class. Our organizations may be required to reexamine their concerns and perhaps find a compromise with rigid intellectual freedom principles.

The Web may appear to be a dangerous place. The giant online toystore does include traps. Children can get too sophisticated and easily outpace their elders. It is also all too easy to get lost from parents or teachers. Children (and, one may admit, some adults) may be so susceptible to games and technical flourishes that they forget why they were online in the first place. A few may be unwittingly lured by product hucksters or to less-than-desirable locations and individuals. Still, the benefits overwhelm the negatives. More important, there are reasonable alternatives to attempting to deny our children access to the general riches of the Web.

WEB FILTERS

Nowhere are the complexities and impact of the Web clearer than in the current national policy struggle to control content on public and school library Internet terminals. Just as in the 19th century, properly concerned individuals and would-be moral arbiters focus on the library as an avenue to restore order within an information explosion.

Librarians approach this new crisis from a more experienced perspective. Since the 1920s, the field has come to embrace a democratic responsibility in keeping with the First Amendment and the lessons of Thomas Jefferson and James Madison. Practitioners learned that the threats from popular literature were more than exaggerated. Great literature should not be withheld from adults to ensure the safety of children—we must trust in the people and defer to individual parental rights. Librarians also found that they were very poor in policing literary productions and consciously blocking selections as censors—especially in the face of the information needs of a clientele ranging from preschoolers to senior citizens. Instead, librarians determined that their energies were better spent selecting appropriate materials and helping people find what they wanted without imposing moral strictures.

COMMUNICATIONS DECENCY ACT

Today's librarians are arguably the most important professional defenders of free access to the Web. They help guarantee its unprecedented abilities to further the open debate so cherished by the Founding Fathers. The American Library Association (ALA), with its Intellectual Freedom Committee, was the major funder of the successful Supreme Court battle (*ACLU v. Reno*) against the 1996 Communications Decency Act (CDA). That legislation tried to reduce readily available content on the Web to the level suitable for a five-year-old. It threatened to send librarians to jail for including book titles with "objectionable" words in online catalogs. A Pittsburgh Carnegie Library study for the CDA case found that it would have to spend over $8 million a year to fulfill the law's requirements.

PARENTAL CONTROL SOFTWARE

In July 1997, ALA also went on record in opposition to parental control software or Web filters for public and school libraries. (The ALA opposition does not extend, however, to home or business use. For a list of filters see Parental Control [www.worldvillage.com/wv/school/html/control.com].) Ultimately, ALA and many librarians feel that they would be usurping individual parental privileges, and that using such software vitiates much of the value of the Web and violates constitutional obligations as well. General use is not considered unacceptable (since much information retrieval would be reduced to that suitable for a child), and even specialized use in children's rooms is suspect.

Filter Assessment: For more complete background information on the very secret world of Web filters, turn to Karen Schneider's 1997 *A Practical Guide to Internet Filters* and the survey findings of her Internet Filter Assessment Project [www.bluehighways.com / tifap/].

Scientific studies demonstrate that no present or likely future software product can successfully block or define all "indecent" materials within the vastness of the Internet. *Internet World* in a September 1996 report revealed part of the limitation—for all major blocking products "fewer than 200,000 Web sites out of more than 30 million pages are rated by these systems." The May 1997 edition of *Consumer Reports* added results of a test sample of four of the leading products on "22 easy-to-find Web sites that we had judged inappropriate for young children." The magazine found that "None is totally effective. The Web changes too swiftly for even a full-time staff to maintain a complete list of adult sites." As *PC Magazine* summarized the Sisyphian task in its April 8, 1997, issue, "a foolproof filter list is impossible to develop because of the subjective nature of what is considered objectionable." Such obvious parental concerns as audio and pictures are beyond any automated fix and left to human intermediaries.

Again, the fact is that the products do not work. Some commonsense illustrations may be in order. Any parent who has faced the impossibility of successfully hiding Christmas packages can see the dilemma. Password security controls are truly child's work to the inquisitive mind. In an informal test in Dutchess County, New York, 12-year-olds needed only seven minutes to take control of their school system's filters. A child can also turn to a site like Peacefire [www.peacefire.org] for online help in disabling many of the current products. Although the products are improving, filtering as a technology for public libraries rests in the realm of science fiction—not as a realistic scientific option.

Libraries could conceivably live with a flawed product but only one that could be individually tailored and engaged by each user. Otherwise, librarians would default to inferior software and unknown, undertrained human operators in far-off locales—elements working for commercial interests and demonstrably lacking the librarians' skills or knowledge of the local community. The results are severely flawed byproducts.

In addition, filters block access to valuable materials. They repeatedly restrict innocent sites that could stand the muster of the most rigid censor. A late 1997 report from the Electronic Privacy Information Center (EPIC) on "family-friendly" search engines [www2.epic.org/reports/filter_report.html] found them blocking access to as much as 99 percent of the material on the Internet that would be appropriate for high school students. The list of improperly blocked sites grows daily. Such affronts range from medical considerations of topics like breast cancer to political action committees and viewpoints on all sides of the spectrum. We meet ever-growing accounts of improper blocking: Essex, England, Superbowl **XXX**, and even the word **"coupled"** in the White House site. The effects are compounded by the filter companies' reluctance to provide lists of their blocked sites.

FILTER USE

Despite the clarity of the technological issues, we face a political reality. The national debate may remove the matter from librarians' hands. In order to try to protect children from some ill-defined "indecencies" or "pornography," school and public libraries may be forced to install parental control software filters. Librarians may see the parallel to their previous compromises in setting up separate children's collections.

If filters are set in place, the institution should at least post signs alerting parents that it cannot guarantee the child's safety. While vigorously protecting constitutional responsibility to unfettered access for adults, you should also try to differentiate between young children and teenagers. Finally, librarians as professionals should be able to evaluate parental control software and heed Karen Schneider's recommendations in *A Practical Guide to Internet Filters*:

- Disable keyword blocking switches, which are notoriously poor.
- Engage different types of categories—such as sex, violence, and nudity. Many of the filter programs have preset categories, which can be scaled for different tolerance.
- Configure filter placement by workstation in a network environment.
- Block by time of day—e.g., to block chat rooms right after school.
- Enable multiple user levels to distinguish among adults, teens, and kids.
- Allow for item blocking by barcode.
- Allow for local access lists to override the filter company's database.
- Provide statistics on searches that lead to blocked categories or sites—without any information that might identify the user.
- Provide for ready user feedback.

SOME LIBRARY CONSIDERATIONS ON FILTERING

- The use of filtering products that delegate deselection to outside agents is in direct conflict with professional responsibilities for collection development.
- Public institutions providing patron access to the free information resources on the Internet incur constitutional responsibilities. Adult users have unquestioned First Amendment rights to legally available information.
- The use of filtering products would professionally obligate librarians to take affirmative steps to remove improper blocks. Such steps could be extremely burdensome in terms of time and money, as well as rendered effectively impossible by the product manufacturers.
- In a technical aside, no current or likely future products work sufficiently well for a library context—nor do they provide legally sustainable guarantees for parents.
- There are options in keeping with professional tenets for dealing with children. These options include privacy protections, formal policies, educational efforts, and virtual libraries with value-added children's and teens' resources.

PICS AND RATING SYSTEMS

Several other types of ratings or labeling systems have also been thrown into the picture. The Recreational Software Advisory Council (RSAC), for instance, instituted voluntary RSACi codings for self disclosure on violence and sexual content from game sites [www.rsac.org/homepage.asp]. Sites listed with the service are searchable by rating level and typically display a RSACi logo. RSACi itself is enabled by the metatag format of PICS (Platform for Internet Content Services [www.w3.org/PICS/]). The World Wide Web Consortium (W3) has created PICS as an open platform, which allows both sites and outside agencies to assign their own classifications and ratings to sites.

Once viewed as a coming panacea and neutral alternative to government intrusions, PICS is being reconsidered for its potentially chilling effects. To some, PICS threatens to set the industry, commercial interests, and select lobbying groups in place as public censors. According to Lawrence Lessig, the Harvard law professor who also serves as the Justice Department's special master in the Microsoft browser antitrust lawsuit, the private regulation offered by PICS "is a greater danger to free speech than public regulation." As our Founding Fathers predicted, the inherent tensions and constant vigilance required to protect the free flow of information will simply never disappear. The lessons from PICS for public libraries thus reflect the cautions against general filters.

ACCEPTABLE USE POLICIES

The traditions of professional librarianship also suggest the development of use policies. You may simply be able to extend selection or intellectual freedom policies already in place, or you may need to resort to a specially targeted Acceptable Use Policy for the Internet (AUP). Once developed such products should be prominently displayed—on the Web page or on a sign posted at the circulation desk, for example.

Any AUP must be carefully considered with respect to the mission of each particular institution, the applicable laws, and the professional ethics of the field. The document does not have to be long, but it should be considered as a training and educational exercise for all the parties. Although you will want to introduce your service in a positive way, you should include some disclaimers on the validity of materials found on the Web and inform the user about copyright.

Unlike public libraries, school libraries act in loco parentis and directly support a curriculum. They are not obligated (like public libraries) to provide the full range of resources. Nevertheless, any institution is perfectly within its rights to establish rules regarding time, place, and manner of Internet use. You have the right to set restrictions to ensure equity of access to all your patrons—and preserve your equipment. Many of the policy questions can only be answered by you. Will you provide such extras as e-mail accounts and access to games or chat rooms? Will you require sign-ups and limit the amount of time for individual users? Will you suspend library privileges for violations? (If so, be sure to include a review procedure in case of any challenges.)

Again, one does not need to reinvent the wheel. Numerous examples of AUPs are available on the Web for adaptation (check under individual library sites, or see School Library Policies [www.enet.edu/tenet-info/accept.html] For Public Library Policies [www.ciloswego.or.us/library/poli.htm]). The sample in AUP Figure 3–1 is partially drawn from The Librarians Guide to Cyberspace for Parents and Kids [www.ala.org/parentspage/greatsites/] and may prove a useful guide for your efforts.

Figure 3–1: Sample Acceptable Use Policy

The ____________ is pleased to provide its patrons with electronic access to the Web. The terms Internet, World Wide Web, Information Superhighway, and Cyberspace all describe the most exciting new learning arena in our era. At the touch of a keyboard, you can read the *New York Times* or the London *Times*. With the click of a mouse, you can watch a volcano erupt, visit Antarctica, read the Gettysburg address, or hear Martin Luther King cry out "I Have a Dream." You can e-mail friends, conduct business, and chat with dozens across the globe. The sheer volume of places to go and things to do can be overwhelming. But this is also the Wild West—without many of the quality controls, basic courtesies, or simple navigational guides that you have come to expect from other media. The Web does not have all the answers—it is a very new arena and, for all its size, still incomplete. Books are still important, and our staff can provide you with information on a range of supplemental electronic resources that the library has contracted for your convenience.

In keeping with the democratic vision of our Founding Fathers, this institution has a constitutional obligation to provide a full range of information to all its clients. Yet the organization must issue some cautions and call attention to your responsibilities and areas of discretion when using a resource like the Web, which takes you far beyond our walls. We cannot vouch for the validity of the material found on the Web. The user must understand that normal copyright and citation protocols are also in order. In exchange for providing Internet access, we require that you observe certain rules to ensure availability to all our clientele and to preserve our equipment.

- No eating, drinking, or smoking near the terminals.
- Felt-tip pens are preferred and pencils are not allowed (the lead and eraser shavings are harmful to the machines).
- [Insert your policy on using personal storage disks (if they are allowed, be sure to provide for virus check).]
- [Insert your policy on computer sign-ups and time limits.]
- [Insert your policy on individual use and group projects.]
- [Insert your policy on e-mail, chat rooms, Webcast viewing, limitations to children's sites, or other use restrictions. (These areas must be carefully weighed. See also the following section on netiquette.)]
- [Insert your policy regarding any parental permission requirement for Web use by those under a certain age. (Such permission may be necessary, but is not recommended. It can easily discourage children from using the library and seeking adult help.)]

Any violation of these restrictions may result in a suspension of library privileges, which is subject to review and an appeals process under the auspices of the director.

Note for Parents: If you are a parent, the Internet can create some special concerns. Parents alone have the right to exercise control over their children's viewing habits. But, the Internet is becoming inescapable—kids who are not Internet literate will be lost in the 21st century. Teaching and working with your child to make wise choices about the Internet and its Web options are simply among the most important things that a parent can do.

This facility is eager to work with you and has made every effort to help prepare the way for children and the Web. Using the unparalleled skills of professional staff, we have built in links to our own Kids Page to help guide children to the most age-appropriate sites. Please feel free to comment on this and other services.

NETIQUETTE

Libraries should reach out directly to their Web users—especially the children. Your patrons may need to be informed of the dangers, but they also need to be aware of their rights to privacy and safety. Our institutions need to work with parents and offer training—or even provide prepared written guidelines or contracts for their kids. For example, you may want to create something similar to the sample child's agreement shown here.

Figure 3–2: Sample Child's Agreement for Web Netiquette*

- I, ___________________, understand that the Internet is a great place to get information and have fun, but that I need to be careful and can go to my parents, teachers, or librarians for help.
- I will always act politely when communicating with others through e-mail or forms. Flaming others with insults—even if I was just flamed—spamming other sites with junk mail, and hacking into sites is just not right.
- I understand that I should not give out personal information—my address, my telephone number, my parents' work address/telephone number, the name and location of my school, or my photograph—without clearing it with my parents first.
- If I come across any sites that make me feel uncomfortable or seem too strange, I will inform my parents and the teacher or librarian.
- I am smart enough to realize that not everything I see on the Web is true. I need to question the sources and seek help from my parents and the teachers or librarians if necessary.
- I will never agree to get together with someone I "meet" online without first checking with my parents.
- I understand that the school and library may need to set up some rules for using the Web. I should also work out similar arrangements with my parents in regard to the time of day and how long I can stay online, as well as the areas that are okay for me to visit.

*Adapted from *Los Angeles Times* reporter Lawrence Magid's "Child Safety on the Information Highway"

INTERNET LITERACY STANDARDS

School and public libraries also share the new responsibility of ensuring that our children are prepared for the Information Age. Thus, ALA has published The Nine Information Literacy Standards for Student Learning [www.ala.org/aasl/ip_nine.html]. These information literacy standards also offer an opportunity to create a skill-building partnership between public schools and libraries.

Figure 3–3: The Nine Information Literacy Standards for Student Learning

Standard 1: The student who is information literate accesses information efficiently and effectively.

Standard 2: The student who is information literate evaluates information critically and competently.

Standard 3: The student who is information literate uses information accurately and creatively.

INDEPENDENT LEARNING

Standard 4: The student who is an independent learner is information literate and pursues information related to personal interests.

Standard 5: The student who is an independent learner is information literate and appreciates literature and other creative expressions of information.

Standard 6: The student who is an independent learner is information literate and strives for excellence in information seeking and knowledge generation.

SOCIAL RESPONSIBILITY

Standard 7: The student who contributes positively to the learning community and to society is information literate and recognizes the importance of information to a democratic society.

Standard 8: The student who contributes positively to the learning community and to society is information literate and practices ethical behavior in regard to information and information technology.

Standard 9: The student who contributes positively to the learning community and to society is information literate and participates effectively in groups to pursue and generate information.

Excerpted from Chapter 2 "Information Literacy Standards," in *Information Power: Building Partnerships for Learning.* Chicago: ALA and Association for Educational Communications and Technology, 1998, used with permission.

IN-HOUSE PRIVACY AND SAFETY RIGHTS

Similarly, libraries can act to help guard the privacy rights of their younger patrons. At the moment, Americans have little legal recourse regarding Web privacy violations. But public and school libraries may be able to play an interesting and little-explored role in protecting community values and individual rights from such abuses. Library records are already protected by privacy laws in most states. And librarians have been vigilant in their defenses—even challenging the FBI's attempted intrusions under the Library Awareness Program in the 1980s. In addition to educating children and parents, your virtual library can theoretically extend some protections by providing an extra layer of anonymity between the user and the Web. The cookies pile up against the virtual library's Internet address, not those of its patrons.

Cookies: Text files generated by a user's Web browser at the request of a visited site. Cookies can track what the user does when visiting the site and record it. The site may use this information the next time the user visits, for example to choose banner ads that fit the user's apparent interests.

Those offering in-house Web access also have internal responsibilities. Your Web policies should be set to employ "cookie cutter" software and eliminate patron history files from public browsers. Just as the institution does not typically tolerate onlookers harassing or interrupting its readers, you may need to consider privacy screens [www.mmm.com] or recessed desks [www.novadesk.com]. Terminals may be placed in such a way as to block accidental viewing by passersby, or screen timers (WebKiosk or Cooler, for example) may be installed to blank out screens and erase the history file of sites visited. In such a fashion, you help avoid offending passersby and subsequent users.

Staff Note: By helping to guarantee the physical privacy of your users, managers also alleviate a growing area of staff complaint. By eliminating the need to police Web use by adults, you help remove occasions when staff might feel insulted or outraged. Inappropriate Web searching by staff represents another problem. You may want to include a statement in your personnel policies regarding appropriate use of online time.

ADDITIONAL PROFESSIONAL ASSISTANCE

Following recommendations for its Intellectual Freedom Committee and other units, ALA has taken its own strong interest in promoting children's electronic services. ALA has gone from an initial listing of 50 great sites to a full-blown Librarian's Guide to Cyberspace for Parents and Kids [www.ala.org/parentspage/greatsites], which has expanded to some 700 entries. Similarly, ALA's American Association of School Librarians has a KidsConnect effort, which is underwritten by Microsoft and features direct student access to media specialists [AskKC@iconnect.syr.edu].

Carolyn Caywood maintains Guiding Children through Cyberspace [ww6.pilot.infi.net/^carolyn/guide.html]. The amount of individual library commitment is also expanding: for example, the New York

Public Library has A Safety Net for the Internet [www.nypl.org/branch/safety.html]; Pennsylvania's Delaware County libraries offer Kids Rules for Online Safety [www.libertynet.org/^delcolib/pweb.html]; and Oregon's Multnomah County Library has a Kids Page and related site for teens [www.multnomah.lib.or.us/lib/kids or /outer].

Jerry Kuntz from New York's Ramapo-Catskill Library System has taken an active role with his KidsClick! [sunsite.berkeley.edu/KidsClick!/]—a Library Service and Technology Act (LSTA)-funded project that Mid-Hudson endorsed. Kuntz's site is based on the SWISH-E search and database maintenance procedures developed by Roy Tennant at the Berkeley Sunsite. Kuntz maintains:

> KidsClick! is comprised of almost 1,800 records for Internet resources of interest to kids that have been selected, annotated and categorized by a team of librarians. KidsClick! aims to provide flexible and fast access to the best that the Internet has to offer kids of all ages. Records can be browsed in major categories, sub-categories, or specific subjects. Searches can be limited by a controlled subject vocabulary, reading level, and amount of illustrative material. Each record contains a descriptive (rather than evaluative) annotation; in many cases, these content notes were taken directly from the web sites themselves.

You will also find commercial alternatives for children's electronic resource services through companies like the SIRS Corporation [www.sirs.com] with its Discovery product.

PRESERVATION CONCERNS

A portion of your preservation concerns should be managed in conjunction with use policies and rules for patrons. Chapter 8 covers some of the technical aspects for protection using backups and a mirror site. To maintain your historical record, we recommend benchmark editions to capture major changes, that is, saving the site at various stages of development, and an annual download of the layout and internal content of your site. But be aware that the medium of the Web largely excludes traditional preservation concerns in its policy making. Unlike a book, which you purchase, own, and have the right to repair, the Web is a source from which data is borrowed.

Unlike a manuscript, digital products have no artifactual values. They only come alive when engaged by the operating system. Rather than caring for the original storage vehicle, electronic preservation thus

Digital Libraries and Archiving Note: The transformation of documents into digital formats for posting on the Web should not be confused with efforts to digitize statistical files, moving images, and audio recordings for preservation. Generally, under the provenance of national libraries and members of the Research Libraries Group (RLG), these expensive endeavors are currently working toward universal preservation formats.

engages an ongoing cycle of enhanced storage media—scheduling, refreshing, and transferring the data to increasingly compact and affordable platforms. But the Web is not designed as a preservation medium. It is a presentation or publication forum. Instead of physical care or restoration, preservation for external sites is altered to monitoring links and worrying that valuable locations will disappear. The technical alternative lies with expensive storage caches or major efforts like the Web Archives project [www.alexa.com].

END NOTES FROM MID-HUDSON

Since it does not serve patrons directly, Mid-Hudson is freed from direct concern for an AUP. MHLS merely provides reference materials for its members and an educational statement for parents in its special resources center for children. The MHLS Web site also avoids privacy policies by not collecting personally identifiable data. We have, however, been careful in considering copyright questions during site development and in the selection of materials. The site also includes the following (Figure 3–4) copyright disclaimer as part of a broad intellectual freedom introduction.

Figure 3–4: MHLS Intellectual Freedom Statement, excerpt

THE PUBLIC LIBRARY, COPYRIGHT, AND INTELLECTUAL FREEDOM

Users should be aware that information is made available as part of the long-established role of the library, which has more recently been codified under the "Fair Use" allowances within the 1976 Copyright Act [See: Stanford's Fair Use fairuse.stanford.edu; Intellectual Property, www.utsystem.edu/ogc/Intellectual Property/cprtindx.htm]. Like buying the books for our library shelves, this location makes a good faith effort to determine ownership, but cannot fully vouch for the reliability of sites to which it links. Individuals should also realize that they are bound by copyright law and must seek appropriate permission to make any substantive reproduction of materials found through this site. You are free, however, to use the ideas put forth by this particular site for non-profit purposes as long as proper recognition/citation is indicated.

4 VISUALIZING THE VIRTUAL LIBRARY

Linda Crow and Fred Stielow

With policy considerations in hand, you are ready for the nitty-gritty of the organization and design of an effective virtual library. Such efforts can be quite challenging, but we can build from a crucial observation. Rather than facing the chaos of a communications revolution, librarians and archivists begin with a real advantage. Virtual library development can flow naturally from established library and archival services. As the following discussion demonstrates, that base translates directly to one type of model for effective construction in cyberspace. Using the logic of systems analysis as a further check, this approach helps produce a blueprint of the functions and organizational structures for your virtual library.

THE LIBRARY METAPHOR

Although easily taken for granted today, the revolutionary contributions, conventions, and order wrought by libraries in the late 19th and 20th centuries still provide a powerful framework for organizing portions of the Web into virtual libraries. In particular:

- The daunting challenges of organizing human knowledge and facilitating browsing are already largely in hand.
- This context includes precedent for focusing or limiting the scope of the endeavor to manageable subsets, with interesting potential for you to highlight local or unique resources.
- Library functions naturally translate to a virtual library. Your patrons have learned at least some of the conventions for doing research in your institution. Instead of needing to reinvent conventions for navigation, they are prepared to look through an array of dedicated spaces—government documents, local history, reference, an information desk.

USING ESTABLISHED CONVENTIONS

Given the newness of the Web, we want to stress the last point. Marshall McLuhan and others have firmly established how a new communications medium must borrow formatting from its predecessor. The library metaphor can greatly enhance the power of the Web for browsing and navigation at a sophisticated level. In computerese, it facilitates "transparency" or "discoverability." We provide further examples of such transference later in this chapter in a discussion of general Web libraries. For now, note the readily comprehensible, yet intellectually robust features of the virtual reference desk model from the University of Michigan's Internet Public Library [www.ipl.org/ref/]:

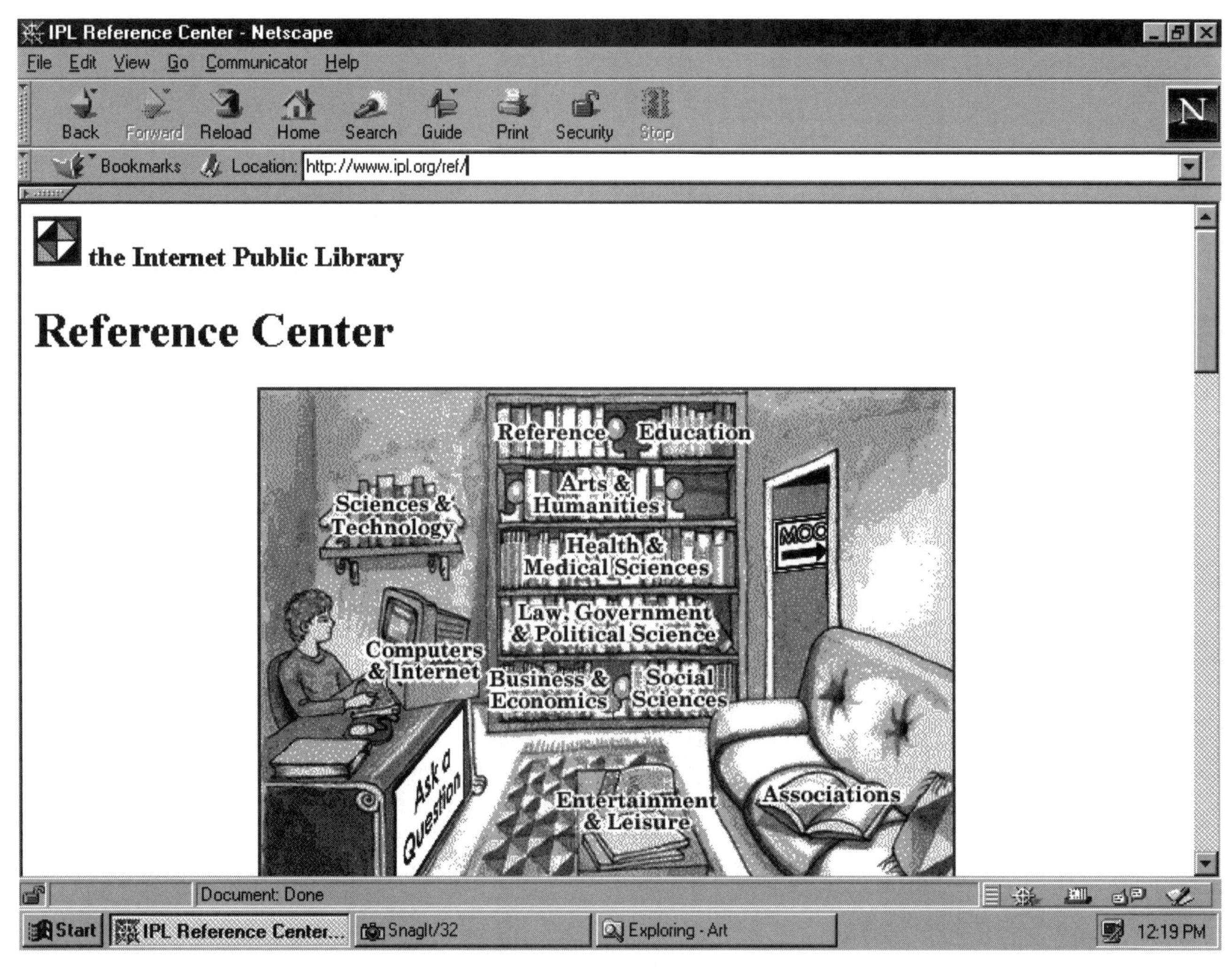

Figure 4–1: Internet Public Library Reference Desk

DESIGN TEAM

THREE DESIGN GUIDELINES

This chapter invites your Web team to act as virtual architects or interior designers. As you gather around the drawing board, you are reminded of several factors:

1. Since you are in cyberspace, initial design follows in a top-down fashion. This is in keeping with the hierarchical nature of the Web, which supplies your structural framework.
2. Navigation and traffic flow are among different levels or planes within the site and out to the Web.
3. Construction should be modular so that portions of the site can be easily expanded or contracted.

BUILDING MODEL

Your work will require a good deal of data gathering and analysis. Graphically, however, your problem set can be reduced to filling a very porous virtual library with three stories as depicted in Figure 4–2.

Figure 4–2: Virtual Library Design Framework

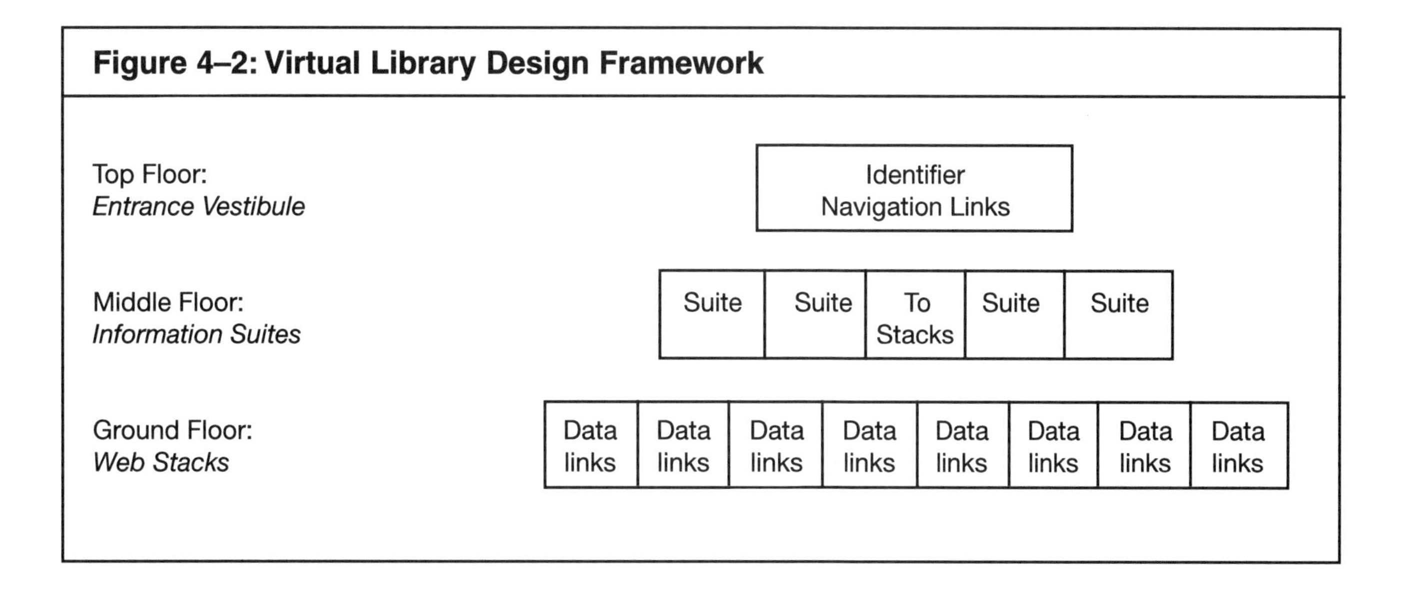

Three Types of Information for the Top Floor

The top floor represents the primary entranceway or vestibule into the virtual library. As described in the discussion on home page design in Chapter 1, you can conceive of three major blocks of information:

1. **Identifier**—Shows people where they are and who you are. With the exception of developing an aesthetically pleasing logo, the elements are straightforward. The institution's address information should be clearly displayed as follows:
   - Institution's name
   - Mailing address
   - Telephone and fax numbers (including area code)
   - E-mail address (optional)
2. **Narrative Introduction**—May introduce the institution as a whole and/or concentrate on the virtual library and use instructions. Text should be grammatically correct and readable. You are well advised to include policy information or a link to such, and an e-mail option.
3. **Navigation**—Set (as with elevator buttons) to provide navigation directly to the most important materials and to the functional clusters of links or "information suites" in the middle floor. Navigation is the most difficult element and requires some further discussion.

Initial Data Gathering for Navigation

Creating the navigation elements calls for special concentration. In effect, you will find that you are again reviewing the project's definition of its projected activities. You will also want to look at other virtual libraries and library Web sites. Do you see any patterns or similarities?

Traditional Library Service Areas

More important, your work calls for a concentration on your institution's current internal offerings. What particular range of information services does your institution provide for its users? These services help define familiar categories for your virtual library; they may include the following:

- book and serials catalog
- reference collection with quick ready-reference resources
- book stacks
- reserve collections
- government documents

- interlibrary loan
- magazine or newspaper reading room
- children's room
- teen or young adult area
- audiovisuals
- displays
- local history/genealogy room
- other special collections (e.g., business information, employment, grants, health, homework, and library information centers)

Sample Library Electronic Services

Your research should hone in on extant electronic features and those in the planning stage. You may need to be expansive and innovative in this section of the data gathering. In addition to formal resources and established services, what supplemental materials lie in electronic form within staff computers? Examples include:

- in-house online public access catalog
- other libraries' OPACs
- serials database, or union list of serials
- AV booking module
- magazine services (e.g., EBSCO, IAC, UMI)
- database services (e.g., Dialog, Westlaw)
- trial subscriptions
- CD-ROMs
- community/school/university information services
- Internet stations and their current uses—be sure to note their default start-up address
- bookmarked links to Web search engines and reference sites
- preexisting descriptive materials in electronic form (e.g., exhibit contents, finding aids, pathfinders)

In practical terms, your analysis focuses on the major functions and information resources that you want to display in the entrance or top floor. You may not need to think very hard about the inclusion of certain elements. As you look at other sites, you may notice that two direct links (or elevator buttons) are common on the top floor:

- an introductory narrative about the institution/site, which may extend to current hours, location, calendar, or board members
- access to the online catalog, as in Figure 4–3.

Figure 4–3: Introductory Screen Mock-Up

	Logo
About Institution	**Institution Name**
	Address
Online Catalog	The Sample Public Library is located in the heart of a gorgeous setting. Founded in 1892 by an association of local citizens, the library now contains 124,567 books and videos. The library offers state-of-the-art electronic access to its collections and the Web through this virtual library site. We invite your comments and participation.
Information Suite	
Information Suite	
Information Suite	
Information Suite	* Library Hours * Site Policies
	* Contact a Reference Librarian

The Middle Floor

Information Suites

The other major navigational elements on the top floor can be tied to the information suites one level below. This middle level serves as the main working area for public contact. Its "suites" are information collectives, or subject nodes. The decision to include them will flow in part from the type of institution and collections that you represent. For example, academic or school libraries would likely have homework centers and ties to specific courses or assignments. Public libraries should demonstrate their special interest in uncovering and sharing community information. Further discussion on these possibilities is held for Chapter 5.

For the moment, we need to concentrate on organizational structures. For ease of implementation and site continuity, we recommend modular construction with suites that correspond to the suites that can be reached from the top floor. Your task for each suite will include the following:

Four Steps to a Functional Middle Floor

1. Identify the suite through a descriptive and clearly understandable title and perhaps logo or other graphical devices.
2. Indicate main functional categories or services.
3. Provide instantaneous navigation to the appropriate information resources under those categories.
4. Provide electronic feedback or contact options (optional).

The Basement

The future effectiveness of your virtual library also calls for organization and categorization at the bottom level. In our model, the ground or basement floor contains a highly ordered set of rooms. These represent the building blocks or categories of information being sought. They are equipped with direct connections to information sites on the Web or to internally developed resources.

The library metaphor comes to the fore again to help organize these blocks. Established classification systems can provide coordinated development, browsing capacity, and the potential for ordered expansion.

Database Note: Classified virtual stacks also map as "data elements" within a database construct. The actual codes do not have to intrude or even be visible to the user within the various suites.

Virtual Stacks

The use of library classification can also be visualized as fostering virtual stacks. Powerful and flexible placeholders (which I will call buckets) contain a variety of sites on the same topic or assigned "shelving areas" to hold groups of Web selections and internally generated materials. Instead of reentering individual URLs for each suite, link to a shared resource in a separate directory. The results are thus more easily updated, partake of standardized vocabulary, and require less physical overhead. They can be reconstituted into an unlimited variety of other intermediate-level rooms or special resource centers (see Chapter 5 for a detailed discussion).

The actual construction of virtual stacks can be quite sparse and require a minimum amount of energy to maintain (see Chapter 7 for details). Classification codes and terms from printed authorities or the Web will spare you the burden of inventing and maintaining control terms and codes. This also directly applies to the database and metatagging approaches described in Part III. It can extend to hypertext concepts for duplicate listings or the cross-linkages with interactive "see" and "see also" references tied to the classification.

Label Notes: While labels can be as spare as the classification number, you are better off to embellish them to include an accompanying descriptive phrase—rather than 300, use 300 Social Sciences, for example. Although labels can provide an alternative search strategy in the basement, they do not need to appear per se within a special resources center. They can be replaced by terminology better suited to a particular audience. No one at the intermediate level needs to be exposed to your codes.

ITEM-LEVEL CONSIDERATIONS

Virtual libraries call us to examine and somewhat redefine traditional library methods. In particular, libraries have long sought control right down to specific materials and their locations. At least two parts of this item-level work may already be complete for your virtual library:

- Online databases include tagged fields along with enhanced field searching capacities.
- Because of MARC (Machine Readable Cataloging) protocols, the library world entered the electronic description scene at a

very early stage. Starting in the 1960s, libraries systematically began to build the largest reservoir of individually identifiable information in electronic form in the world. Today the Z39.50 protocol, with its HTML compliance for Web access, allows you to expand your virtual library with the contents of online catalogs around the world.

NAVIGATING FROM MARC RECORDS

DOI is a type of data element that can be embedded in a record to allow the user to travel automatically to that resource.

We have some good news and some bad news. MARC tagging structures are being expanded to include Web sites within extant bibliographic records. Tags, such as the 856 field, can be opened for DOI (digital object identifiers) to link automatically to related Web sites. The bad news is the impermanence of Web sites with an overall reported half-life of 45 to 78 days—hence, your added need for monitoring and database maintenance after implementation.

CATALOGING WEB SITES

A few brave souls have looked lovingly at bringing MARC cataloging across the Web. OCLC, with its Internet Cataloging Project [www.oclc.org/oclc/man/catproj/catcall.htm], took the lead and remains in the forefront. OCLC also stimulated efforts for a new virtual title page for Web pages. The Dublin Protocols [purl.org/metadata/dublin_core] provide a special set of tags added to HTML that could be applied to such purposes. In addition, OCLC's NetFirst is available for subscribers through its FirstSearch services [gilligan.prod.oclc.org:3052]. NetFirst now contains over 100,000 listings of Web sites. In late 1998 OCLC announced a CORC initiative (Cooperative Online Resource Catalog) [www.oclc.org/oclc/research/projects/corc/]. CORC intends to automate HTML page production for library portal sites. It hopes to mix local and national records, as well as facilitate link maintenance and support metadata creation.

Some products are beginning to appear to help those interested in doing MARC cataloging of Web sites. OCLC has made available Cataloging Internet Resources: A Manual and Practical Guide [www.purl.org/oclc/cataloging-internet], which is aimed at less-experienced catalogers, and Nichols Advanced Technologies markets a rudimentary and low-cost MARCit module [www.marcit.com].

ITEM-LEVEL ANALYSIS AND WARNING

For the present, the bulk of our readership should, however, shy away from the item-level cataloging of Web sites. The extra time and effort is not fully justifiable, for the following reasons:

- The library does not own most of the Web sites it lists. There is no analogy to the purchase of a book.
- In a related sense, you face the bad news of impermanence. Thus ongoing monitoring is required, and internal controls for weeding are lost.
- MARC itself is best suited for describing published materials that have clear titles and authorship.
- The bulk of the Web simply does not follow a title-page convention, nor are there "publisher-supplied cataloging" and shared bibliographic databases.
- The addition of sites as distinct entries now demands labor-intensive original cataloging. Unless some method appears to reconvert the hundreds of millions of sites already in existence, complete cataloging is practically impossible.
- In keeping with archival appraisal and information science guidelines, not every site is worth the time and money for its cataloging.

Catalog Resources Note: The January 1998 issue of *American Libraries* included the following list of resources for organizing the Internet:

- Dublin Core Home Page [purl.oclc.org/dc]
- Foundations Project [bridges.state.mn.us]
- Minnesota Metadata Guidelines [bridges.state.mn.us/metadata.html]
- Content Standards for Geospatial Metadata [www.mews.org/nsdi/revis497.pdf]
- UK Office for Library and Information Networking [www.ukoln.ac.uk]
- OCLC CORC Project [www.oclc.org/oclc/research/projects/corc]
- Coalition for Networked Information [www.cni.org]

ORGANIZATION FOR GENERAL WEB LIBRARIES: 19TH-CENTURY REMNANTS

Finally, your data gathering on the Web may alert you to a dirty little secret—library classification disciplines are remarkably well established on the Web. Many of the Web's technological gurus and most of the leading general Web libraries and portals knowingly, or unwittingly, resort to the library order to ease browsing. Netscape, for instance, comes equipped with a library-like taxonomy for Web resources under its bookmarking options:

- Search
- Directories
- Banking and Finance
- Business Resources
- Computers and Technologies
- Education
- Entertainment
- General News
- Hobbies and Lifestyles
- Local Information
- Shopping
- Sports
- Travel and Leisure

Newer start-ups are also following in this direction. For example, Northern Light [www.northernlight.com] attempts to bridge between a search engine and a commercial library. It features special collections in news, current events, public affairs, business, finance, science, technology, health, medicine, social science, education, arts, humanities, recreation, and lifestyle. The major search engines and leading ISPs, like AOL, offer similar library-like organizational structures. Their ultimate goal is to be your single, all-encompassing portal site—to lock you in and get as much of the advertising dollar as possible with a combination of searching, content, e-mail, chat rooms, shopping, and other services.

NONPROFIT COMPARISONS

Many nonprofit organizations and libraries employ similar patterns. The leading general Web libraries often rely on adaptations of the Library of Congress classification scheme for their browsing. For example, the Argus Clearing House for Subject-Oriented Internet Resource Guides [www.clearinghouse.net/] provides an alphabetic listing of related headings, while the WWW Virtual Library [www.w3.org/hypertext/DataSources/bySubject/LibraryOfCongress.html] borrows even more directly, with the following scheme of categories:

- Agriculture
- Auxiliary Science of History
- Bibliography, Library Science
- Education
- Fine Arts
- General Works
- Geography, Anthropology, Recreation
- History, America
- History, General and Old World
- Language and Literature
- Law
- Medicine
- Music and Books on Music
- Philosophy, Psychology, and Religion
- Political Science
- Science
- Social Science
- Technology

END NOTES FROM MID-HUDSON

Following is a quick overview of Mid-Hudson's thoughts and decision making to give more in-depth examples. Please remember that each situation is different and requires individual treatment. Because of the cooperative nature of the MHLS, for example, the MHLS home page did not open directly into a virtual library. Rather, our model had to be a level or click below. It was designed for entry through the Mid-Hudson Library System [midhudson.org] or through the home pages of our independent member libraries. Most important, Mid-Hudson is primarily a service bureau and not a library. With the exception of electronic services, we lacked the comfort of established areas to help define our project. Fortunately, we still had general library theory and practical experience to help build our structures and interfaces.

ELECTRONIC RESOURCES LIBRARIES

The primary purpose for establishing electronic resources connections was to localize and provide one-stop shopping for MHLS's catalogs and databases. This practical measure was intended to facilitate the addition of new services, but could assist our smaller libraries without DOS or Windows-based menu managers, such as CARL's Site Builder. The goal was to include the full range of electronic information resources within a single, information-driven Web interface. We worked at the same structural and functional examinations discussed earlier in this chapter. First we surveyed to identify the electronic resources then available to us. They included:

- FASTCAT, an online GEAC catalog system, not HTML-compliant
- an area serials list, which was scheduled for HTML access
- a magazine database, which promised HTML access
- a CD-ROM tower of databases, which were not HTML-compliant
- the Mid-Hudson home page with links to its operations and 65 member library sites
- Video Health Information (VHIP), a site directed by MHLS
- access to the general resources on the Web

To that list, we added several desirable components. Theoretically, these components were all intended to be viewed separately from within the general Web library. Equally important, we were planning for future flexibility to tailor specific subsets for our region. Thus, we also prepared for:

- an area to mount trial HTML databases from vendors
- links to other key libraries or area library systems
- a limited general Web library with a ready-reference subset
- access to Web search engines
- "white," or mediated, sites for children and perhaps teens
- parental information on intellectual freedom
- a librarian's page of useful professional information on the Web
- the facility to add other special sites such as grants as the need arose

We determined to try to incorporate the bulk of these two groups, with a few exceptions. Since Mid-Hudson's home page was already one level up, the virtual library page only needed a return button to it. The CD-ROM tower was a balky piece of equipment and raised some potential copyright and licensing questions. We eliminated it for the first stage and focused on the free resources of the Web. Since the serials database was not really ready, we also chose to ignore it for the first go-around. Still, the number of resources was far too large for display without some further breakdown. We settled on three large categories with subsets that could potentially be shoehorned onto a single browser screen:

- Mid-Hudson's electronic resources (FASTCAT, Video Health Information Project [VHIP], Web site magazine database, trial databases), which could be somewhat logically linked to other libraries and their resources
- general Web resources—a general Web library along with a ready-reference collection and search engines
- special services tied to local resources (e.g., librarian's page, children and teens areas)

CONSIDERATIONS ON DEWEY CLASSIFICATION AND THE WEB

The Dewey Decimal Classification System (DDC) provided a ready-made solution for the internal sections of Mid-Hudson's virtual library. Evolving with professional oversight since 1876, DDC is a flexible and extremely adaptable choice for the modern era. Although DDC was conceived with the purpose of organizing books, it can fit an online library. You can browse the "shelves" by scrolling and clicking instead of walking. As the most widely used cataloging system in the world, it is universally recognized. DDC also helped MHLS plan for the future. The system provides content buckets that allow content integration in our electronic resources library. The taxonomy even ac-

Figure 4–4: Dewey Decimal Main Summary of Categories

000	Generalities
100	Philosophy & Psychology
200	Religion
300	Social Sciences
400	Language
500	Natural Sciences & Mathematics
600	Technology & Applied Sciences
700	The Arts
800	Literature & Rhetoric
900	Geography & History

commodates some local customization for subjects not provided for in the schedules.

Dewey also has preexisting rules and explanations to help work through some of the tricky organizational problems of the Web. With ten major categories, Dewey exceeds our rule of seven choices; yet it can map to a single-screen frame, and it is reportedly easier for people to intuit than most other systems.

Unlike many of the commercial models on the Web, the DDC hierarchy is infinitely expandable and depends on real experts for its maintenance. Each major class or discipline can be divided into subclasses that are conceptually linked. Elements can be further subdivided to go from the general to the more specific—for example, the 500s, one of the main ten categories, which has the subdivision Mathematics, has a subdivision Geometry, which in turn has a subdivision Analytic Geometries. It is a framework that readily extends beyond the prepared categories found with typical portals.

Rather than using item-level or individual descriptions for each site, we chose to use the Dewey numbers as buckets or collective virtual shelf-location symbols for our visitors and for data entry. In particular, we wanted to try to increase user satisfaction by offering visible alternatives to search engine access. Dewey's conceptual categories alleviate the frustration naive users have with keyword matching and its annoying "zero hits" from simple spelling errors. We also supplied an alphabetical list of topics for those who do not understand Dewey. By supplying multiple access points we hope to maximize users' chances to find what they need. In addition, as the implementation described in Chapter 9 demonstrates, the Dewey framework allows for metatagging.

GENERAL WEB LIBRARY

With the Dewey model in hand, a portion of Mid-Hudson's time and energy turned to building a prototype for a general Web library. Given a finite staff and the reality of our resources, we needed to reach a workable compromise on its potential scope and size. We knew that no one could even begin to examine or classify every site on the Web; furthermore, our users would be overwhelmed if we succeeded. So, this portion of the project was intended more as a training device to provide the technical wherewithal for the construction of special resources centers.

We initially came to a reasonably comprehensive number of sites for the typical patron in our region. In our calculations, Mid-Hudson's general Web library would begin with around 1,000 selections. Ideally, it would be limited to about 10,000 sites—still a significant figure. With our design guidelines in mind, we also opted against long lists that would require scrolling through screen after screen—a practice that only a computer could enjoy. Instead, we opted for the postcard screen or a Miller Number selection limit of seven choices. As we found to our chagrin, even these guidelines were not simple enough. Unlike books, Web sites are so ephemeral that over 40 percent of our seemingly well-chosen selections vanished within a few months, leaving significant gaps in coverage. Moreover, our member libraries did not yet have the expertise to come to our rescue.

SPECIAL RESOURCES COLLECTIONS

More important, analysis pointed to some unique prospects for the cyber-librarian or information entrepreneur. Just as in special library collections, we envisioned subdividing our virtual library into sections tailored for more advanced and localized use. Indeed, we believe that selecting such sites will emerge as a basic part of modern collection development for librarians and archivists. Our opportunities surfaced largely from grant initiatives in the health, employment, and education areas. In addition, we needed to respond to our own continuing education mission for member librarians and to our proactive stance to help children and teens get to the materials that they needed.

FINAL ADMISSIONS

Our design motif began with the image of a card catalog in a reference room. The first view was a cabinet with a set of nine drawers. Ideally, one would click on the familiarly titled drawer and virtually pull out files with key listings and additional tabs for more navigation.

No attractive picture should deny some false starts and mistakes. The proposed design construct was itself technically ambitious, and we had no adequate model. The closest immediate inspiration came from an information table or button grid (now replaced) within the University of Michigan's Internet Public Library. Our prototype has undergone several design changes and may never be finished.

While a Dewey database discipline still seems right, the thoughts of maintaining a general Web library were far too ambitious. Even the selection of appropriate numbers proved problematic. We erred on the side of simplicity by limiting Dewey's potential. At the start, we used only whole number references (for example, 281 for Eastern Orthodox churches, not 281.9, or 281.947 to indicate churches in Russia). For the all-important local differentiations, we tried to keep to natural language or mnenomic codes, rather than adding on the geographic extender (thus 917 Geography & Travel, North America for New York became 917-NY). The expanding nature of the Web and our interests, however, soon called for redress and a stricter set of classification protocols. We had to go back to our DDC manuals and true library roots.

5 BUILDING VIRTUAL LIBRARY SUITES

Joshua Cohen, Susan Hauserman, Mary Keelan, and Fred Stielow

The system must be designed to operate for each possible selection, not just the one which will actually be chosen, since this is unknown at the time of design.

—Claude Shannon, "The Mathematical Theory of Communication"

Turning from the in-house concentration of Chapter 4, this chapter focuses on adding external data from Web resources, and increasing the audience. The goal is to complete the planning for your vestibule (top floor)—to project an initial set of virtual library rooms of "information suites." This chapter stresses simplification and reducing the amount of in-house labor needed for your installation and maintenance. While your planning should look out in a broad and all-encompassing manner, the chapter strongly recommends that newcomers not bite off more than they can chew and certainly avoid reinventing the wheel. The first parts of your virtual library should be easily erected and kept to a manageable set.

SPECIAL RESOURCES COLLECTIONS

The range of information suites is limitless. However, the true opportunities for most archives and libraries rest with their unique strengths for tailoring portions of the Web for their patrons and locale. The current climate is favorable to a new brand of information entrepreneurship—one that actively markets and opens windows through electronic access and also unlocks doors into community networking. The window of opportunity for nonprofits, however, may be limited. Should libraries and archives falter in their quest for localization, active commercial interests will be more than willing to install fee-based services.

OPPORTUNITIES

To meet the challenge, libraries and archives can call on their particular talents, scholarship, and experiences in collection development and outreach. Such skills reflect on current service areas and should take extra note of experiences with special collections. Additional incentives may arise at any moment from one or more of the following:

- tourism and economic development offices
- area entrepreneurs and civic leaders
- interested college students and professors
- an eager teacher or school administrator
- people searching for jobs
- a special holiday or event
- a change in community demographics
- local history or community clubs
- the opportunity to network with a nonprofit or for-profit organization
- a grant application

Each item on the above list could be the subject of a Web site. The key is to identify the appropriate area by considering what changes are occurring and what questions people are asking. Equally important, such determinations point the way for making bridges out to the community and for sharing resources.

Your traditional library outreach skills will help you add the specifics. Suppose a library responded to a groundswell of interest by establishing a chess club. A Web page devoted to chess would enhance the club and increase the activity's visibility. What if your community is experiencing an influx of an ethnic group? A Web site on that culture might be of interest. Librarians in particular have long practice with targeting special collections for specific clientele. They regularly organize print and archival collections on particular subjects and in dedicated spaces (for example, the local history room). Their experience extends to art and multimedia, as well as to the marketing and reference functions behind creating a display, bibliography, or pathfinder for an event or program. Whether it is Banned Books Week, Black History Month, or a researcher's interest in fly fishing, librarians must locate, organize, and present a list of resources to meet the need.

WEB RESOURCES

Instead of going off to conquer the world, start small. A survey of virtual libraries and library home pages suggests some realistic limits and a couple of default options for your vestibule.

ELECTRONIC RESOURCES CONNECTIONS

This integrative facility is extremely important and should be automatically included on a Web site. If you only have a single resource, you may wish to link to it directly from the vestibule; with multiple resources, an information suite is in order. The technological matters are presented at the close of Chapter 8. Your main managerial problems will lie with securing the funds to bring in these resources and the public's annoying tendency to think that everything available through the Web is free.

QUICK WEB

Library and archival sites tend to provide access to standard Web search engines, which is especially useful for their in-house users, as the seach engines tend to be familiar and speed up contact and downloading. Web search engines could stand alone as a suite or be combined with other Web resources, which may include a range of ready reference and library or portal sites from the Free Web.

READY REFERENCE

The Ramapo-Catskill (N.Y.) Library System (RCLS) addresses standard reference questions with a visual gallery in its DeskRef area [ansernet.rcls.org/deskref/] as shown in Figure 5–1.

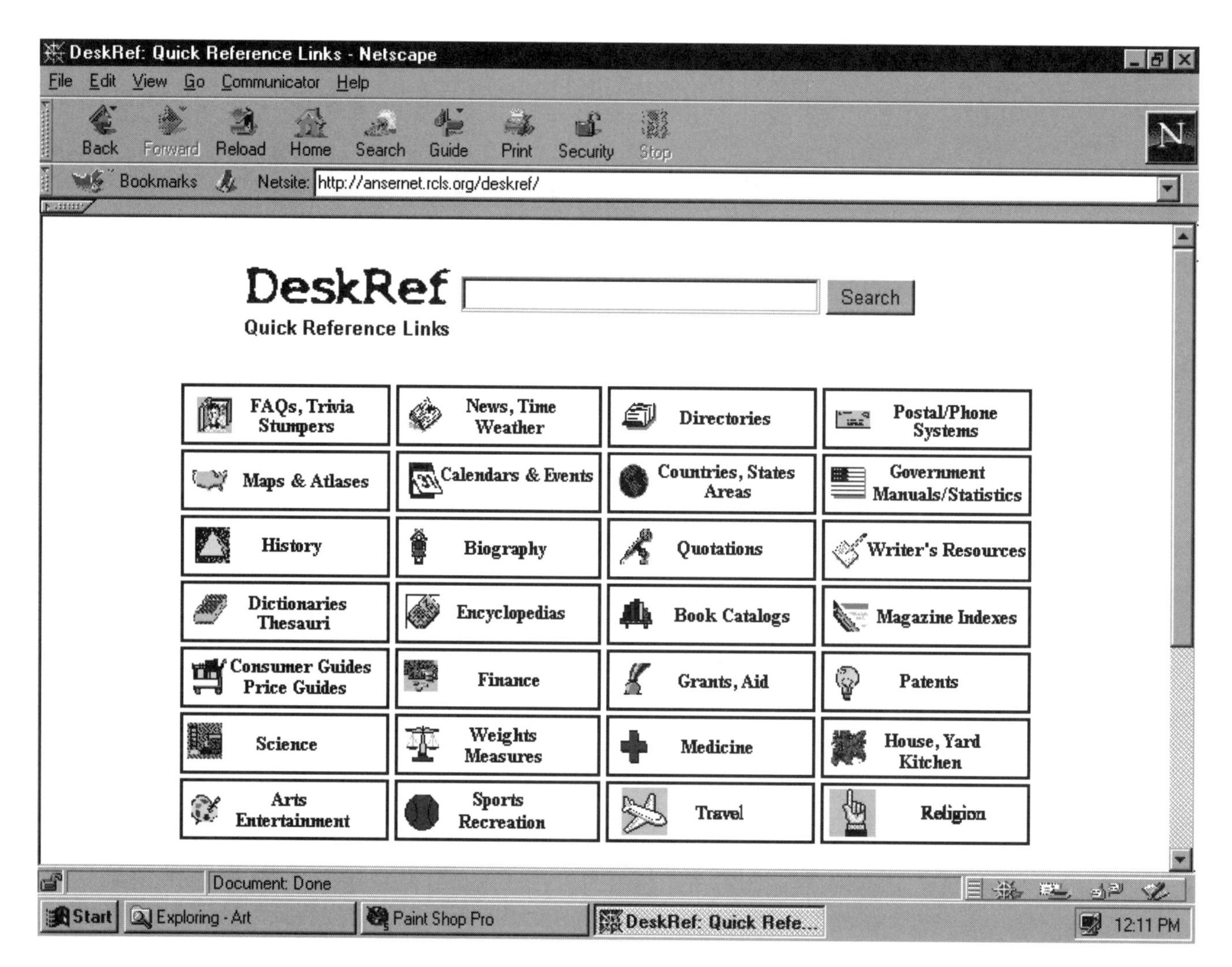

Figure 5–1: DeskRef Icons, Ramapo-Catskill Library System

Thanks to RCLS and similar sites, most other repositories can save money and do not need to build their own ready reference sites. If electronic ready reference is needed in your community, the simplest method is to create a link to an established site.

MAJOR LIBRARY LINKS

Similar approaches are applicable should your analysis reveal a need to include national portal sites, which may require a fee for subscription. Equally important, in your external data gathering you should have encountered related free library or archival sites for possible inclusion—like the Library of Congress [www.loc.gov] or the National Archives [www.nara.gov]. You may also want to link to major academic libraries—especially those within your region.

Figure 5–2: Sample Web Default Suite

Quick Web	**Introduction to Quick Web**
Area College	*Welcome to the Sample Library's Quick Web resource center. Just Click on a selection in the left-hand column to go directly to the site or a list of options.*
Library of Congress	
Ready Reference	**Web Search Engines—Sample List**
Web Search Engines	* Alta Vista * Excite * Lycos
Web Portals America Online Microsoft.com	* Magellan * Yahoo * Others

Alternate Resource Note: Private ventures have appeared on the scene in Ohio and elsewhere and are marketing their abilities to maintain individual virtual libraries—albeit for hefty fees.

WEB SUBJECT LIBRARIES

Despite its newness, the Web is already so well developed that any library would think twice about launching a broad Web subject collection. Indeed, other librarians have collated their own mediated lists to most conceivable topics in general Web libraries as Infomine [lib-www.vcr.edu/Main.html] and the Librarian's Index to the Internet [sunsite.berkely.edu/InternetIndex]. Simple identification and linking will likely solve any internal need for the extra level of specificity beyond commercial search engines.

FOUR KEY AUDIENCE FACTORS

Library collection development studies demonstrate that audience factors are crucial to your task. In our model, very few institutions plan to design for every potential user. Your virtual library should be built to consider the following points:

1. In-house patrons and staff will use the site repeatedly.
2. The site offers a venue for remote use by that same clientele.
3. Individual information suites can be fine-tuned to reflect special clientele.
4. Any service to other general users emerges as an extra benefit.

Collection development techniques also call for community analysis and an awareness of specific factors to help hone portions of the site. The results of a community analysis should also help determine the appropriate terminology and necessary navigational aides for the virtual library. The planners can then tailor for specific audiences within the general user base. Ask yourself these five questions.

1. **Age:** Is this a site designed for teens, kids, adults, or users of any age?
2. **Computer Literacy:** Will your primary users be computer literate or will the site need to be accessible at the simplest levels?
3. **Reading Level:** Are most of the users good readers or should the vocabulary be simple?
4. **Specialized Terminology or Searching Strategies:** Does the target group have a unique vocabulary that should be employed to facilitate interaction?
5. **Physical Needs:** If the target group specifies physically challenged members or non-English speakers, does the site provide suitable alternatives or adaptive technologies for them?

Survey Notes: Any community study will likely uncover that your patrons have come to expect access to the Web as a normal library service. It is also highly likely that many will overestimate what is available for free and may be confused by the interplay with fee-based online systems. As a result, your collection development leads beyond materials to the importance of providing supplemental online and written guides.

The makeup of the target group may inform every aspect of your site from choosing content to creating categories for that content. Despite featuring the same topic, for instance, a site designed for a comic book study group should be different from one for comic book artists. A determination of the target group also defines the parameters for a directed marketing strategy, networking with other community groups, and other buy-ins necessary to see that the site is actually used.

Web Support: The Web itself can help with data gathering. You can use its monitoring capacities to determine actual use patterns for both the initial topic selections and later fine-tuning of the site.

CHILDREN AND SAFE SITE

The creation of a special resources center for children should take priority over all age groupings and extant services. Given the legislative and professional issues discussed in Chapter 3, such a facility is a practical necessity and another realm of opportunity for public and school libraries. Public and school libraries have the duty, opportunity, and skills to ensure an unbiased, but sensitive attention to local community needs while still protecting the rights of the individual users. This positive approach also offers the library's best technical, professional, and ethical response to filtering. Instead of censoring, deferring to inappropriate external agents, or usurping parental prerogatives, librarians extend their proactive collection development to the Web through mediated sites. No better settings, guides, or software exist for the productive orientation of Web users.

A "Kids Page" can incorporate subject or curriculum-based sites, non-English language sites, and community-based local resources. It might also be used to enhance deficiencies in a library collection. For example, a library without space for a large geography collection could connect to the CIA Fact Book. A children's Web page offers libraries a practical tool for accomplishing one of the most fundamental services of our profession: to provide access, organization, and easy-to-retrieve information in a manner that the client can handle. Such creations can serve as a foundation for Internet information and evaluation skills instruction for the youngest patrons. In addition, a children's Web page:

- Offers novice users (from children to grandparents) a starting point to learn technical and intellectual skills for the Web.
- Can provide guidance on resources to assist users to find needed information quickly and efficiently, as with homework help and high-interest topics.
- Forces librarians to stay current on information resources available on the Internet, to improve information retrieval skills, and to monitor trends in this rapidly changing environment.
- Provides users the ability to move freely about in keeping with their information needs, but follow only selected links to avoid exposure to materials that they would choose to avoid.
- Opens the prospects for networking with parents and schools, as well as with granting agencies.

Downloading Option: WebWacker and other software packages offer the possibility of downloading an entire suite of sites within your computer. Those with highly protective instincts could thus allow children or restricted classes of users (such as convicts) to play in the browser environment—but be blocked from access to the Web. If this somewhat suspect approach is taken, you should make certain to notify and gain copyright permission from the downloaded sites.

COMMUNITY INFORMATION CENTER

Most public libraries should feature some sort of community information on their virtual libraries—the community must be a primary focus. The suite can be quite flexible and expansive. It should be a marketing agent that reflects the library's potential as a cultural resource center and portal to the entire community. Featured items might include:

- a calendar of local and library events
- local history background and resources
- tourism information
- links to the local government site
- information on area business nonprofit organizations
- special information services (e.g., community health, employment, hobbies, homework, social services)

As a manager, you want to link to extant resources and try to avoid creating or maintaining such resources on your own. National resources (such as the community pages distilled by Microsoft and Yahoo) may offer some content. More important, you should be aware of the opportunities to use your Web site listings to meet community needs and to build or reinforce networking prospects within your community.

FOUR PRACTICAL IMPLEMENTATION FACTORS

Once you reach consensus on the initial set of information suites, you can add technological enhancements. Based on the data gathered to date, your analysis should point to four categories of enhancement: Free Web, internally developed content, internally developed interactive services, and private services/electronic resource library.

FREE WEB

This rapidly expanding universe can be roughly divided between content sites and search engines. Technically it is the simplest enhancement. After identifying the site, you use a Web editor to grab the address (URL) and place a corresponding anchor to link it in your site. Such approaches are in keeping with the managerial ideal of minimizing internal staff and time commitments.

INTERNALLY DEVELOPED CONTENT

In addition to the introductory narrative, this category includes any special databases, digital archives, or descriptive information that you will need for the site. With a Web editor, this enhancement can be almost as easy as linking to the Free Web, but it does demand considerable thought. Anything currently in the electronic hopper should certainly be considered ripe fodder. Exhibit material, for example, is of great interest and comes ready for mounting. While database conversion can be complex, word processing text is readily converted from a number of standard programs into HTML. Your major consideration will be the creation of digital archives, which can demand considerable resources.

INTERNALLY DEVELOPED INTERACTIVE SERVICES

Such services include electronic reference services or interactive forms. These implementations range from the inclusion of e-mail addresses to the more complex inclusion of interactive forms. More important, you should remember that such a presence calls for constant monitoring and a never-ending staff commitment.

Easiest First: An automation rule of thumb is to tackle the easiest applications first and delay the most difficult problems. Your knowledge and the available software and hardware applications will likely improve during the project.

PRIVATE SERVICES/ELECTRONIC RESOURCES LIBRARY

These resources are partially differentiated by licensing agreements and may include both HTML and non-HTML coded materials from your CD-ROMs and online catalog to fee-based commercial databases. Implementation can run the gamut from creating simple anchors to

Packing More Links: As your site expands, it will become apparent that there are design restraints on the number of initial navigation buttons you can have. As Chapter 8 describes, there are alternative methods (e.g., "pull-down" menus) for adding or "packing" more links on the screen.

working with complex communications protocols. Unlike the other selections, these resources offer the luxury of letting others do your maintenance and updating. In addition they offer item-level retrieval and greater controls than any of the other factors.

TOWARD SOLUTIONS

From the analysis to this point, we can project what may become the normal or default set of suites for a public library's presence on the Web. For example:

Figure 5–3: Public Library Introductory Screen Mock-Up

About the Institution **Online Catalog** **Community Events** **Kids Room** **Magazines Online** (in-library use only) **Quick Web**	**Logo** **Institution Name** **Address** The Sample Public Library is located in the heart of a gorgeous setting. Founded in 1892 by an association of local citizens, the library now contains 124,567 books and videos. The library offers state-of-the-art electronic access to its collections and the Web through this virtual library site. We invite your comments and participation. *Library Hours *Site Policies *Contact a Reference Librarian

STREAMLINING SUITE DEVELOPMENT: MANAGEMENT HINTS

Designing for Teachers: Our survey of educational resources suggests that teachers, as an audience, respond well to a grid or matrix designs.

The information suites or special resources centers are ripe arenas for the modularization and simplification of your overall virtual library project. Continuity, integration, and simplicity should become the bywords for Web project management. As Chapter 1 suggests, you can begin by limiting the number of design options for the team. In particular, we are led to the split-screen model (Figure 5–3). Such default removes a good deal of time and conjecture, as well as interminable meetings discussing minor design features. As a result, too, you bring more continuity to the overall site and provide fundamental frameworks, which are familiar and easily mounted by your technical staff.

THREE QUESTIONS FOR DETERMINING THE OPENING IMAGE

With a classification discipline and single design model, the most rigorous portion for team analysis is determining the elements on the opening screen. This work includes identifying the appropriate language levels and a simple set of organizational questions for the suite. Consider the following:

1. What identifying/graphic information needs to present?
2. What are the major functions—what terms should be set in place for the left-hand navigation buttons and what coordinating classification numbers apply or need to be opened for them?
3. What opening information should appear by default in the right-hand screen? Do you need to produce any introductory narrative or directional material? Should you include a functional category and its operative links?

Design Note—Directional and Information Links: While it is important to maximize the navigation within your site through set buttons, you should relinquish screen control as soon as the user ventures outside the site. External sites should paint across the entire screen and not be relegated into a partial screen or frame. Any internally generated content, however, can be designed to fit within your right-hand frame with the navigation side intact.

NOTES FROM MID-HUDSON

Mid-Hudson employed a default design screen and three questions for building its information suites. The opportunities and demands for MHLS's special resources centers emanated from three sources:

- One set of questions was almost unavoidable. It occurred with the creation of the original home page and such logical features as a librarian's section and Web suite. Similarly, advocacy and the need to request state funds made a listing of political links natural—and incidentally a well-received marketing flourish. We felt it necessary to have a Kids Page, which quickly branched off to teen and parent offshoots.
- A second arena arose rather deliberately from our financial and institutional nature. Like many other nonprofits, MHLS sought new ways to attract funds for previous projects and to gain a competitive edge for other grant initiatives.
- A third area emerged organically in response to local library needs and the approaches of outside agencies, which are being attracted by our newfound expertise.

The rest of this chapter illustrates actual MHLS implementations and a pragmatic framework. It begins with the activities surrounding our Kids Page. Next comes a treatment of a video program that began prior to the current schema. Following an insert on a service site for librarians, the discussions retreat to briefer listings of some of the special resources centers that Mid-Hudson has erected over the past year and a half.

MAKING THE KIDS ROOM AND ADJUNCTS

Mid-Hudson's responsibilities to children were clear. According to the most recent statistics, the system serves a total population of just over 574,000, with 269,000 registered cardholders. Recent studies indicate that three out of five public library users are children or young adults; thus an estimated 162,000 young people use the services of member libraries in the Mid-Hudson Library System area. Youth needs are clear, and MHLS specialists already provide services in conjunction with a children's services committee and wide participation by every member library.

With the onset of information sharing and communication via electronic media, the Mid-Hudson Library System is changing into a more active electronic information intermediary, and even a producer of Internet services for its member libraries. MHLS sponsored an ongoing series of Internet workshops and cosponsored a Putnam/Northern Westchester Counties School Library System grant to help "Log on with Your Family." We also posited that a children's page could become a vital service both to young patrons and to member librarians, who were just beginning to provide Internet information services.

As a first step for our site, our children's specialist was assigned development responsibility. She followed from management guidelines to define a target audience: 7- to 12-year-old children in the MHLS service area (the range of children who could read on their own, but were younger than the intended users of the Teens' Corner). We then listed subject areas we thought would interest this age group, in conjunction with the services we and member libraries provide to young patrons. We wanted to provide the traditional information services of a public library—to promote reading and literacy, provide access to local community resources, and help to meet homework and educational information needs. About 15 broad areas were identified as being of potential interest.

Following from the system's site development rules, the next and most difficult step was to narrow these areas into seven or eight categories—a scientifically predetermined limit for design and utility purposes. We envisioned our Kids Page to contain a series of pages with all information appearing on a single screen—no scrolling, no paging down required at least until the piloting was completed—and with a limited number of clicks or selections needed to reach information. As Web users know, it is easy to spend time trailing from link to link to link without reaching actual information. Children have little tolerance for endless selection, especially if their time is limited by computer use sign-up, homework deadlines, or the need to keep to a schedule or to be home for dinner. Ultimately, eight categories were decided on and fit into appropriate Dewey sequence, but with a special "—kids" extension on the numbers. Selecting any category would lead a user to a list of hyper-linked sites; a selection from that list would take a user to a site containing information.

Exceptions to category lists included LOOKOUT and an area FOR PARENTS ONLY. LOOKOUT initially took users to an electronically published version of *Child Safety on the Information Highway*. This much-noted brochure, describing the risks of online and electronic communication and how parents and children could responsibly minimize those risks, was the model for the section on netiquette in Chapter 4. FOR PARENTS ONLY originally led to a statement on access and intellectual freedom, which was prepared as part of the general introduction to Mid-Hudson's home page. These two areas were intended to address issues of education about electronic media and communication via the Web and issues of intellectual freedom.

As you can see, we found a number of functional choices based on what the staff had determined might most interest kids. LOCAL STUFF is the area where children can find information unique to the Hudson Valley. We believe that it is very important to lead children to their local public library, so here we linked to member library Web pages for children. In the future, with more staff time, we will include information about library programs for children. We also linked to local newspapers and information about Hudson Valley sporting events. We also plan to link to local organizations such as recreation departments, scouts, museums, nature centers, and theaters. The other categories dealt with all-important homework and recreational needs. The sites themselves were primarily assembled from reviews in professional journals, favorite picks by kids via Internet projects like K.I.D.S. (Kids Identifying and Discovering Sites), and Internet training sessions for librarians being conducted at Mid-Hudson. In all cases, we made a conscious decision to avoid any forceful disclaimer—*You Are Now Leaving the Kids Page*—in favor of not overly intruding on users' voyages around the Web. We also tried to be aware of technological issues in sites selected for inclusion, such as Web browser requirements and load time for hypertext links. Lengthy document files and large image files take a significant time to load. Many people become impatient if they must wait more than a few seconds, and their frustration is directed at the home site, not the site being loaded. We wanted the Mid-Hudson page to be a convenient point-of-access tool for Web resources that patrons would return to time and again.

The next phase in developing the Kids Page involved librarians' review of the page, solicitation of "wish lists" of types of sites young patrons wanted and needed, and training librarians to use the Internet for youth services. We conducted a series of Internet training sessions called "HotHits," covering a variety of topics requested by member librarians, including children's authors and illustrators, homework helpers, parents and preschoolers, and home schooling resources. Several member librarians volunteered to work with kids to evaluate our site.

We developed paper evaluation forms, using some of the great Web site evaluation forms available online. Very few evaluation forms were returned, however; librarians reported that kids preferred to vote with their mouse buttons. Furthermore, young users like to surf the Net, but don't want to spend time evaluating why they liked or didn't like a particular site. We recommend that you evaluate your site by observing users or by talking to them. E-mail response forms may also be helpful.

The Kids Page prototype soon evolved into Electric Kids. Sites were added and removed, and categories were redesigned. At the moment, we have temporarily abandoned some fancier design attempts for the basic default design, as shown in Figure 5–4.

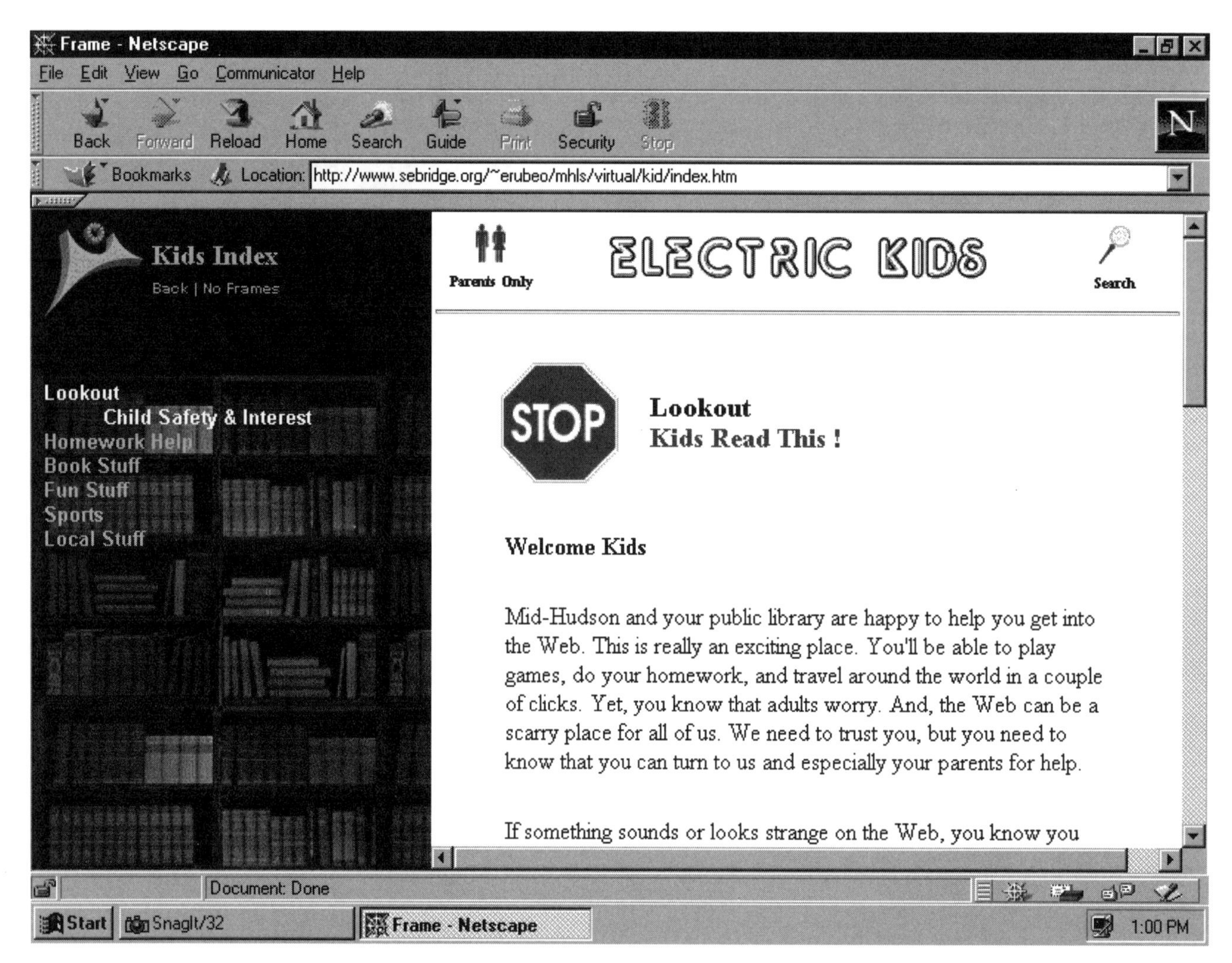

Figure 5–4: MHLS Electric Kids Page

TEENS' CORNER AND OTHER VARIATIONS

The work on children led to other notable expansions. Teens are easily the most at risk on the Web. They are the most likely to engage in chat rooms and to follow the natural hormonal interests of their age to sites that many parents may find offensive. Rites of passage may be unavoidable, but sitting at a computer terminal is obviously a positive alternative to hanging out on the street corner. Still, providing Web education and helping teens find their way is crucial. As soon as Mid-Hudson staff member Mabel Lopez was assigned to work on the Kids Room, for example, she argued for the immediate creation of a Teens' Corner. This work was therefore logically delegated to her.

After a while, we somewhat expanded the project in conjunction with member librarians, and established a young adult committee.

Children and young adult users evaluate the MHLS pages for usability, content, and design and suggest directions for future development. MHLS also brought in an outside expert to lecture on the subject of teen Web resources and provide additional input for our venture. Moreover, we hope to benefit from the wisdom of our off-hour computer operators, who come from a partnership with the local high school.

Our functional analysis has been eye-opening. Although recreation was important, the teens actually wanted to use the Web for their homework, personal advancement, and checking out colleges.

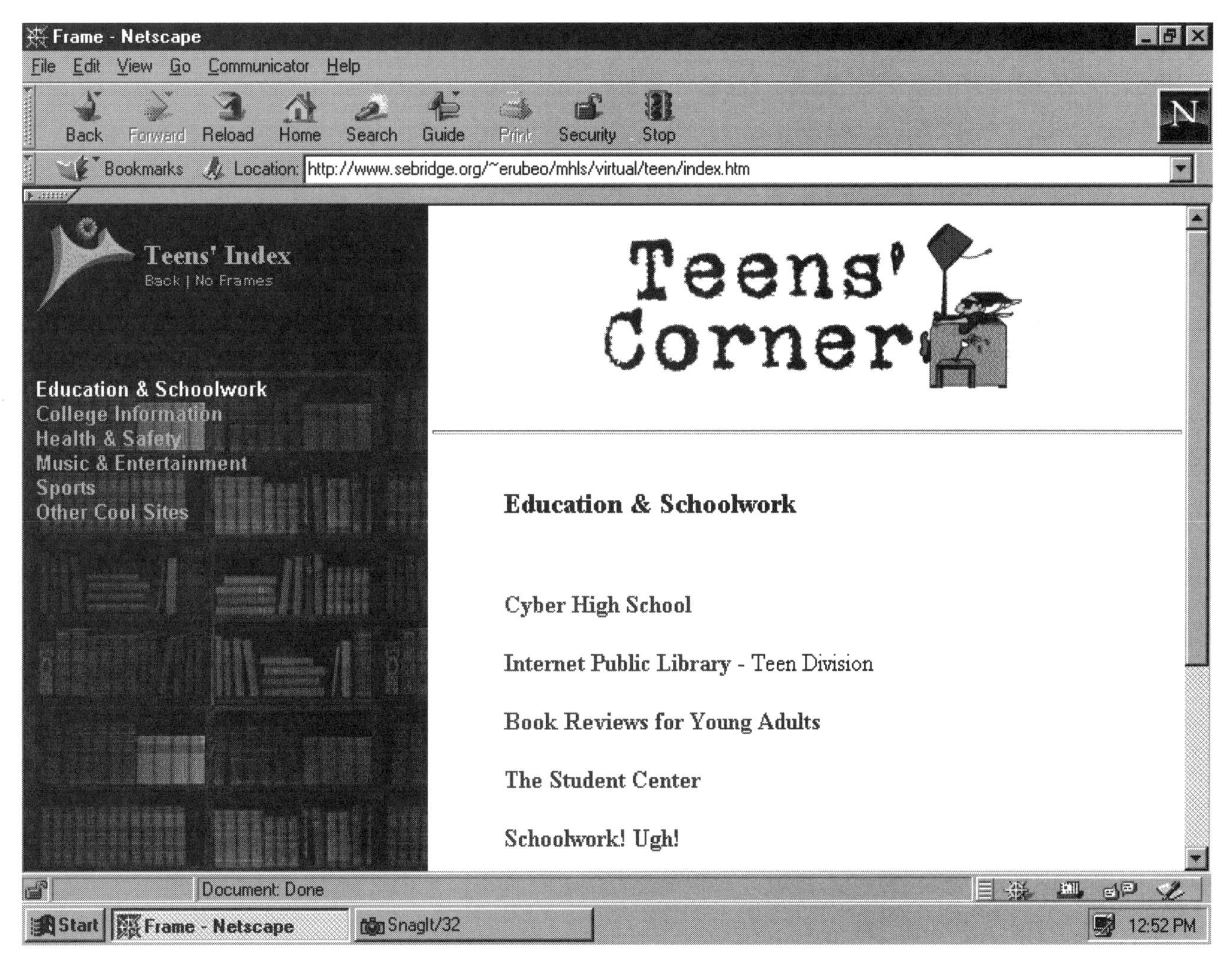

Figure 5–5: MHLS Teens' Corner

PARENTS' PAGE

Similarly, we expanded our earlier "FOR PARENTS ONLY" area into a full-blown special resources center. In addition to including commentary on intellectual freedom and democratic values, we inserted up-to-date discussions on filtering in libraries. But, the site also went on with links to parenting information, and home schooling—the last is fairly active in our region.

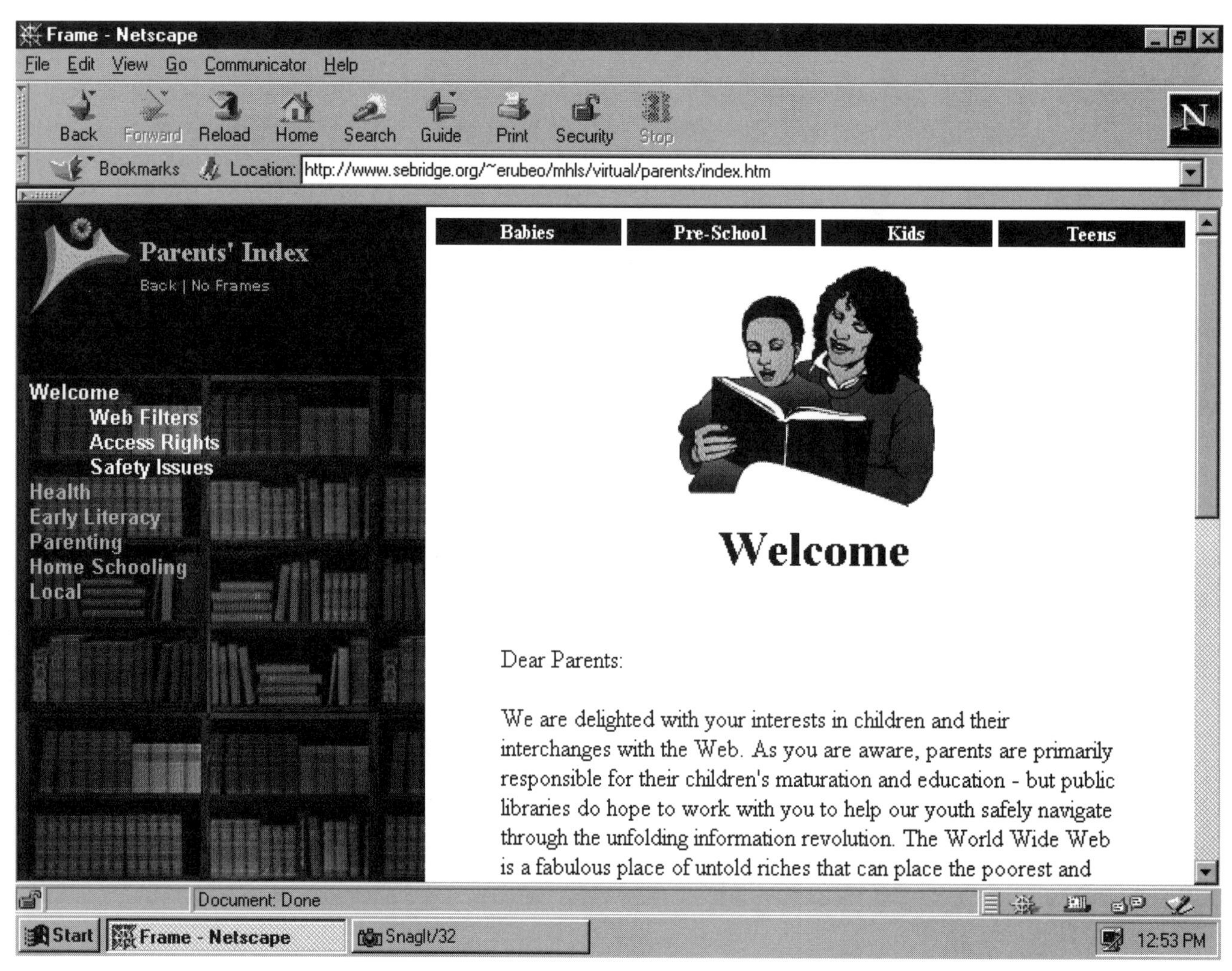

Figure 5–6: MHLS Parents' Page

BABIES AND BOOKS

Mid-Hudson has also created a preschool Web area, as part of its "Babies & Books" program, which is funded under a federal Library Services and Technology Act grant. The goal of Babies and Books is to work with area hospitals to reach out to newborns and their parents with vital lessons on the importance of parents reading to their children and the services that libraries can provide. The welcome page is shown in Figure 5–7.

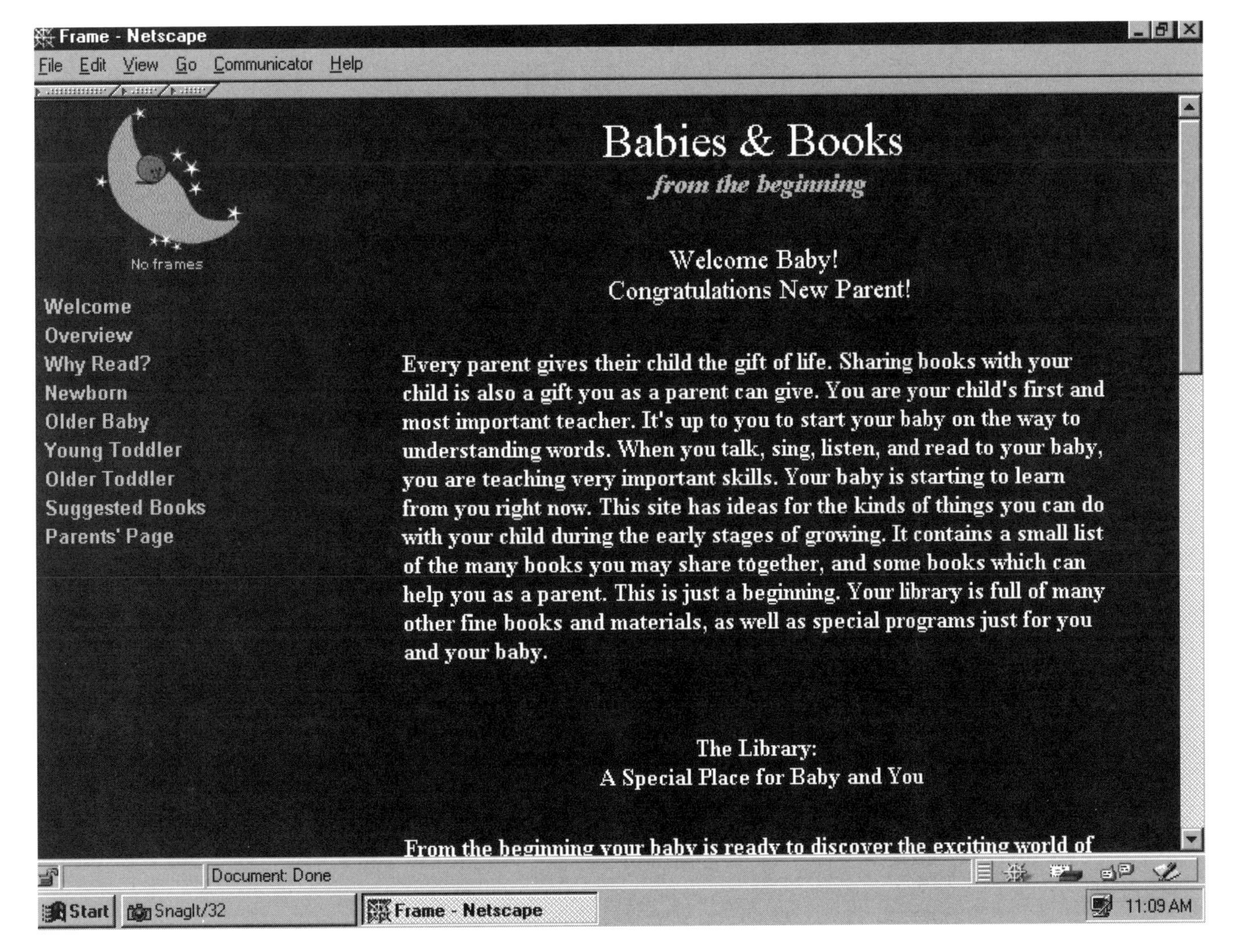

Figure 5–7: MHLS Babies & Books Page

VIDEO HEALTH INFORMATION PROJECT

Mid-Hudson's initial special resources center, the Video Health Information Project Web site, predates any systematic management address of the Web. VHIP evolved as a special initiative of a project that had been in place since 1987–1988. Funded through the Drug Free Schools and Community Act and the Task Force on Integrated Projects for Youth and Chemical Dependency, a collaboration among the New York State Education Department, the Office of Alcohol and Substance Abuse Services, and the Office of Mental Health, the VHIP mandate was to provide educational/informational materials in video format through the public library. The primary content issues are wellness and substance abuse with a focus on the teenager and young adult.

Over the years, VHIP emerged as a unique statewide service. It made videos available directly to social service agencies and through local libraries and the other 23 public library systems across New York. Components of the project included training in the use of video, publishing subject-specific mediagraphies, establishing collection development guidelines, designing exhibits, making presentations at professional meetings, and developing cable spots to promote the public library as a source for these materials. The Web initiative itself arose in conjunction with several external players. By 1995, the New York State Education Department was interested in setting up a pilot site on the Web. SENYLRC (Southeastern New York Library Resources Council) had added an Internet gateway, Sebridge [sebridge.org], and wanted to explore their potentials. Sebridge also tied to interests from collaborative efforts with the John D. and Catherine T. MacArthur Foundation Library Video Project, which contracted its own site design through Northwestern University for mounting on Sebridge. The MacArthur Foundation Library Video Project welcome screen is shown in Figure 5–8.

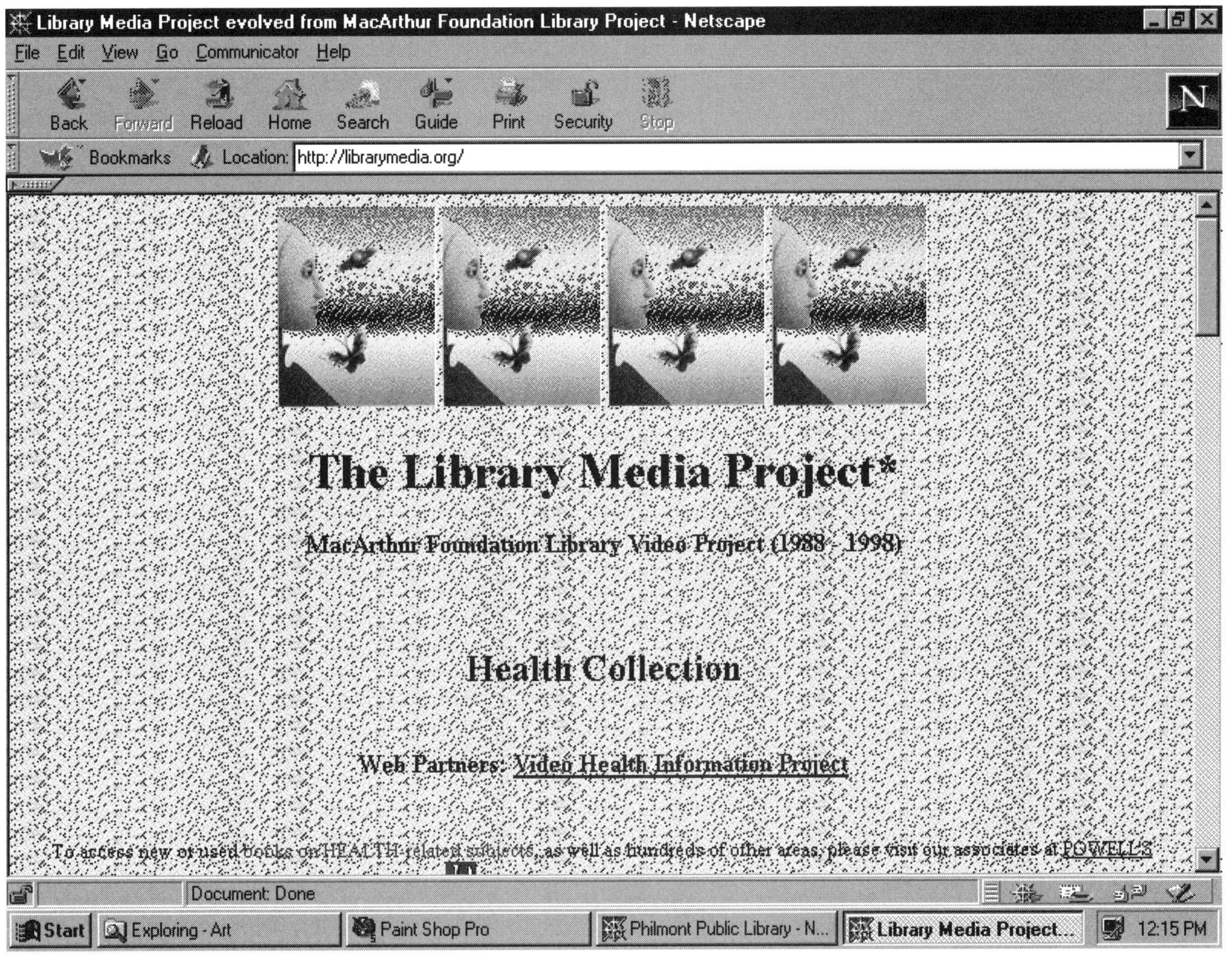

Figure 5–8: MacArthur Foundation Library Media Project Page

As previously indicated, technical Web expertise did not exist at Mid-Hudson in 1995. Time constraints from the VHIP grant and other automation priorities also did not encourage internal development. Yet, VHIP did have a track record of contracting for services as a preferred modus operandi. After review and discussion with management at both Mid-Hudson and SENYLRC, a contract was drawn up between the two systems. SENYLRC would coordinate any subcontracting and Mid-Hudson would be included in any critical decision-making issues. All moneys were provided for in the VHIP grant as "piloting new technology."

After eight months of discussions and noting the steepness of the learning curve on the Web, SENYLRC drew up a contract and Mid-

Hudson signed. As the saying goes, "hindsight is 20/20 vision"—in retrospect we might have done some things differently. However, no one had a Web track record—we were blazing new terrain. The urgency and expediency driving delivery dictated some decisions. The biggest flaw was we had no precise timeline. The biggest plus was *we did it.*

We engaged a graphic artist through a subcontract with the host site at SENYLRC. Rejecting an earlier logo, she redesigned the VHIP page to appeal to teenagers. Her resulting paint splash with large type and a jazzy motif were designed to attract the surfing teen. The underlying video database was accessible through alphabet links to a rough subject thesaurus. The site was up and operative in the spring of 1996.

Though Mid-Hudson was invited to participate in the approvals with the graphic artist, we were unfortunately not privy to the details of the subcontract. In light of difficulties that arose later, it might have been helpful to have an open-ended contract and not absolute closure on design elements. The graphic artist also raised issues of copyright ownership, her recognition on the site, and post-site development and sign-off questions. Such concerns should be handled in advance and clearly stated in the contract—the contracting firm must ensure a transfer of copyright by written codicil for any work for hire.

In fact, the designer did not have a track record with MHLS and was not familiar with library practices. Because of SENYLRC's intermediary position, communication problems were almost certain to arise. As a result, the designer did not have a clear idea of the intended audiences or functions of the site. While the interface was acceptable for mounting, it did not comport well with the rest of Mid-Hudson's presence, nor were we able to work out differences in later discussions. Instead, we lost some of the aesthetics and turned in-house to the original logo and a functional treatment as shown here.

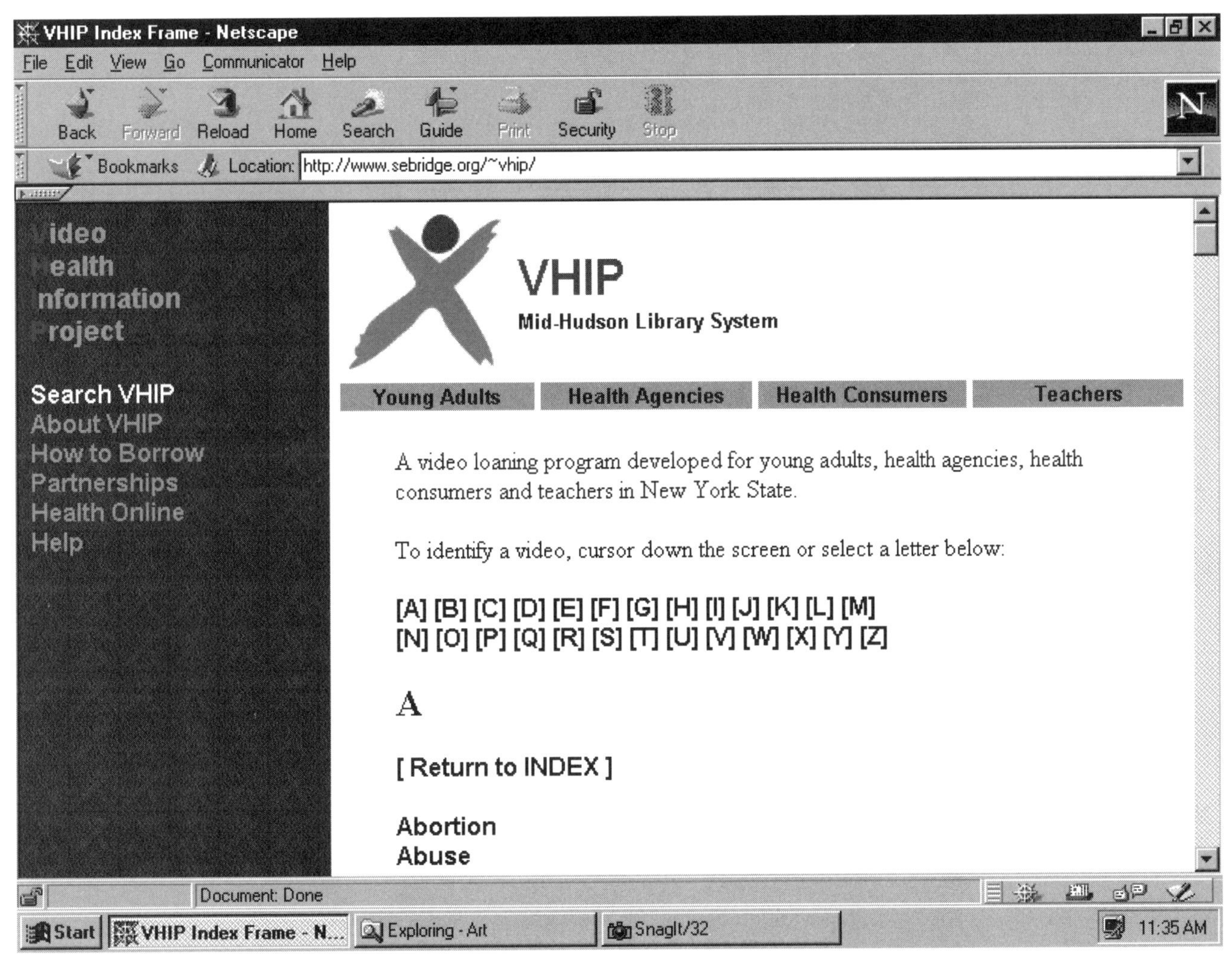

Figure 5–9: Video Health Information Project—Working Site, 1998

LIBRARIAN'S PAGE

Theoretically, the opportunities for providing Web information enhance the value of the rest of the collections and increases institutional visibility to the community. A site for library staff addresses a different, yet equally important set of needs. Creating a page for the librarians in your organization or system is a form of continuing education. It can improve internal communication and lead to professional discussions of library issues. The page is a staff development tool that can lead to improved services and time savings. Unlike patron pages which require extra research, a librarian's page is remarkably comfortable and reassuring to construct. Feedback and evaluation is as close as a staff meeting. Our librarian's page originated out of the initial home page development but separately from the virtual library team.

In keeping with the principles set forth earlier (Chapter 1), a librarian's page should be designed with intuitive categories that reflect the target audience's profile. While far from sui generis, the MHLS categories are still tailored to a particular environment. This site was originally modeled to follow the button grid of the member sites, but it will soon be changed to a split-screen design.

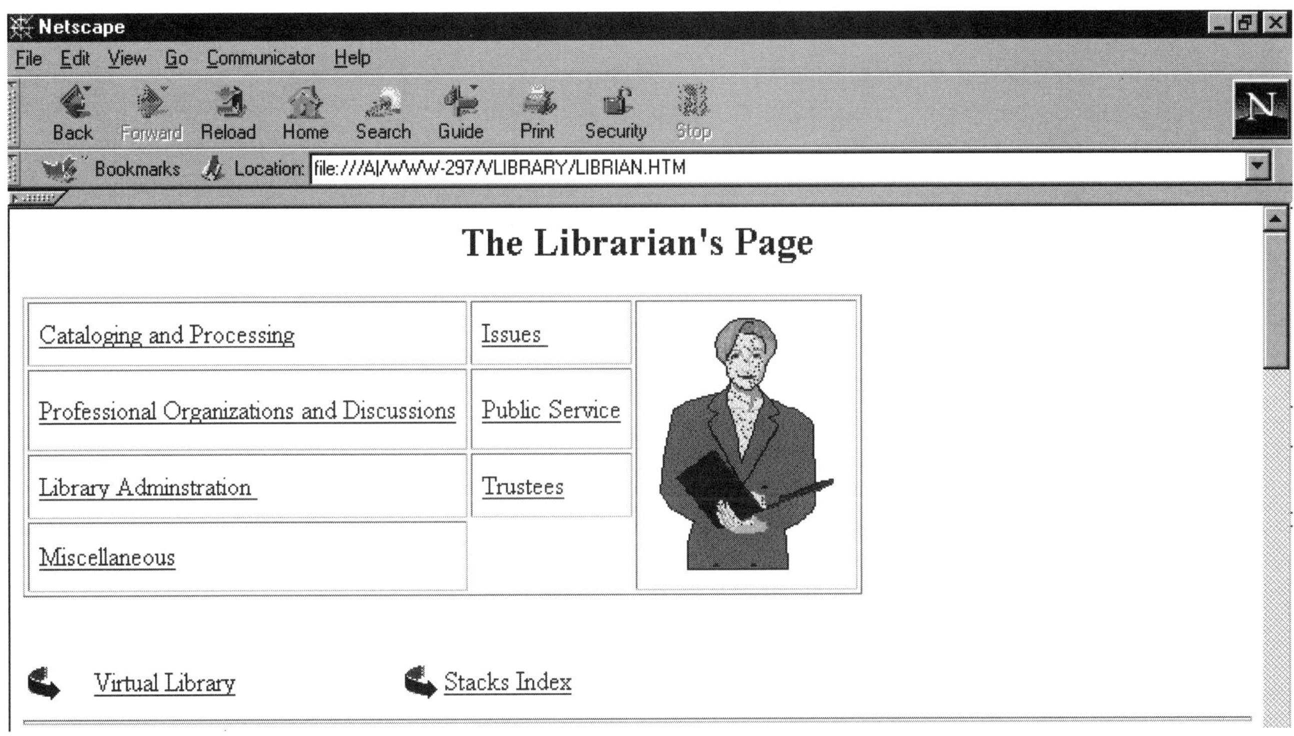

Figure 5–10: MHLS Librarian's Page

READY REFERENCE OPTIONS

At roughly the same time that RCLS was developing the DeskRef site, Mid-Hudson staff was recognizing the possibilities for a ready reference suite to answer definitional or encyclopedic questions. Although now gratefully defering to RCL5, we opened with a Dewey frame and numerical guidelines:

- Address Directories (DDC 383)
- Atlases (DDC 912)
- Calculators (DDC 518)
- Calendars (DDC 904)
- Dictionaries & Thesauri (DDC 403)
- Encyclopedias (DDC 031)
- Quotations (DDC 802)

CAREER INFORMATION CENTER

With the explosion of Web sites, the ability to provide career assistance not only increased, but the Web became the primary method of job seeking. Since Mid-Hudson had had a series of grants to establish job referral services in semirural areas and needed to apply for additional support, the idea of a special Web site fit well. Our earlier work was a great incentive, but we were also motivated by a sense of grantsmanship to keep the funding stream alive another year.

The first step was to identify job seekers as the primary clientele. Our concerns were also to build a page that was easy to use and would provide the user with the most reliable information in the shortest time. Even before the Web existed, we had had experience with gopher sites to aid job seekers. We had worked with the online career center and telnetted to the New York State Department of Labor Workstation and similar departments across the country since the early 1950s. The Department of Labor Workstation had long been engaged in providing alternative ways to find jobs without having to search newspapers or pound the pavement. Thus, even before the Web, the Internet itself was recognized by job seekers and employers as a cost-effective vehicle of choice.

Beyond the basic task of locating a job opening, the Internet had also quickly unlocked a vast array of supplemental information for job seekers that most libraries could not previously have thought of offering. People seeking company or industry information, economic or demographic statistics, and national or international information could find help through the Internet; before this such information would have been impossible for a medium-sized library to offer. Once you have the basic site, the expertise of the librarian is needed. Enhance your site with as much local information as possible. There are many sites with job information, but people look for employment close to home. You will have difficulty finding a local site with job ads, but you can provide links to local newspapers and businesses. Do not forget the sites for chambers of commerce and other local organizations. Becoming a good source of county, city, or town information will make your site a must for any job seeker.

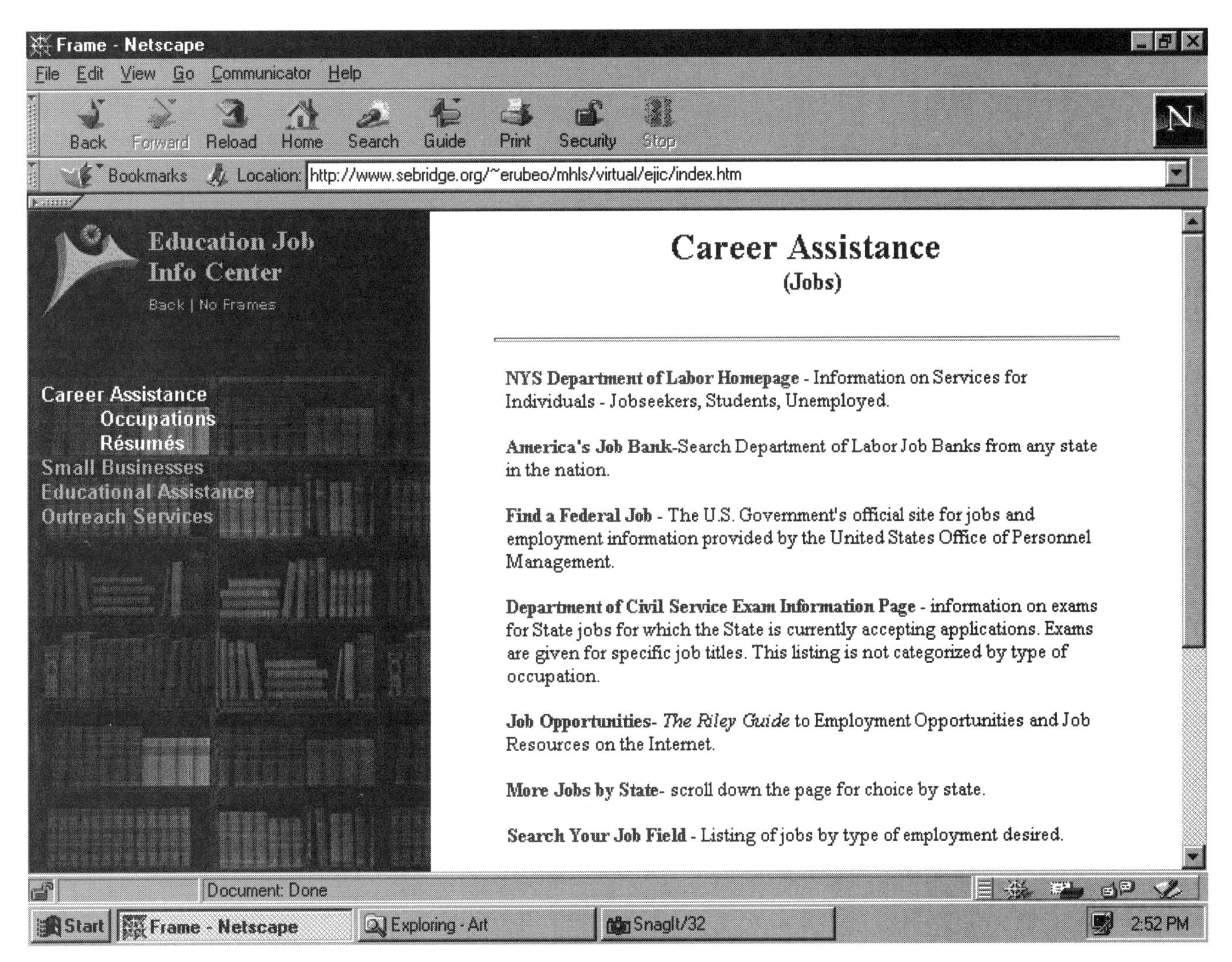

Figure 5–11: MHLS Career Assistance Page

BUSINESS INFORMATION CENTER

This grant project followed from the Employment Center program. The clientele of those centers expressed a growing interest in information about beginning their own businesses. As their inquiries increased, the number of our links began to expand beyond the comfort range for easy navigation. Demand suggested a cross-link to a separate site that would discuss business start-ups along with providing general business information.

Our challenge was to understand the needs of a target audience that does not traditionally use the public library. First, we identified some potential information categories and developed a survey. Our survey of the business community helped in paring down the number of possible categories to fit site-design standards. We also found that, for business people, time is of the essence. Creating a site that can be navigated quickly becomes a primary concern. Specific topics of interest included taxes and regulations. We found sites to assist a searcher find information on human resources, labor law, and OSHA regulations. In addition, we included local information on regional economic trends. Finally, we used this opportunity to build ties to local organizations and thus position the project as part of community economic development.

Started with a Library Services and Technology Act (LSTA) grant in 1997, this project has attracted additional private foundation support. The site features a large interactive graphical image, but users must scroll down or click for an introductory narrative. It is the first MHLS site to include annotations for Web listings along with extensive in-house information supplements.

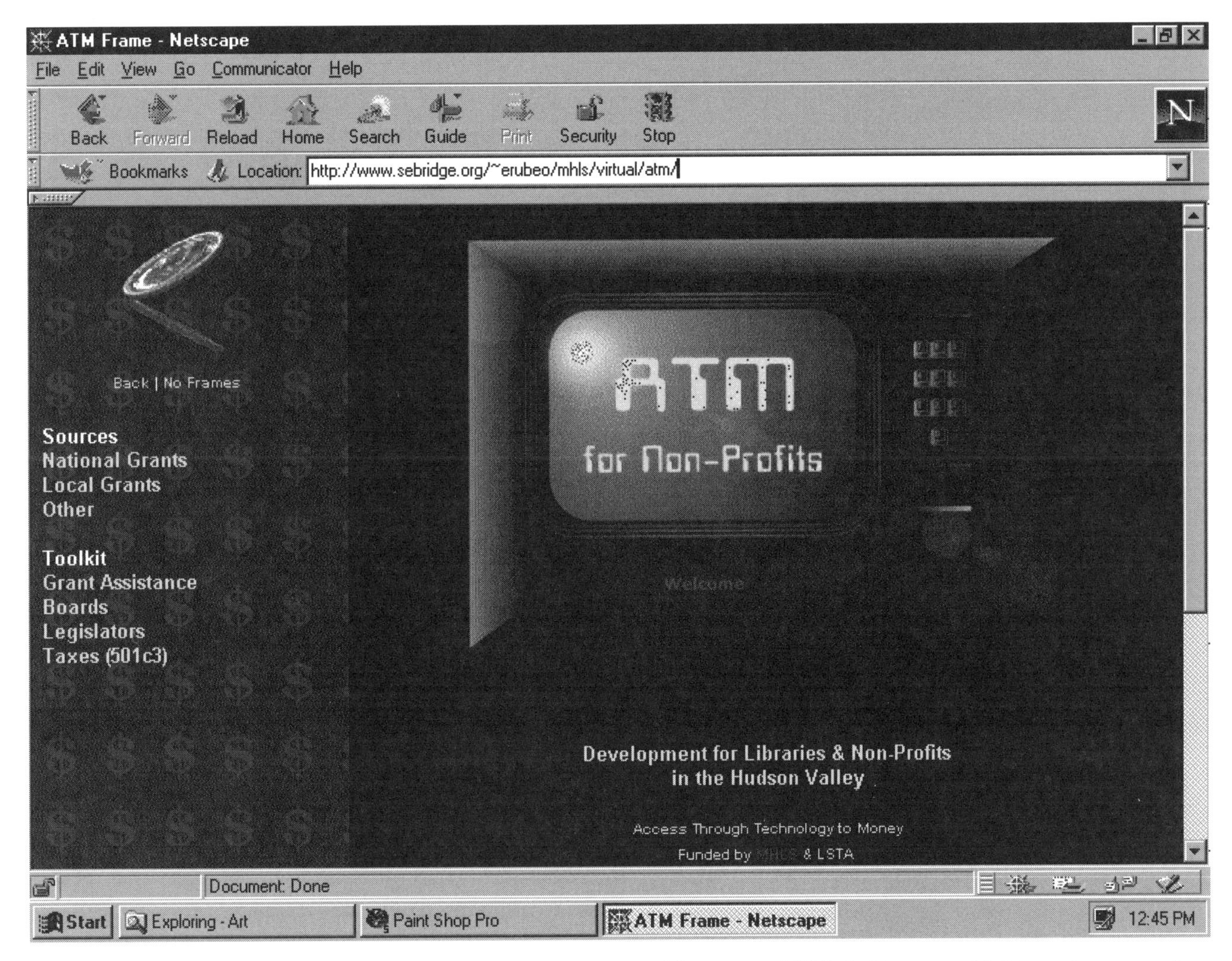

Figure 5–12: Access through Technology to Money—MHLS Nonprofit Development Page

NON-PROFIT DEVELOPMENT—OR ATM SITE

Building from the original LSTA grant in 1997, this project has succeeded in gaining additional private foundation support. The site features a large interactive graphical image with a scroll down or click to its introductory narrative. It is also the first site in which we included annotations on the Web listings and added extensive in-house information supplements.

PROJECTS UNDER DEVELOPMENT

Budding expertise and entrepreneurship have also led to several other projects that are now underway or in the hopper:

- We have taken the lead in building a Web presence for an early literacy homework center. This is in conjunction with a three-year grant initiative with the local county school administration.
- Pending grant funds, Mid-Hudson will take the technical lead in a United Way pilot networking site for the nonprofit agencies in Dutchess County.
- In addition to periodic requests for help with local problems with our online bibliographic system, we encounter ongoing and sustained inquiries into basic computer repair. We are addressing this area with a Web information center of hints and links, which we may eventually upgrade with an intelligent response agent.
- Finally, we have used our basic approaches to try to create continuity among our special resources centers and the online catalog. In addition, a new bookings module is being produced under an outside contract.

6 SELECTING VIRTUAL RESOURCES

Joshua Cohen, Marie F. Smith, and Fred Stielow

The structural framework and policies are now in place. The remaining questions are about content. This chapter presents collection development methods to help populate your virtual library's basement. These skills include principles for the selection of Free Web sites and an analysis for internally produced materials. This chapter also suggests refinements to standardize the information suites and concludes with a call for evaluation and the integration of the site within your institutional context.

COLLECTION DEVELOPMENT AT THE ITEM LEVEL

Ultimately, even the best production line will fail if your virtual library lacks good content. Library experience again comes to the rescue. Just as classification systems are vital to organize your site, collection development skills are equally basic to the content goal. For instance, managers must approach two overlapping stages:

1. Prototype/Piloting: The introduction of a virtual library demands a specialized seeding period similar to that required for any new material or collection.
2. Maintenance: With time and establishment, evaluation methodologies turn to maintenance and comparative criteria for additions and weeding as a never-ending process.

COLLECTION FACTORS

As suggested in Chapter 5, initial site development centers on four categories of electronic materials. Two of those categories, internally produced interactive services and an electronic resources library, are dealt with as technical services in Chapters 7 through 9. The concentration in this chapter is on the heart of your work load—the selection of sites for inclusion as external links and the production of internal resources.

FREE WEB

The Web realigns a portion of traditional collection analysis:

- Instead of evaluating potential selections against extant holdings and applying various evaluative criteria within a limited budget, one faces an undifferentiated grab bag floating in cyberspace.
- The presence of Internet terminals opens the entire Web as a resource, but a virtual library requires specialized professional selection from that vast resource.
- Selection is not limited by costs, but arises from an almost overwhelming array of choices. The temptation for overreaching becomes a real danger along with the uncertainties of relying on a still unformed and transitory medium.
- In such an environment, it is easy to reach beyond your immediate constituency and mission. Institutions may be lured into attempting to provide resources for the world.
- Searching for sites to select can lead you through a dizzying maze of loops and links, which can easily make a reviewer unsure of what has or has not been seen.

SITE SELECTION TOOLS

With a library model, you obviously do not need to reinvent the wheel. Libraries have established advanced devices for their collection analysis—such as the Research Libraries Group (RLG) Conspectus process. OCLC's NetFirst is a good resource, but at this evolutionary stage of the Web you still need to rely on your own resources and analysis. Some other generalizable approaches and tools are available to assist your selection process:

- **Content Specialists:** The best way to guarantee quality for a virtual library is to include reference librarians or area content specialists as key players in the Web team.
- **Other Recommenders:** Although final selections belong in the hands of the content specialists, other members of the team will have an interest in building content and should be invited to share their findings. In addition, the site itself should include a

suggestion "box." Institutions that provide training in Web searching can also contribute material from their sessions.

- **Print and Media Sources:** Print is one of the best sources for uncovering sites. Expert and not-so-expert commentators are building a growing genre of texts proclaiming selections of the best sites. Although these (and our) suggestions can become quickly dated, they do constitute a major jumping-off spot. Somewhat less time-sensitive are computer and Web periodicals (like *Yahoo: Internet World* and *PC Magazine*), specialized trade magazines, and professional library publications. Airline magazines are, oddly enough, ironically often a good source of news notes. The Web has also made its way into the national press, with Web articles appearing in the national runs of the *New York Times* and *Washington Post.* Local papers—such as our *Poughkeepsie Journal*—may contribute even more appropriate features. And, keep a notepad handy; the Web is on television, with recommendations flowing from syndicated programs and related services, such as MSNBC News.
- **Library and Subject Collections on the Web:** Although the wide expanse of a general Web library will likely surpass the experience of even the most active reference librarian, one can turn to resources compiled at other library sites (for example, check the Public Library Server page [sjcpl.lib.in.us/homepage/PublicLibraries/PublicLibraryServers.html]). There are other general subject resources to consider. The World Wide Web Virtual Library [vlib.stanford.edu/Overview.html] provides a point of entry with some insurance of a modicum of stability and adherence to standards. With somewhat less quality assurance, Ringworld [www.webring.com] may prove a valuable beginning place. Such meta-sites represent a special site category for your inclusion—they exponentially multiply the power of your site.
- **Search Engines:** In addition to other virtual libraries, Yahoo and Magellan and other search engines provide their own hierarchical directories or bookmarked collections, which may map to your general or specific applications. A set of criteria has already been applied to make these selections. Once you have reviewed the directories, try some search engines. Alta Vista, Excite, and Hot Bot will locate sites that may not be listed in their directories. Meta-search engines like Dogpile or Metacrawler should also be used. Choose a variety of keywords and see what appears. Try following the links in the sites you find to identify other sites.
- **Special Search Engines:** Look for special search engines built for a specific topic (for example, GILS [search.com and www.fedworld.gov/gils]).

INDIVIDUAL SITE EVALUATION

Site selection is a coming art form for the modern librarian and archivist. Be open and let free association take over, be sure to document your findings, and keep alert for specialized terminology and unforeseen organizational patterns. You might find some interesting things in unexpected places. As a reminder, you should not be shy to build from, or tie into other successful sites. Despite the lack of control over the sites and media differences, you can also use traditional professional review criteria. For example:

- **Audience Factors:** Take your intended audience into account. Does the site speak to the appropriate age range and level of technical competency? (See Chapter 5.)
- **Layout:** Is the site attractive, easy to load, and easy to navigate?
- **Reviews or Recommendations:** Are awards or outside reviews available?
- **Source/Location:** Is the site from a respected body and apparently free of copyright infringements? Is it an academic resource, a student creation, or a commercial product? Does it display the creator's credentials or present important ties with a key developer of the material? Does it have special values because of its proximity to your local area?
- **Special Features:** Does the site call for registration, payment, or special browser features? Does it include some of the advanced features discussed in Chapter 9 (dHTML, XML, EAD, GILS, metatagging, search engine enhancements)?
- **Stability, Currency, Duplication, and Accountability:** Can you determine when the site was established and how frequently it is updated? Is there an e-mail address to contact? How much does the site duplicate information and navigational links from other sites?
- **Subject Relationship:** How responsive and to what depth of delivery does the site respond in relation to the subject matter in question?
- **Type/Genre:** Categorizing the site and determining whether it is in keeping with your policy guidelines is a growing challenge. Is it primarily of content or navigational value? Does it have a specialized format—subject virtual library, ring, ready-reference, dedicated search engine? Is it a recreational or commercial site? Is it highly demanding of resources—(for example, is it an interactive game, radio or video, chat/palace, mud room, or Webcast)?

Review Note: You have entered an ongoing process and will need to evaluate and renew your links regularly. Web sites are never finished. As sites disappear or change, or as new ones are created, your page needs to be revised. Beware that some sites may change their nature. Not only do you need to be searching the Web regularly for new relevant sites, but you must revisit old sites.

FOUR MORE EVALUATION QUESTIONS

During your searching, the subject you thought you had narrowed may well grow exponentially. Whatever the case, you need to keep track of the sites you have checked. You can do this with a manual checklist, by creating a separate directory in your bookmarks, or by creating a word processing or database file. Your analysis should extend to mental and physical notes on such questions as:

1. Can you identify major sites through frequent cross listings?
2. What locations offer a complete view of the subject and are not likely to be gone the next time you log on?
3. Do the sites have particular formats or employ specialized terminology that should inform your navigational choices?
4. Which hits from a given search make sense to you and which will make sense to the target audience you identified earlier?

INTERNALLY PRODUCED CONTENT

In addition to uncovering appropriate sites on the Web, your virtual library will call for internally produced content. The managerial rule of thumb is to exercise caution and limit such projects in keeping with realistic staffing requirements. But producing content in-house may prove the most exciting and positive arena of your virtual library. Material might include:

- **Narrative** or thematic introduction to the information suite or a particular message that you wish to get across to the user. (See Chapter 6 and the Parenting Site example on Intellectual Freedom.)
- **Annotations** or additional explanations about a Free Web site listing.
- **Content information** to provide additional explanatory data to complement your links to other Web sites. For instance, a site on nonprofit development may include functional links to a site with information on planned giving, but you might also include a supplemental link to your own definition of that term or to a list of contacts.
- **Digital Archives.** You may choose to add digitized archival or other special data to some suites. Again, remember the importance of policy development. You must consider potential copyright factors and the possibility of negative tradeoffs from exposing your treasures to view.

Note: Annotations take valuable space and may cost navigational flexibility. If used, you may want to make annotations an option on the link for those who want this additional information.

Note: Supplemental information should be distinguished from links to external sites. You may want to develop your own conventions or graphical symbol as a standard indicator.

ADDITIONAL DISCUSSION ON DIGITAL ARCHIVES

With digital archives, history could be repeating itself. As in the manuscript era before Gutenberg, the strength and identity of libraries may once again come from their unique local holdings. For now, you should be aware of the two data entry methods for adding such material to your Web site:

- **Analog Scan:** One technique is to capture an analog or photographic-like input. Most information found on paper can be easily managed with the assistance of an inexpensive scanner. Capturing three-dimensional images calls for a digital camera. That equipment is also becoming quite affordable. Either approach typically requires a large amount of storage space and may demand considerable amounts of time for your viewers to download.
- **Rekey/OCR:** In addition to, or in place of, an analog image, textual materials can be rekeyed or scanned and converted to text using OCR (Optical Character Recognition) software. The results take far less space and loading time than analog images and can be displayed as special texts.

Teasers and Other Protections: Your site does not have to provide access to the full content of your archival holdings. The costs and time involved could easily become prohibitive. You have the option of using key parts or teasers to arouse additional interests in your materials. Rather than including a full picture, we recommend thumbnail sketches, which require far less space. You can easily link the sketches to the complete files for those interested in detail. Given the nature of cyberspace, however, such a step may cause you to lose control of the image or may even, for all practical purposes, eliminate your copyright. For those who need such extra protection, we recommend including some mark of ownership within or across the image when you can scan it (e.g., "Property of the X Library, All Rights Reserved").

Hypertext Options: In addition to space savings, OCR gives the developer the possibility of enhancing the document with explanatory materials, or even adding navigational hypertext links to other materials. The use of hypertext in this way must be carefully considered for its policy implications and its impact on the intellectual integrity of the original materials.

TOWARD A NEW PRINT DEPARTMENT

Those interested in continuing development can push to another level of project maturation. The managerial goal is to distance content and navigation from technical detail. The creation of information suites can thus become akin to producing a handout with the help of a print department (for example, you may work with the designer to ensure a pleasing layout, but you probably do not ask about how to print the page, collate contents, or bind the item). Current experience suggests that automation presents a great deal of distraction for content specialists on the team, who feel compelled to delve into HTML operations. With standardized approaches, they are free instead to concentrate on what they do best and on the real needs of a good Web site—content, content, content.

REVISED STEPS FOR THE PROJECT TEAM

As the process for setting up special resources collections matures, project management should thus evolve into a standard path:

1. Develop initial group consensus on the scope, subject area, and place of the suite within the overall site plan.

2. Identify your primary and secondary audiences. Be careful to avoid the trap of designing for a general audience unless you have the proper credentials, mission, and support.
3. Keeping steps 1 and 2 in mind, begin to collect sites and develop any needed additional content.
4. Identify the functional categories and analyze how your users would approach searching for this type of information. Lay out the major navigational categories and any needed subcategories with their user-appropriate terms.
5. Tie the navigational terms to your underlying organizational structures (e.g., the assignment of Dewey Decimal numbers).
6. Determine any graphical and/or narrative elements that you want to appear as the site's opening image. Keep in mind, too, any links to other areas within the overall site.
7. Pass the design and content information to the Web implementation crew—but be prepared to make some compromises.
8. Evaluate and redesign—an ongoing, regularly scheduled process during the life of any site.

FIVE CRITICAL EVALUATION QUESTIONS

As you prepare to mount and pilot test the site, you should plan one last review. Are the level and terminology truly appropriate for your headings? How much jargon has snuck in during the process? Just when you think you have the site ready, invite some members of the target group to evaluate the site. (Such evaluation also serves as a marketing device.) Encourage them to make as many mistakes as possible and provide a solid critique. Their feedback will be useful since, if they cannot use the site on the first try, many people will simply never try again.

You also need to elicit feedback from users of the site once it is mounted. Surveys or online feedback from users can keep you informed of how the site is being used, as well as provide invaluable qualitative data to supplement your mechanical cookie counting.

Finally, remember that your analysis must be constantly grounded in the institutional context and must speak to realistic management questions:

1. What is the overall pattern of your information services and which would you want to include—now or later—in your virtual library?
2. What are the other management implications? In particular,

how can you integrate electronic publishing on the Web into your regular work flow?

3. What are the professional/legal considerations, especially if services to children are involved?
4. Do you have anything special to contribute to a virtual library? Does your clientele have special demands and needs that can be met in a virtual library?
5. What can you realistically construct and maintain?

END NOTES FROM MID-HUDSON

DIGITAL ARCHIVES

Our experience with digital archives is quite sparse at the moment. We expect that this area will grow exponentially, but primarily MHLS will only provide some technical background and equipment for its member libraries. For instance, MHLS consulted with the Philmont Public Library on a successful grant project to mount parts of a collection on World War II (Figure 6–1).

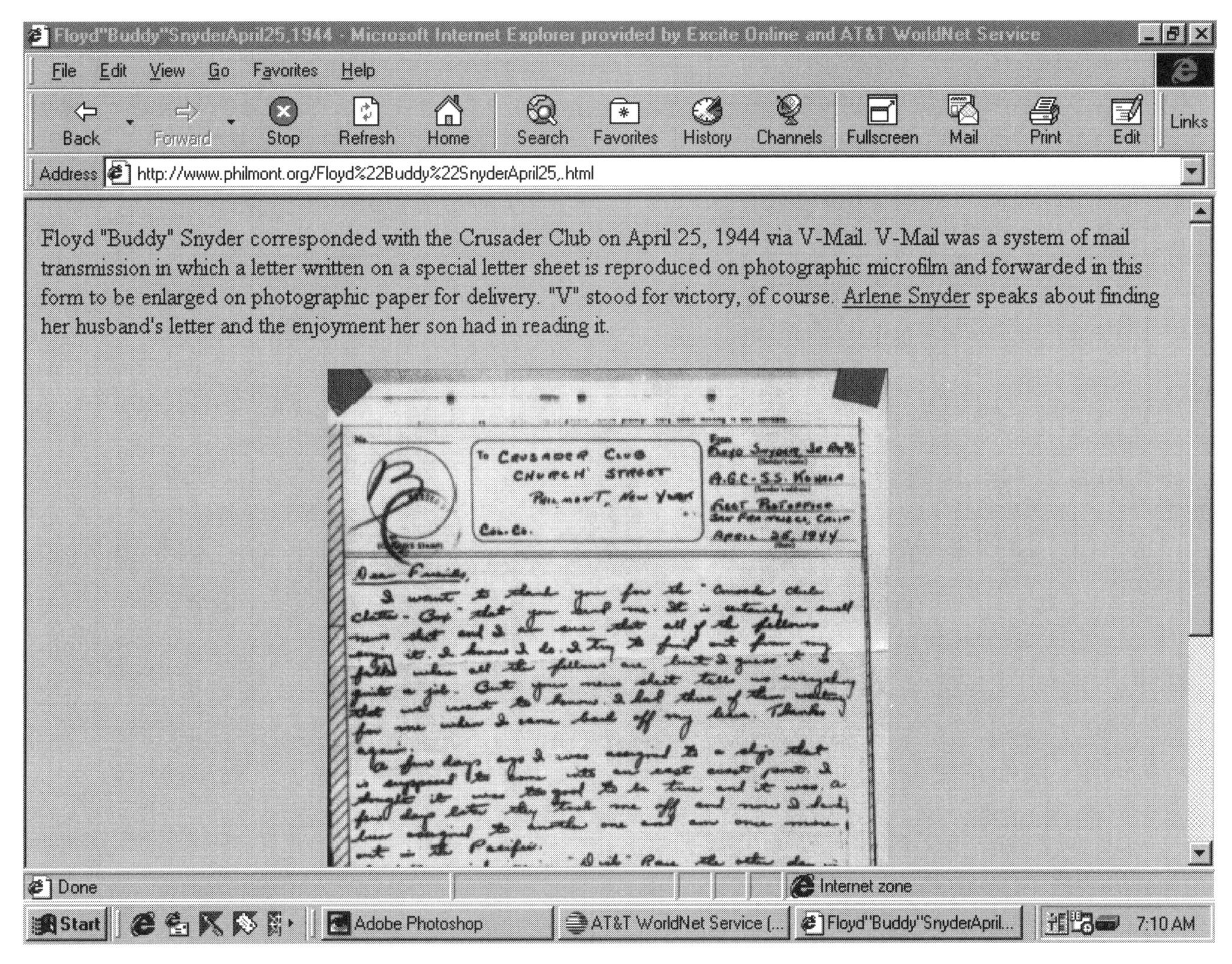

Figure 6–1: Excerpt from the Philmont Public Library World War II Project

FEEDBACK MEASURES

While the quantitative analysis of a site is largely a straightforward technical matter (as discussed in Chapter 8), qualitative analysis is always harder. Our special resource centers do have some user evaluation tools in place or under development. At the moment, the extant MHLS committees are taking over a portion of the site evaluation (for example, the children's committee will have say on content for the Kids Page and the outreach committee has some influence regarding the Employment Site. Furthermore, the MHLS site includes e-mail feedback and an electronic survey form. The hard-copy evaluation form shown in Figure 6–2 was also available. However, it was not really that helpful.

Figure 6–2: MHLS Virtual Library Evaluation Form

Mid-Hudson Library System
Virtual Library Content Form

Library Name: Date:

Site Name	URL	Dewey #	X Delete

Additional Special Collection/Comments:

7 MOUNTING THE VIRTUAL LIBRARY ON THE WEB

Edward J. Rubeo, Tom Bialek,
and Mabel Lopez

Based on the trial and error of sometimes painful experiences, Chapters 7, 8, and 9 help you understand the physical construction of the prototype or pilot for placing your virtual library online. While we will try to tone down the jargon, your immersion in these chapters will come with an injection of terminology. Such introduction is necessary for the manager's awareness, but the rapid changes suggest that any in-depth knowledge can be deferred to the specialists.

This chapter examines both the software to assist with HTML coding and the practical realities of the current scene. It will enable you to erect a basic virtual library and proclaim its existence to the outside world. The text, however, begins by calling your attention to alternative methods to reduce your capital outlays.

MOUNTING OPTIONS

Before proceeding with implementation, managers should conduct a cost/benefit analysis on the physical options. Do you need to invest in the software or, especially, the hardware for a Web site? Options are appearing in tandem with the third generation of integrated library automation software with its object-oriented program and graphical OPACs. DRA with Taos, Sirs-Mandarin's M3, and other integrated library systems are being tuned for the Web. They bring the ability to add community information services and other special resources centers to your online catalog. Similarly, UMI's database service offers its subscribers a Site Builder front-end, which holds exceptional promise for virtual library integration, while Librarycom [www.librarycom.com] offers libraries a special Web hosting service.

Local colleges or other nonprofits may also be willing to host your site. Most of the national portals and ISPs, such as Netscape with FortuneCity [www.fortunecity.com], and Yahoo with Geocities, offer free or inexpensive home page mounting that could work for many institutions. Local ISPs are also sprouting up, eliminating the need for an onsite Web server, and they may be eager to work with the library.

Note on ISPs and Site Setup: Given the probability that most readers already have a Web presence, we have chosen to avoid start-up questions. How to get an appropriate address or how to select server software and an ISP can be answered by other books in this series and your own networking. For other assistance, you can go directly to the Web (e.g., How to Select an Internet Service Provider [web.cnam.fr/Network/Internet-access/how_to_select. html], the ISP Checker [www.ispcheck. com], An Information Provider's Guide to Web Servers [www.vuw.ac.nz/who/Nathan.Torkington/ideas/www-servers.html], and WWW Web Server Software [www.w3.org/pub/WWW/Servers.html]).

Such agencies tend to have dedicated staffing and equipment that is superior to what most of us could afford. The ISP takes care of the trouble and much of the expense of site maintenance, and may also provide design services at little or no cost.

Management thus has three options when pursuing the physical creation of the virtual library:

1. With your active library or archival expertise in place for design, organization, and policy purposes, you can outsource the physical operations and HTML coding.
2. You can maintain design and coding controls in-house and contract for the site and periodic transfers of your data.
3. You can do everything in-house.

INTRODUCTION TO THE TECHNOLOGY

For those interested in engaging the second or third options listed above, there is a lot of promise. You do not have to be a computer genius. If you can work with word processing software, you can create a virtual library. In general, you will find that everything is getting easier. You may still need to be aware of HTML standards, and "Web graybeards" do love the feel of coding. But, modern editing software has all but eliminated the need to know the actual language. We can thus outline the technical portion for a version of a general Web library in a single paragraph without divulging any coding strings. In just a few more words, we can present the physical steps for creating the interface for an electronic resource library.

We must once again warn that your actual building will be a learning process. Even today's powerful and simplified editors call for some reserve. You will need to make ongoing compromises and use personal innovations or "workarounds" to reach your goals. Above all, you should remember to keep it simple and avoid the temptation of the cutting edge—especially given the uncertainties surrounding the current "browser wars."

BROWSERS

The World Wide Web Consortium (W3) proclaimed [www.w3.org/MarkUp/MarkUp.html] a new HTML 4.0 standard in 1997. Broader

Browser Note: Those with an unquenchable interest in alternatives or the ongoing evolution of browsers can conveniently turn to BrowserWatch [www.ski.mskcc.org/browser watch/].

Lynx and Legacy Note: Those with dumb terminals may still need to consider extensions for pre-browser software. Backward compatibility means design for Lynx—the Internet's earlier text-based browser (e.g., no graphics and perhaps no mouse controls). With its low overhead, such technology does enjoy the benefits of fast screen loading. The normal option is a text-only alternative, which demands careful planning and site layout to avoid unnecessary work and duplication. You could also employ high and low bandwidth versions of new pages. A good practice to address these issues, and to assist those users who choose to turn off their graphics, is to include a descriptive caption for any image. In the end, however, you may decide to abandon any adaptation for the outmoded format.

market forces are now at play that leave that standard and future advances in question. In 1994 Netscape appeared and effectively launched the Web revolution. Depending on the outcome of its marketing efforts and a forthcoming federal court decision, Microsoft's Explorer may overwhelm the pioneer. Fortunately, both are free. Explorer is bundled with Microsoft's operating system or is available from its Web site [www.microsoft.com]. In January 1998, Netscape announced a similar offering and even opened a source code for its Navigator product [www.netscape.com].

The interplay between Microsoft and Netscape effectively delimits your design potential. It also suggests the need for a good deal of caution at the moment. Despite formal HTML standards, Netscape and Internet Explorer may differ significantly in the way they support or interpret HTML tags. It is conceivable that you might create a nicely designed page for one browser that would appear as an unformatted jumble of text and symbols on the other. Your job is to support *both* Navigator and Internet Explorer with a reasonably similar feel. Do not take anything for granted; you need to coordinate and test the look and feel of the site between these two models and their various releases. You also need to test how your pages appear on Macintosh and IBM equipment.

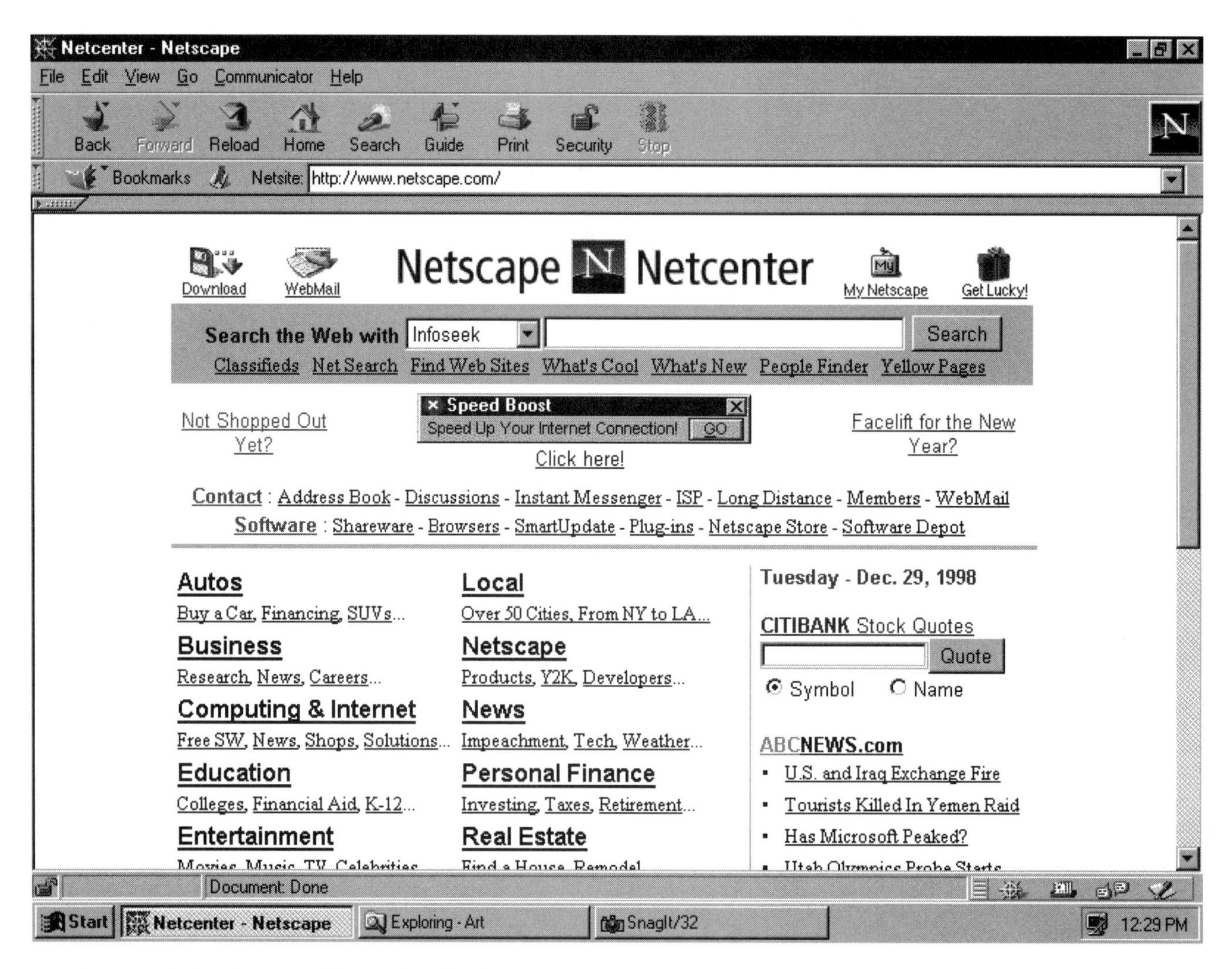

Figure 7–1a: Home Page for Netscape

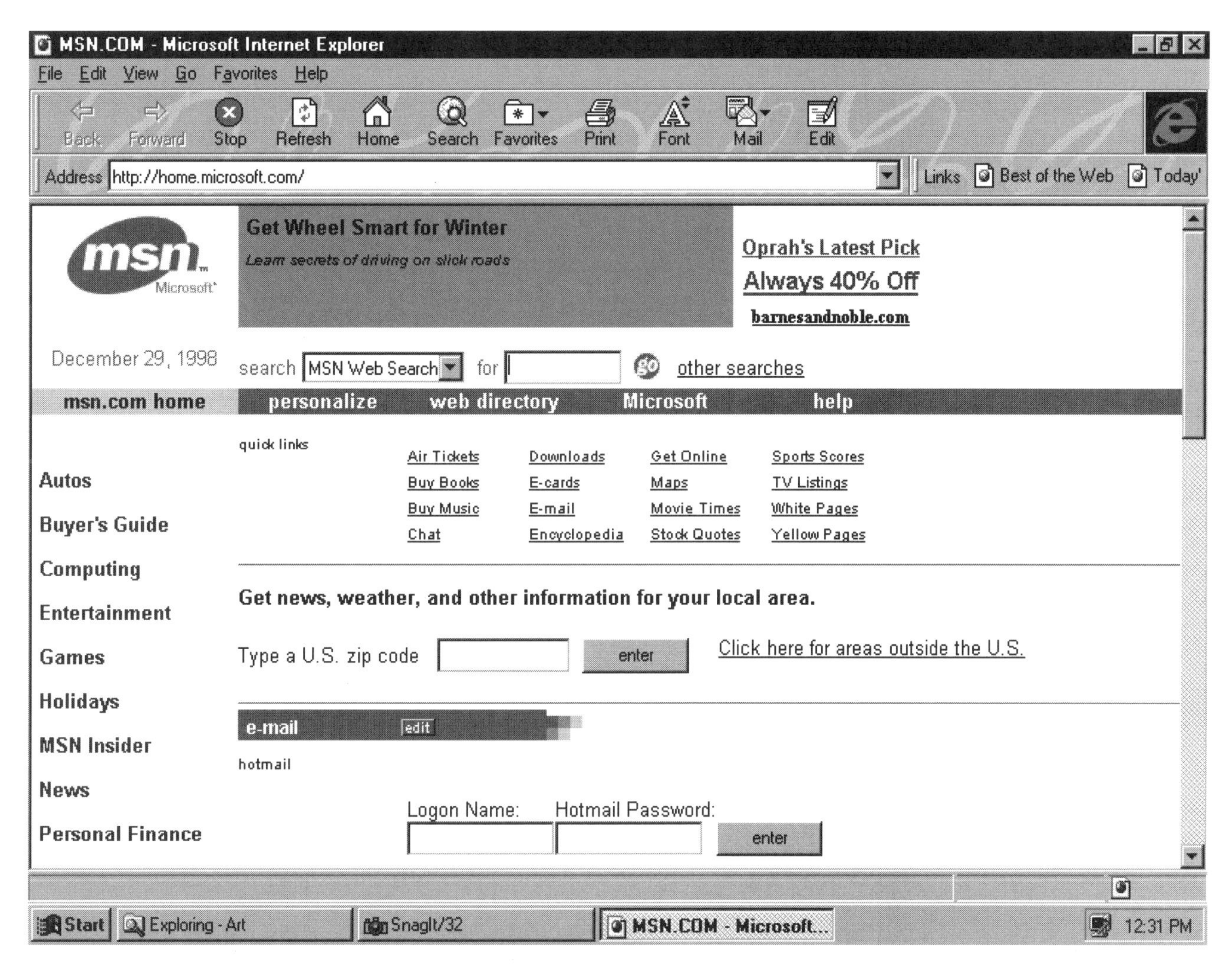

Figure 7–1b: Home Page for Microsoft Explorer

PROGRAMMING IN HTML CODE

Web pages rest in HTML coding. You could learn the language and directly enter the appropriate brackets and code terms (see A Beginner's Guide to HTML [www.ncsa.uiuc.edu/General/Internet/WWW/HTMLPrimer.html] or HTML Quick Reference [www.cc.ukans.edu/~acs/docs/HTML_quick.html]). This laborious process is not unlike working with the line editors of yesterday (such as those embedded in the DOS system) and is not recommended. Fortunately, the browsers themselves come equipped with rudimentary HTML editors to make your life a little simpler and reduce errors. Unfortunately, these editors do not support coding for all HTML functions and they may produce files that cannot be properly imported if you upgrade software. Rather, the browser's greatest strengths for your coding lie in cutting and pasting and in the View function (Figure 7–2). The latter reveals the source code for a successful site, which you can then copy and insert for your own project.

Copyright Reminder: If you borrow HTML coding from another site, acknowledgment of the parent site is courteous and ethically in order.

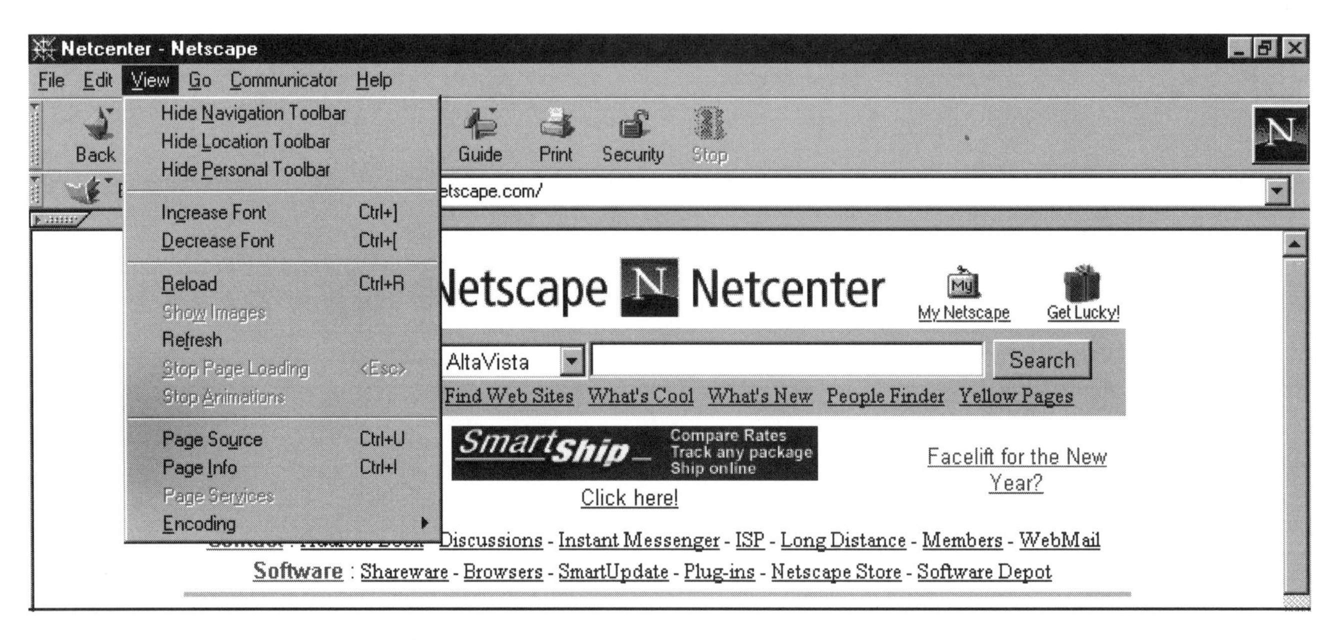

Figure 7–2: Netcenter with View Menu

Other alternatives exist for the coder. For example, you can create simple pages as a downloading option from many standard word processors and spreadsheets. Push a button and an intermediary program converts the output to HTML. You can also use your server software. An httpd server can interpret an external file as an http document type request (that is, one with an .htm or .html file name extension) and then can view the file as Web pages. The Apache Web server program [www.apache.org], which is currently the industry standard and used by 44 percent of all Internet domain names, provides such a facility.

DEFAULTING TO WEB EDITORS

In fact, the preceding options are no longer needed. Instead, specialized Web editor software is now available and it has evolved into true turnkey approaches. You can now pick from dozens of packages that automatically inject your codes. For instance, the MHLS Web team had the opportunity to review three fairly representative products (NetObject's Fusion, Microsoft Front Page, and SoftQuad's HotMetal Pro), during the first phases of Mid-Hudson's projects. Their analysis revealed that these HTML editors could easily meet the demands of a virtual library. Such software comes with essentially the same editing features as other HTML editors, but it does differ in terms of ease of use and application. Since these evaluations were made in early 1997 and were not comprehensive, you should review the current literature and perhaps experiment to find what best suits your needs.

NetObject's Fusion (Figure 7–3) proved a high-end page layout program in compiling output into HTML. We found it easy to create impressive pages with relatively little effort. Fusion made it difficult, however, to alter from its predefined templates since it uses a proprietary file format. Microsoft Front Page (Figure 7–4) has an extremely intuitive interface, which reminded us more of a word processor than an HTML editor. Though it was a joy to use, we produced many pages that did not display properly in Netscape Navigator. HotMetal (Figure 7–5) was arguably the most difficult of the three to use, but Mid-Hudson already had it and Netscape in-house, and it offered us much

Figure 7–3: NetObject's Fusion Features

- user can create Web pages without having to know code
- offers drag and drop manipulation
- includes templates
- imports existing sites with all links
- offers enhanced code generation for different browsers

Figure 7–4: Microsoft Front Page Features

- user can create HTML pages without having to know code
- imports and converts existing text files into HTML
- supports the latest HTML Web standards
- automatically converts images into GIF or JPEG format
- uses drag and drop to create hyperlinks
- includes wizards and templates
- WYSIWYG editor

Figure 7–5: HotMetal Pro Features

- user can create HTML pages without having to know code
- imports and converts existing files into HTML
- supports the latest HTML Web standards
- includes built-in graphics editing package
- includes rules checking and validation
- includes wizards
- user can preview pages in multiple browsers
- WYSIWYG editor

more control of the code. All three programs met the team's simple initial requirements. They offered tool bars or pull-down menus with sufficient features to build a virtual library. For example, they included:

- header-tag size selection
- basic word processing features with buttons for such type features as italics, underline, and bold.
- formatting features, including the establishment of new paragraphs and insertion of blank lines or breaks
- content control features for creating bulleted or unordered and ordered (alphabetic, numeric) lists and tables
- hypermedia controls for adding and keeping track of external URL linkages and for targeting and linking to internal areas within the site
- table functions with controls for the number of rows and columns

BUILDING AN INTERFACE IN SIX EASY STEPS

With any good Web editor the construction of a serviceable virtual library is remarkably easy. No longer does a basic or intermediate workbook need to reproduce page after page of coding.

1. The editor prompts you to start with a Title for the official listing to be captured by the browser (for example, Test Virtual Library).
2. You will then be led into the Body, where you should replicate your descriptive title as the largest Header size (<H1>) and use the Target or Anchor function to define this as the home link to your virtual library. The program allows for the direct entry of any narrative description and launching to the site listings.
3. The organizational scheme—special collections, Dewey, or whatever—can be indicated by smaller Headers (<H2>, <H3>, and so on).
4. Any Header can be hot linked to locations across the Net or to other resource pages within your site.
5. The only minor flourish in Figure 7–6 is the use of the editor to call up an Unordered List feature and hot link the items in the list to external URLs or to targeted locations elsewhere in your site.
6. Finish the listings and close.

Congratulations! You have started a virtual library.

Figure 7–6: Sample Stacked Model Virtual Library

TEST VIRTUAL LIBRARY

This facility is delighted to facilitate your access into the World Wide Web. Feel free to browse and send any comments to *virtualmaster@test.com.* Click here for **site policies**.

Children's Room

Web Library

Agriculture

- National Library of Agriculture
- State Extension Service
- Joe's Local Farm Services

Bibliography

TABLES TO COLUMNS

Tables are one of the most significant tool sets for controlling the entry of content in a Web site. They represent a significant step up the design ladder and were standardized as early as HTML 2.0. The process of creating a table is quite simple and very flexible. Either by clicking on a Tools menu or special Tables button bar, editors will allow you to designate the number of rows and columns that you want to present. Your controls will extend to the width of the column and likely to the color and border elements.

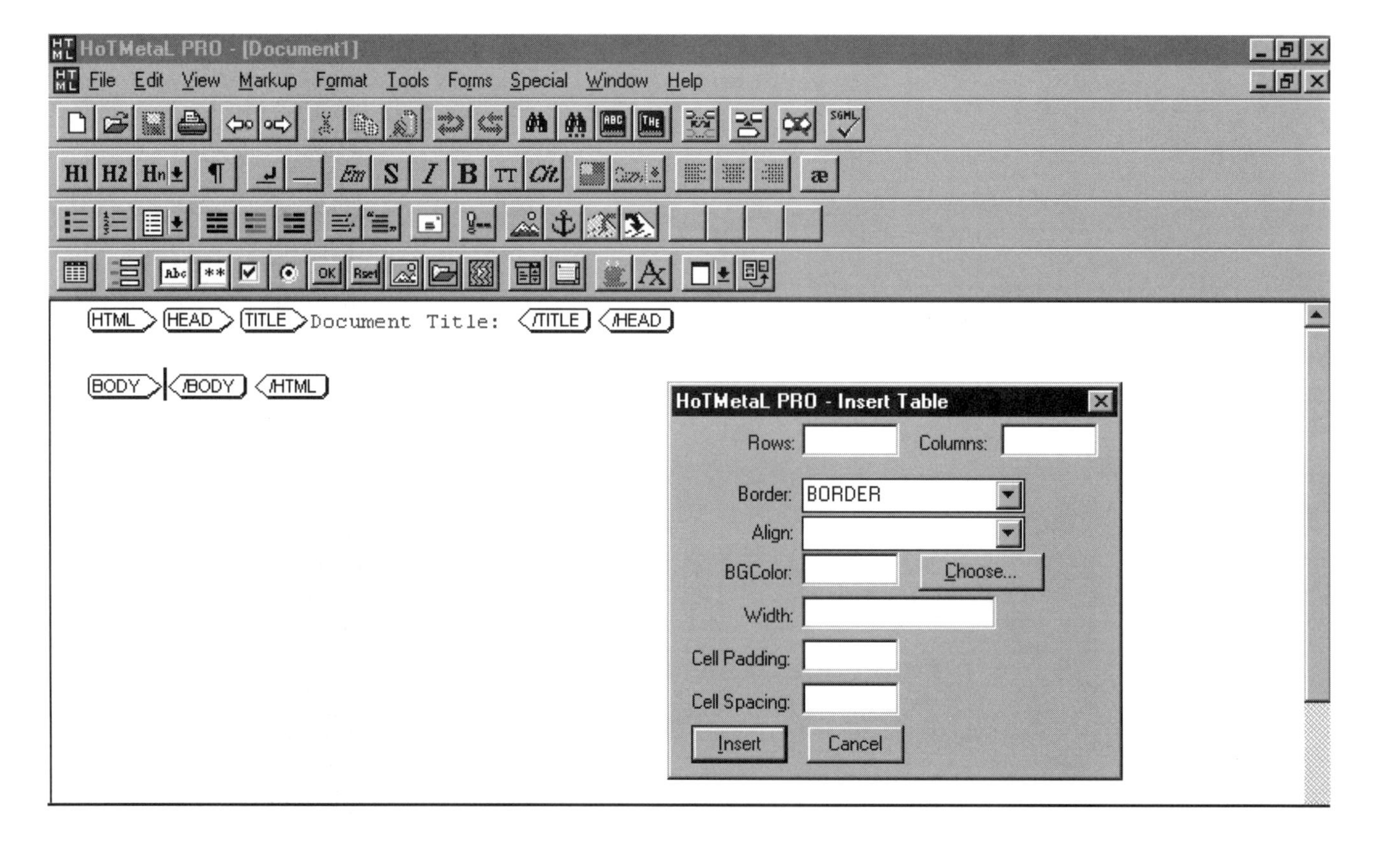

Figure 7–7: HotMetal Pro with Table Menu Engaged

The Table function is remarkably useful for screen design. For example, you can add lists within a cell. One can define a table within a table and use this to manage the placement of objects on your screen in a manner not available with straight HTML line coding. With a table of only one row in depth, the columns become a single button bar for the top or bottom of your opening image. In addition to simulating columns through your regular page layout, the Table command with a one-cell block for the navigation table also offers an easy way to produce the recommended split-screen design.

INTRODUCING FRAMES

Warning on Frames: Ease of initial set-up can be deceptive. This feature should not be used without caution. Given an already limited physical arena, planners must account for the loss of space from the scroll bars and additional loading time. More important, as much as 25 percent of the browsers in use at the time of this writing will not support frames, although this figure is changing. Frames are simply not recommended for the beginner or for most applications; if used they should include a non-frames alternative.

Another way to create the split-screen model involves the Frame function. It allows you to divide the screen into independent viewing areas (something like watching two televisions shows on the same screen) each with its own scrolling bar. Frames are quite attractive for a virtual library. With any good editor, this advanced feature is remarkably straightforward and easily implemented.

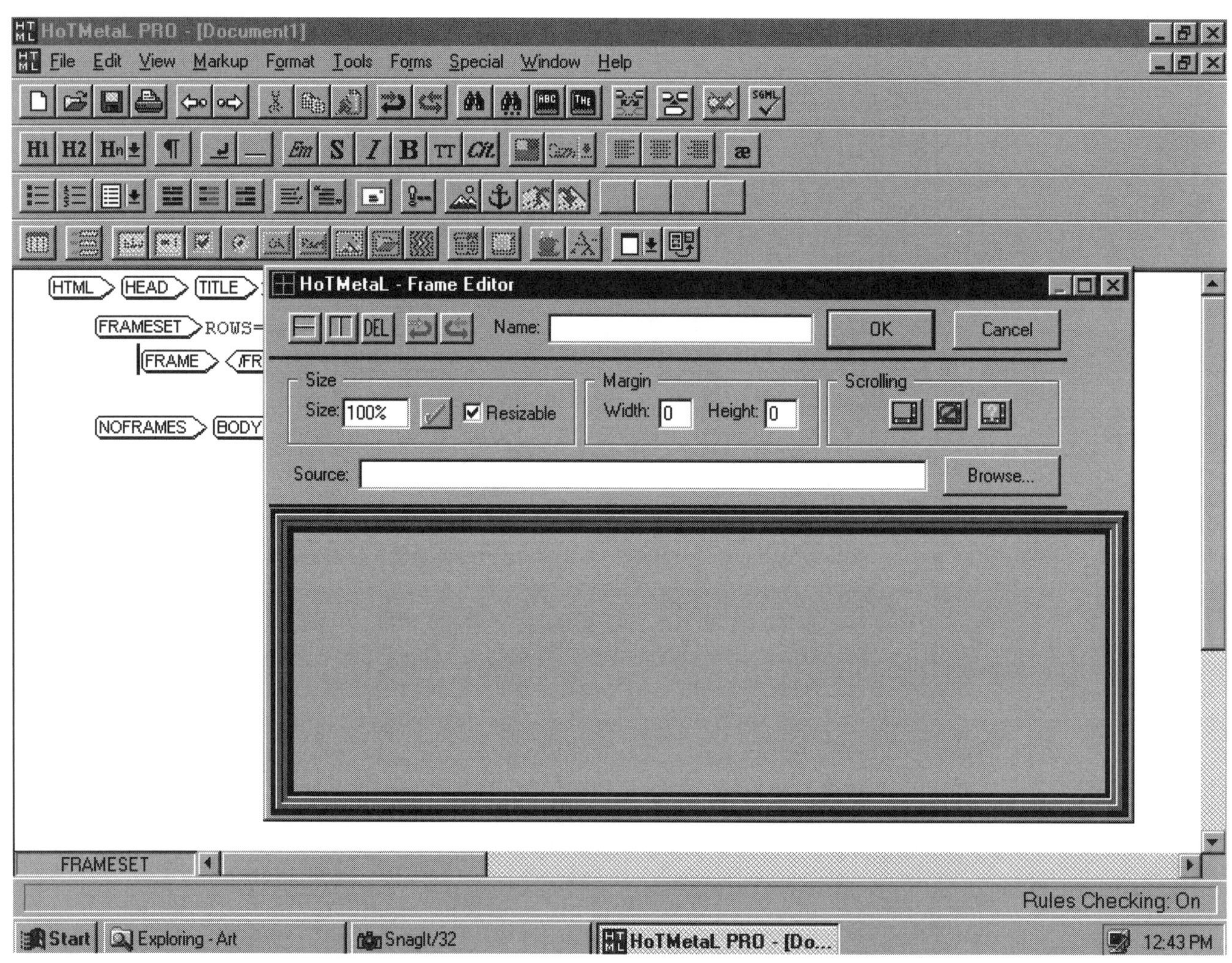

Figure 7–8: HotMetal Pro's Frames Commands

Frames can be supplemented by tables and other features. If used, we recommend only one frame with a scrolling bar on the screen or at the most two at a time. The best compromise model, for example, keeps the left-hand navigation column as a part of the background page. A frame with its own scrolling bar is then inserted in the place of your right-hand column. The following illustration is from a site that a group of our staff developed in their off hours for another non-profit organization's Web site. Another variation appears in the End Notes from Mid-Hudson.

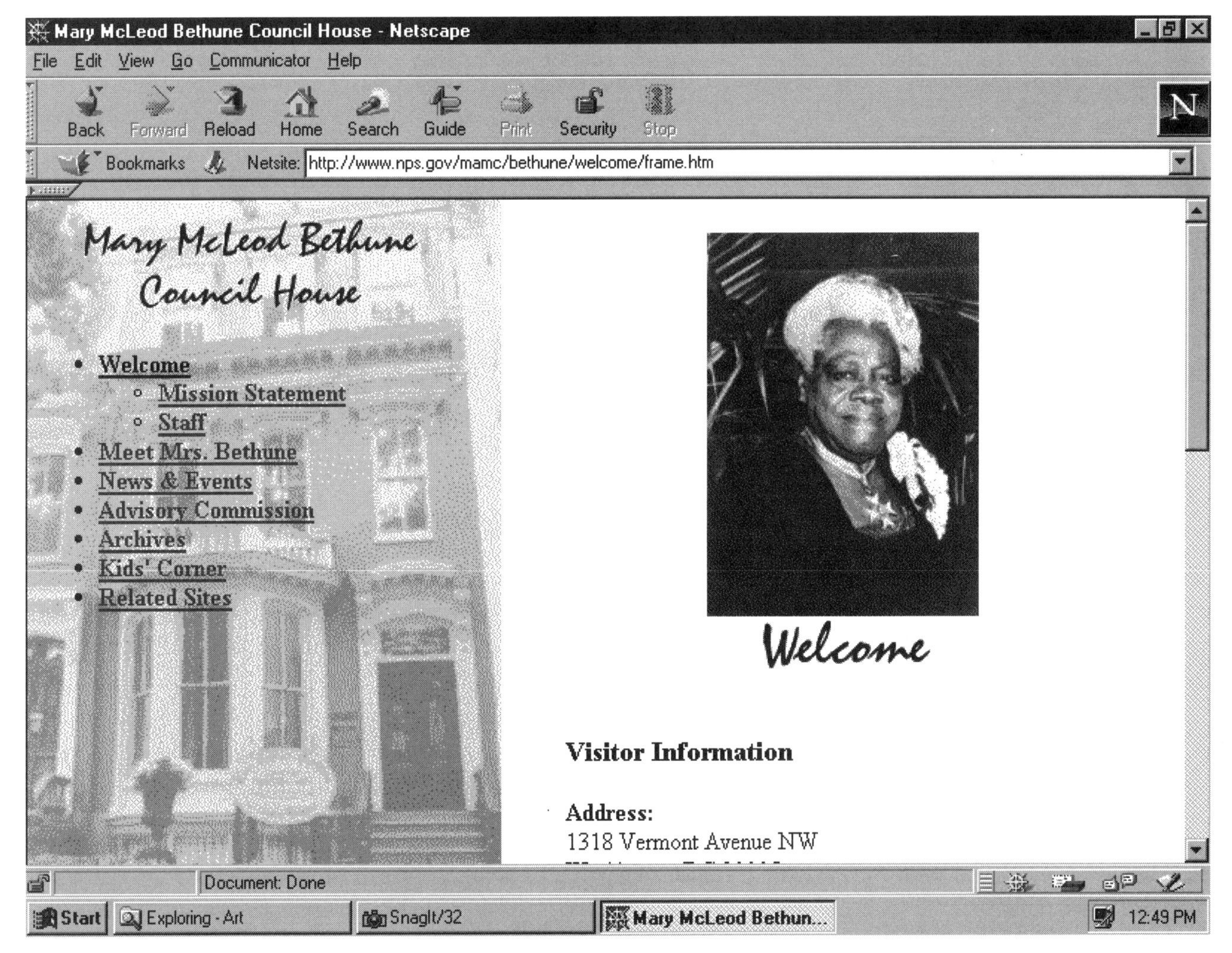

Figure 7–9: Mary McLeod Bethune National House Site

LISTING WITH SEARCH ENGINES

Once your virtual library is mounted, you may want to help the world find it, but another note of caution is sounded. Despite the burning desire to let everyone know about your killer site, management may want to examine some of the implications. Common sense dictates delaying listings until the site is out of prototyping and somewhat polished. If the site is intended as a pseudo-Intranet or Extranet for a small number of intended users, widespread use may be counterproductive. Response times could be negatively affected by your success.

If you are still interested in broadcasting the site's existence, the common course is listing with Web search engines. As always, we recommend keeping things simple. Go to each search site and look for a registration link—usually called "submit a link" or "register your site." Some are easier than others, but once you are done, you won't need to register unless you change your URL. A few sites claim to register with a number of search engines at once. However, we have had some problems with them. You still have to enter most of the information manually, so it's probably better to register with one site at a time, rather than having one of them running in the background. How do you find search engines? Your browser will likely provide many built-in links, but Search.Com [www.search.com/] and How to Announce Your New Web Site [ep.com/faq/webannounce.html] can certainly help.

Meta Note: After a number of Web searches, you might begin to notice that some sites pop up prominently, but seemingly without a clear relation to your search strategy. Some have violated basic "net-iquette" by raising the use of hypertext titles and metatags to a frustrating art form (see Chapter 9 for more detail).

END NOTES FROM MID-HUDSON

MHLS staff faced some interesting challenges in piloting a general Web library. We wanted to insert a commercial search engine to help people find entries from the entire range of holdings. That method, especially without an advanced thesaurus, was deemed potentially too frustrating to stand alone. Rather than providing only a canned message ("Your Search Resulted in 0 Matches—Please Try Again"), we attempted to ensure positive feedback and intuitive methods that built from the library model. Thus, we chose to replicate some of the browsing power of the virtual stacks by adding both Dewey and alphabetically arranged indexes.

BUILDING FOR NAVIGATION

Graphically, we wanted to keep images to the minimum and to have applications transparent to the users. The design of the site followed from the split-screen options and design principles laid out in Chapter

2. In keeping with our guidelines, the Dewey and alphabetic options were relegated to the left column (see Figure 7–10). The right, or larger, working area was reserved to display the individual catalog and specialty pages, such as our query form and help information. Since we expected users to spend most of their time working in the right frame, we also gave it the lightest background color (white). In contrast, we made the left frame light gray and placed descriptive information (such as the label "Dewey Index") in a darker, gray box, and later a tiled box (Figure 7–10), using Frames commands. This design allowed us to display on-screen indexes, which persist as their results are displayed. Consistent page menus also engender a feeling of order and familiarity, so that the user focuses on content, rather than on the layout.

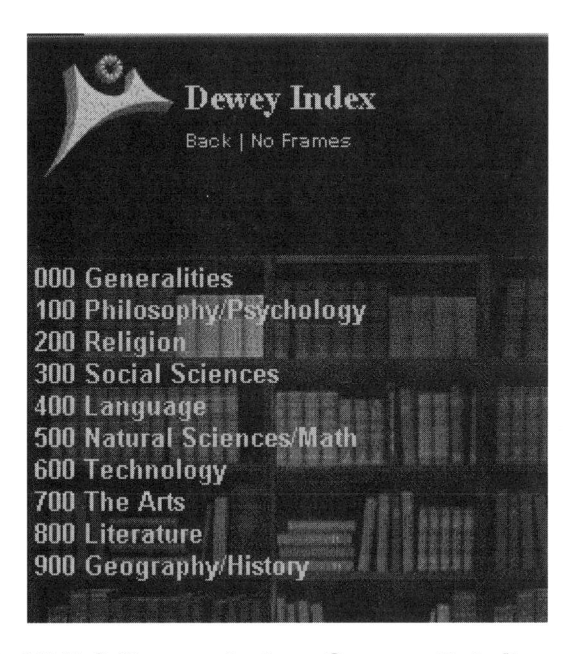

Figure 7–10: MHLS Dewey Index: Screen Detail

For Mid-Hudson's situation, Dewey's ten major subject categories served as the most logical default display for the navigation frame. Rather than requiring the user to link to a lower level to display the choices under each of those ten, we wanted to pack as much as possible into the navigational frame. As Chapter 8 illustrates, when our users click on a main category, a pull-down menu of subcategories appears on the screen. To help focus the user's attention and work within physical guidelines, the active portion of the list appears in bold. Clicking on a subcategory brings up the catalog entry pages in the right frame.

ADVANCED TINKERING

The raw outline could also easily be enhanced with other navigational features. For instance, we included a direct query function with an e-mail option to a librarian from the Ready Reference page. A link in the left frame allows the user to switch to the alphabetical index. One can scroll through the listings, or jump to a particular letter, by clicking on a navigation bar. When the user clicks on a subject within the index, the corresponding Web catalog page is displayed on the right. The user can also browse through the Web catalog pages by using the Previous and Next buttons on the menu bar. Other buttons include links to the Excite search engine, our help page, and our home page. The Index button is used to display the Dewey Index when the Web catalog is viewed with a browser that does not support frames.

Table Note: The menu bar on the Web catalog pages is actually a table, with the BORDER tag set to "0" and the background color (BGCOLOR) tag set to light gray (#808080). This shade of gray was chosen because it can be properly rendered, even with the standard 16-color VGA palette.

There are two advantages to using a table rather than an image map for your menu. One is that it loads faster than a bitmap. The other is that a table can resize itself automatically. Thus, the same Web catalog pages can be displayed properly in all browsers, regardless of their ability to render frame documents. This resizing is accomplished by simply specifying that the table WIDTH tag equals "100%." To "gray out" unavailable choices, we used plain text, formatted with our dark gray FONT COLOR and underlined it with the <U> tag.

Figure 7–11 illustrates a set of compromises in one of Mid-Hudson's early navigational structures. While a Dewey Index required only two frames, an Alphabetical Index with its recognizable string of 26 entries called for three. Clicking on a letter could then cause the frame below to scroll to the listings in that part of the alphabet.

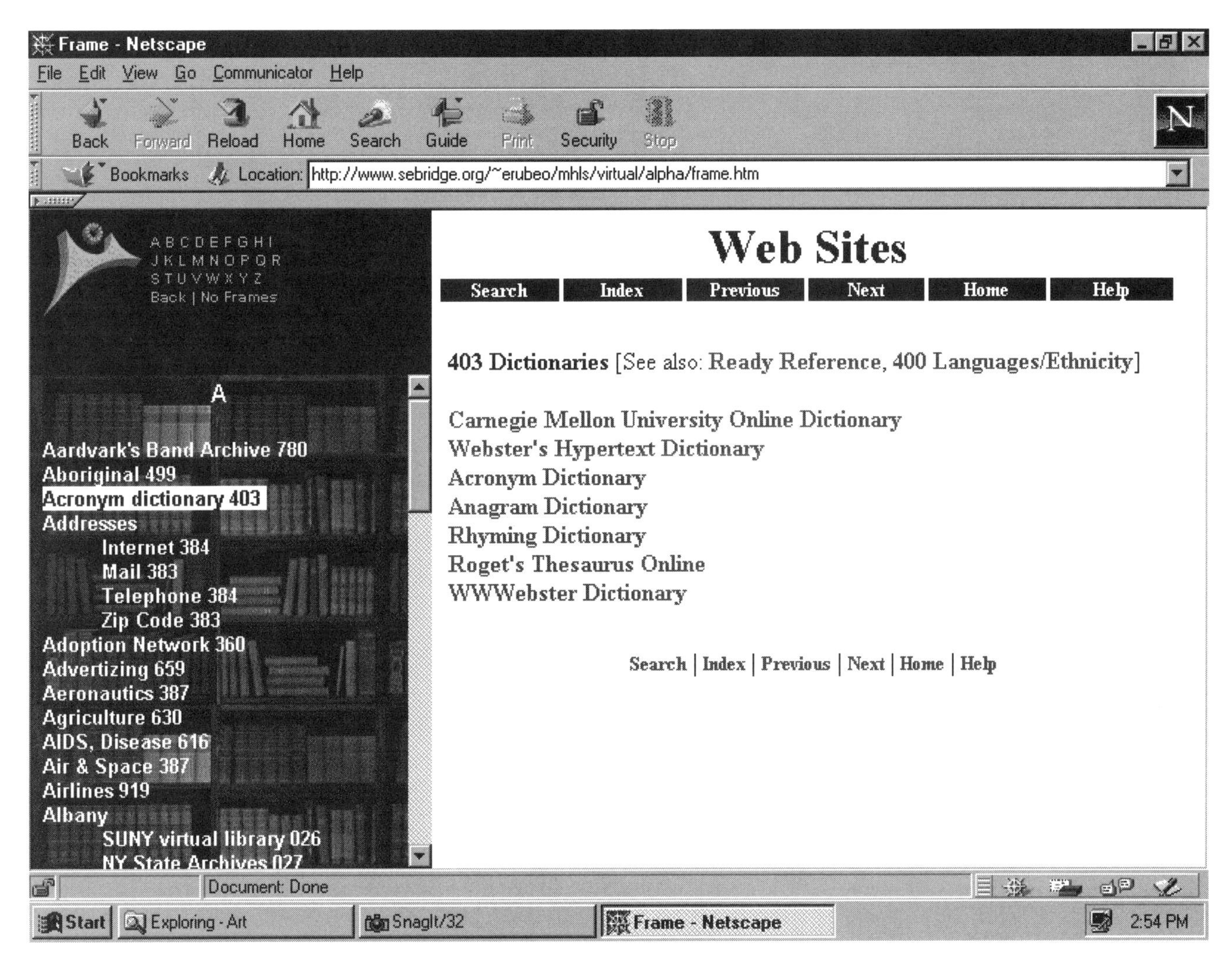

Figure 7–11: MHLS Alphabetical Index

CONTENT FRAME AND DEFAULT

In addition to setting the navigational defaults, we needed to select the initial information to appear on the larger right-hand frame. Such choices are a crucial element of site design. We had several options:

- Let the image default to the sites listed under the lowest, highest, or an intermediate range of the Dewey classification holders.
- Have it open to the Excite search engine option.
- Provide access to a descriptive account of how to search the site.

Given the freshness of our initial offering, we opted for the final or help option. Even the most seemingly transparent site should not delude its creators into thinking that help screens are superfluous. Some introductory explanation and options for a little training and instruction should always be part of a design.

REFERENCE ROOM MODEL: SELECTION GRID

The production of a suitable graphical interface for the "reference room catalog" model (see Chapter 4) required its own series of compromises and an extended development period. Levels of staff expertise, the type of software available, and the time required to mount a reasonable product all came into play. We began by checking other virtual libraries and related sites for ideas. After some looking and playing, Mid-Hudson staff focused on the use of the HTML Table function to simulate the design model as a grid.

MAKING THE GRID

In developing a grid, we had to determine how many columns and rows would be needed to divide the main categories for presenting our electronic resources. With the editor, we were able to customize the vertical and horizontal text alignment, the width of the column, and the background color of the table or cell. Bulleted and nested bulleted lists provided a useful feature to pack information within a cell and avoid using valuable space for table lines. The Web editor also allowed us to change font sizes. Being careful to retain a legible size, this variable facilitated scaling for a postcard discipline so that all our information could be viewed at once on the screen.

Unfortunately, the original three-part idea became somewhat chopped up in the actual application (see Figure 7–12). The general

Web library sections had to be split apart. Because of the space needed for coding of the cells, we could only fit nine categories on a single screen. After consultation on probable use patterns with our central library, the 100 Philosophy category was grouped with 200 Religion. Since the resulting nine categories took up the right-hand column, we squeezed Ready Reference into the central column and resorted to a bulleted list of reference categories. That design left enough room below for the Kids Room in the left column and Web Search Engines in the center column. Hence, the in-house database, online magazine subscription databases, and links to other libraries were readily defaulted to the left-hand column.

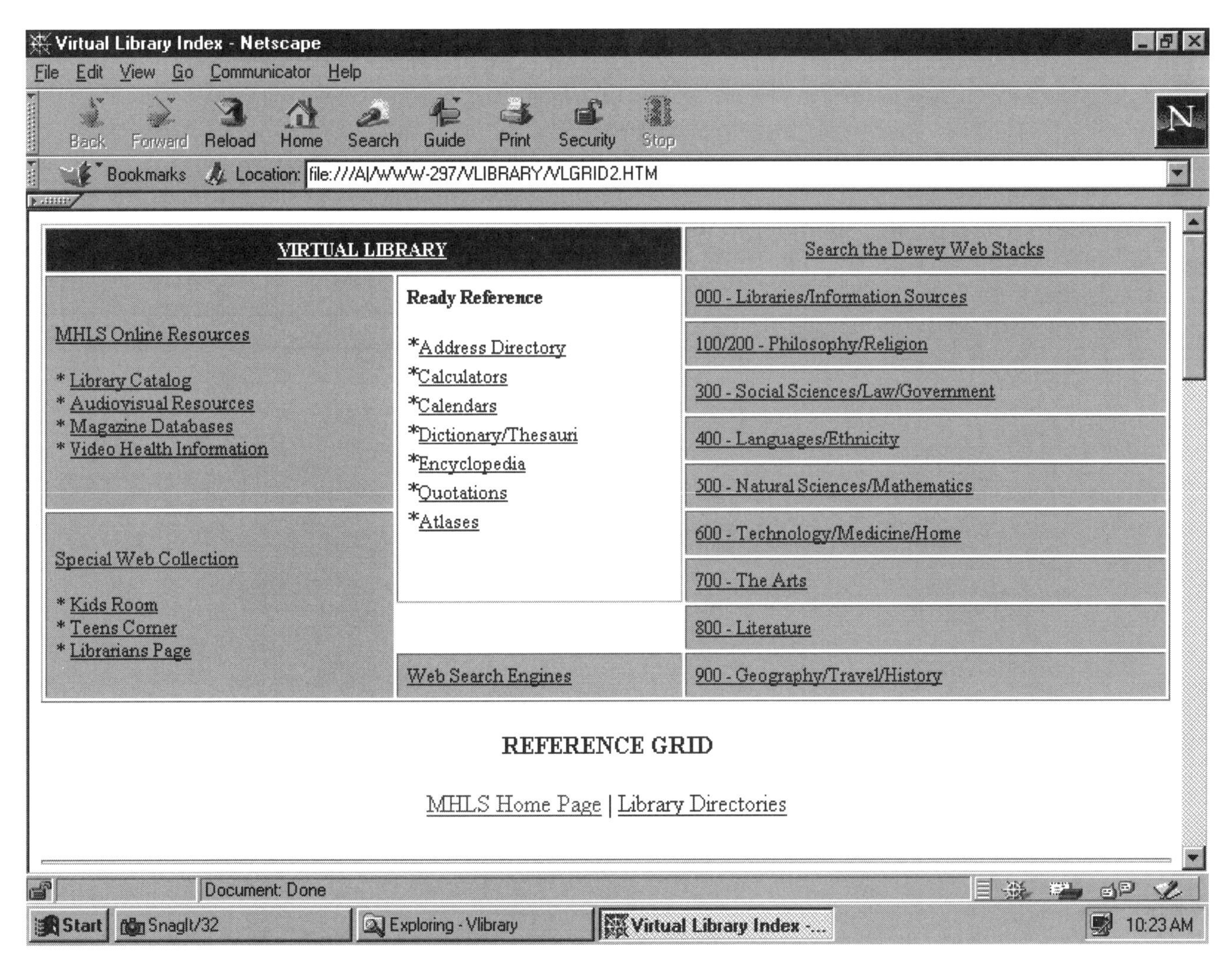

Figure 7–12: MHLS Virtual Library Grid, Original

EVALUATION OF PILOT

As the project turned to the actual mounting on the Web, we conducted a simple evaluation and informal survey of users. While we had successfully kept the information paths to only three levels or clicks in depth, the survey results suggested that the initial interface was too busy for easy use by our intended users. Despite our attempts to fine-tune the use of only nine categories, users did not necessarily intuit the gradations of our grid. Moreover, we had picked up a little more sophistication and resources along the way. Thus, the prototype grid was quickly scrapped. Newly found skills also allowed for a better interpretation of the original design concept. Although the original organizational principles remained, the interface would undergo ongoing refinement and redesign. A second version is shown in Figure 7–13.

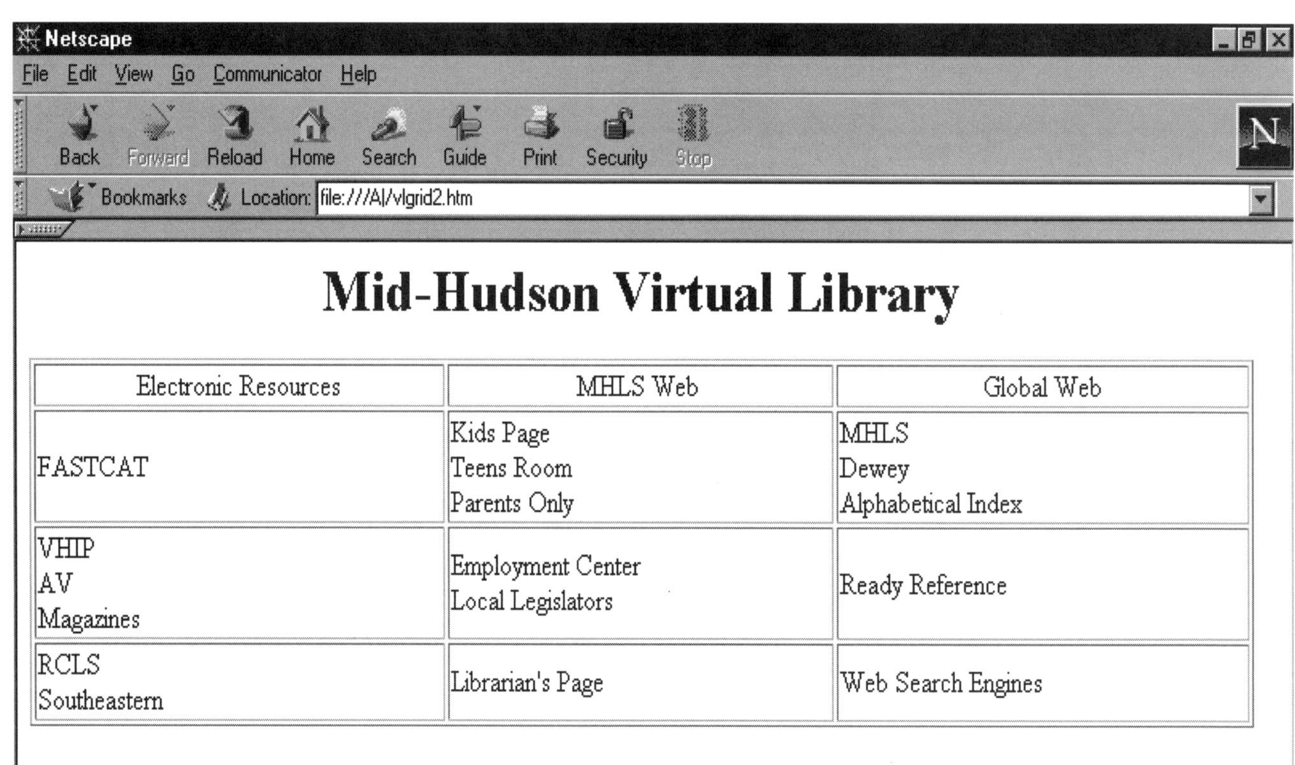

Figure 7–13: MHLS Virtual Library Grid, Version 2

The design was well received and quite functional for over a year. But information needs kept expanding and we did not stand still. With the active interest of the MHLS director, our budding Web implementation expert, Ed Rubeo, began exploring other options. During the summer of 1998, Mid-Hudson unveiled its latest look. The filing cabinet model emerged full-blown to include the entire site, which by now was built on a database model and dHTML. In the process, we abandoned the tripartite design for the simple split-screen layout with left-hand navigational buttons as in the rest of the site. The virtual library was integrated as one of the left-hand drawers of the filing cabinet into the entire site. Instead of pull-down menus, we expanded the virtual library's search options through a file card/tab design with the top layer of navigational buttons in the right-hand column. The new WebCat default screen is now the Catalogs page, as shown in Figure 7–14. Subsidiary files (Magazines, Videos) hold the virtual library functions that are most used by our member librarians. The results are highly utilitarian because we consciously emphasized functionality, organization, and ease of use. Visual enhancements, dictated by the content, will come later.

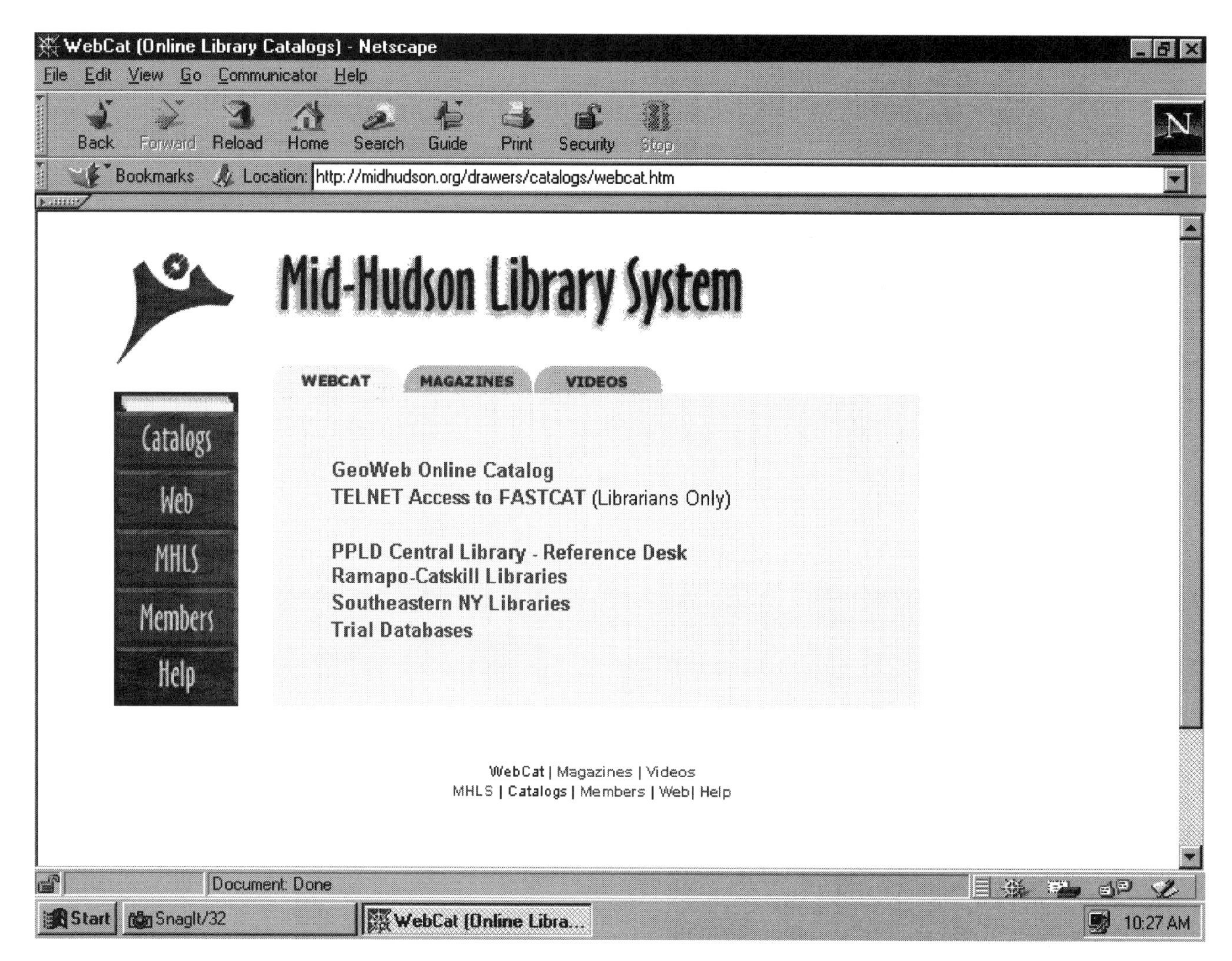

Figure 7–14: MHLS Virtual Library Card File, Fall 1998

3 MAINTAINING THE VIRTUAL LIBRARY

Edward J. Rubeo, Tom Bialek
and Denise Garofalo

The initial fun of selecting sites and building interfaces can dissolve into chaos if there is no underlying order at the start of a project. Although newer Web editing software is designed to help with site management and can lift some of the burden, you should understand some of the rules of the game. Site management begins with clear and consistent protocols for naming the files and directories. The importance of such ordering is impossible to play down. It provides the frame for all future enhancements. Consistent ordering can help improve the speed of your site and will ease maintenance and updating. As will be illustrated, recognizable words, abbreviations, and mnemonics are the guideposts for data element, file, and directory naming. Terms should make some sense to humans—especially those who might follow in later management of the site. You should also use natural language hierarchies whenever possible.

Your naming conventions are rooted in the limits of your operating system. With current Macintosh or Microsoft 95 or later versions, you can string together quite descriptive phrases. But overly long terms can become awkward; moreover, your operating environment may not present such a luxury. In particular, any team working on different platforms (UNIX; DOS; Windows 3.11, 95, or 98; and the Power Mac) will need to default to the lowest common format. This probably means adopting DOS conventions and limiting file names to no more than eight characters, a period, plus a three-character extension (e.g., filename.doc). Eight basic hints will help you select usable names.

EIGHT HINTS FOR NAMING DIRECTORIES AND FILES

1. **Use lower-case for file names.** Since operating systems such as Unix may be case specific and treat a capital letter as a different character, you will be safest using lower-case characters in file names. It is important to recognize that file-name extensions may define specific types of data (e.g., .htm, .html, .gif, .jpg, .txt).
2. **Use appropriate extensions.** Many software applications need such extensions for their operations, so keep them or add appropriate ones to your file names. A practical result of using

Dewey Note: The files for a virtual library are best controlled by relying on the Dewey classification codes. The advantages of using Dewey were explained later (Chapter 4). Hence, the title for the first content-holding file in a Dewey Catalog Web Library should be something like "000 Generalities." Its file name could be "cat000.htm." This convention also makes it easier to troubleshoot errors in a Dewey index or in subsidiary alphabetical indexes—the link to the page titled "000 Generalities" will be "/webcat/cat000.htm," the link to "403 Dictionaries" will be "/webcat/cat403.htm," and so forth.

extensions is that you will be able to identify a document's format quickly without having to open it. For similar visibility, we recommend that you apply a suffix only to file names, not to directory names.

3. **Avoid codes.** Rely as much as possible on natural language, easily recognizable abbreviations, and mnemonics rather than artificial codes for naming files and their directories. For example, the file name for a library's monthly newsletter for October 1999 could either be a cryptic "/library.org/f-10.htm" or something a bit clearer like "/library.org/newslett/97-10bul.htm."
4. **Name your Home Page files systematically.** Depending on your server software, files named "index.htm," "index.html," "default.htm," or "default.html" may load automatically when a user points a browser to the directory that contains them. Using one of these names ensures that browsers will see your home page, rather than a list of directories on your site. To find out which name(s) your server supports, simply rename the file and type its directory path in your browser. If recognized, your home page will appear. If not, you will see a directory tree.
5. **Create reserved names by file type.** Create your own list of reserved terms to help differentiate certain types of files that are common to several directories (such as lists, frames, menus). If a directory contains only one file, the file could even share the directory name. For example, if a list is stored in a directory named "/list" and the directory contains only one file, the file is named "/list/list.htm." If the directory holds a frame document, the frame document should always be titled "frame.htm," the menu "menu.htm," and so on. Using the method above to make a list for a frame page could result in a directory "/list" with the following two files:

   "/list/frame.htm" (the frame document)

   "/list/main.htm" (the content, usually in the right frame)

   One or more of the following files would also be in the directory:

   "/list/menu.htm" (the menu in the left frame)

   "/list/header.htm" (the header over the right frame)

   "/list/lheader.htm" (the header over the left frame)
6. **Keep the root directory clean.** Place your home page in the directory with your domain name. Put all other files in subdirectories of this directory. This convention gives users who access the site through an FTP address a logical starting point and helps them find your home page. A plain text (.txt)

file listing the names of the documents on your site and what they contain can also be invaluable for FTP address users.

7. **Duplicate/mirror the site.** Duplicate your site in a separate directory or stream it to tape or another storage area. Ideally, one copy of the most recent working version is a fail-safe for preservation purposes and a quick fix should your newest version inadvertently crash the system. Do not store this copy on the working computer. In addition, you should keep a historical file of all features or earlier versions (to fulfill your professional responsibilities and as a good management tool for comparison purposes). While the archival copies can reside on your server, keep in mind the danger of accidentally linking to their directories. As previously noted, we also recommend a separate computer as a mirror site and test bed for both security and quality control purposes.
8. **Store files indexed by your search engine separately.** This tip is for those employing the enhanced features discussed in Chapter 9 and prevents unwanted pages (such as templates and indexes) from turning up in your search results. It may also save hard disk space and improve the response time (since your indexes will be smaller). Those who browse through the catalog, rather than searching, will also benefit from this arrangement, because when they click the "previous" and "next" buttons on the menu bar their machines will most likely search the current directory first for the next sequential page.

Code Checker Note: Before mounting a site, always debug it and look for outstanding coding errors. Fortunately, most Web-editing software now automatically resolves such problems. The Web Consortium has also provided an online alternative to verify codes [validator.w3.org].

HOW TO ADD GRAPHICS AND MULTIMEDIA

Although you can achieve a crisp and highly functional layout with the default options in your editor, you will undoubtedly want a little pictorial gloss. Graphics, attractive fonts, and even sound or animation are also increasingly expected by today's netizens. Such enhancements help enliven a site and draw return visitors (especially desirable qualities in sites for children and teens). Once you reach a graphics decision, you will discover that good Web editors have turned the actual task into an easy series of commands. Finding appropriate materials is also not hard. Most Web authoring software packages include copious amounts of clip art and simple graphics applets to make your life easier. Additional artwork is available on the Web (for example, Background Sampler [home.netscape.com/home/bg/], Icons for Web

Pages [www.jsc.nasa.gov/~mccoy/Icons/index.html], and Sandra's Clip Art [www.cs.yale.edu/homes/sjl/clipart.html]). Similar sites and applications, but extra space and downloading demands, are available for animated GIFS. In time, you may even want to design your own images, or at least customize the ones you own. Simple image editors, such as Adobe PhotoDeluxe or PhotoShopPro, are cheap and easy to use. Full-featured graphics programs, such as Corel Draw and Adobe Photoshop, are more powerful but also quite sophisticated applications. They may take a considerable amount of time to master and suggest the need for a dedicated design specialist on staff.

Graphics Warning: Use graphics sparingly. Images can require a great deal of memory and thus slow the loading of pages that contain them. Moreover, HTML is not the most facile language for handling nontextual elements.

Software for creating MIDI music, digital sound, video, and virtual reality worlds also abounds. Use restraint. Such additions require a considerable amount of bandwidth and may severely slow down your site. While state-of-the-art systems attract some users, they exclude many more. Thus we offer the following simple guidelines for graphic images:

- **Keep your graphics separate.** In keeping with data-naming conventions, be careful with your assignments. If you must use images, store them in a separate directory, so that they can be found and updated easily. You can further improve speed by using the same image on more than one page (assuming that it is a logo or an icon). Since the path name will be the same, the graphic will be reloaded from the user's cache, rather than from your server. And bringing the image to the screen through progressive scanning to add detail in waves may speed up the user's ability to recognize the image. These hints may prove useful for loading into children's and teens' facilities, which require a bit of sprucing up to engage their users.
- **Choose your graphic format wisely.** As of this writing, the most common and best image formats for the Web are GIF and JPEG ("jay-peg") files. Both formats are shown in lower case as the extensions on the file name (e.g., xxxx.gif). GIFs are best suited to drawings and charts. They produce cleaner, sharper lines, and can be interlaced for faster loading, but they only support a limited number of colors. JPEGs are best suited for continuous tone images, such as photographs, or when more than 256 colors are needed. You can use graphics programs (such as Adobe Photoshop and Corel Draw) to convert files into these formats. The normal recommendation is to design original images in .TIFF or vector formats (such as Corel's native .CDR type), save them, and then experiment with converting copies of the image to .GIF or .JPG (JPEG standard). JPEG usually produces a smaller file (the amount of compression can be specified in your drawing application). The size of GIFs can be limited by restricting the

number of colors used. For moving images, you can use animated GIFs rather than scripting in JAVA or other languages. The GIFs are the most stable formats available at the moment. In time JAVA or new graphics formats, such as .PNG, may reach the level of sufficient standardization for cross platform use. It is also hoped that they will combine small file size with increased sharpness, color palettes, and color fidelity.

- **Choose your color palette wisely.** Netscape Navigator and Microsoft Internet Explorer each recognize a palette of 256 colors. Yet your users may well see something quite different from your intended selections. Variations in video cards and monitors interfere, along with the fact that the 256 colors are not fully standardized, but are instead drawn from a palette of 16 million. How these colors are selected depends on many factors. If more are needed for an image, the missing colors are made up by dithering the existing ones. For practical purposes, you don't need to worry about color in JPEGs. When you convert a file to a GIF, specifying an *optimized* palette of 256 colors usually produces the best results. If file size is a problem, limit your optimized palette to less than 256 colors. Trial and error is currently the main method for determining how much you can limit the palette before the image quality becomes unacceptable.
- **Use descriptive names for the graphics.** Since some users turn off or do not have graphic capacity, you should include an understandable title at the place marker (that is, not "image1," but "Mid-Hudson logo").
- **Consider the wallpaper option.** One semi-advanced touch beyond color is to add wallpapering or special designs "behind" your text. This can be done for part or all of your screen. If you are a novice, you should be aware that most editors will let you pick a background image from a predefined template. But almost any graphic can be used for a background image. Background images (GIFs, JPEGs or whatever) can be specified along with the global color values. The smaller the image's file size, the faster it will load. You can either use a single, large image (not recommended unless you greatly compress it), or a tiled image that is repeated such as in the bookshelf image behind our Virtual library's navigation buttons (Figure 8–1). Just about every HTML editor and graphics program is bundled with images designed to tile seamlessly. Some editors also come with applets that allow you to generate your own tiles. Again, the general process is quite simple with the typical HTML editor. The wallpaper feature is usually under Document Properties or specified on the Page Layout menu.

Resource Note: You will find an extensive discussion of color in Web site design through Microsoft [msdn.microsoft.com] in its Site Development area. For other solutions, note the scripting options in Chapter 9.

Clarity Note: When choosing a background image, take care that your text can be distinguished over it. If not, your writing becomes camouflaged. We have discovered a few tricks for avoiding this problem:

- Use a simple, tiled pattern for the background image.
- Lighten the background image and darken the text; or darken the image and lighten the text.
- Use boldface for text that appears over a background image.
- Use one of the specially designed Web fonts.

Sample Fonts Note: Our virtual library uses two Microsoft fonts that are optimized for the Web: Georgia and Verdana. These fonts are usually bundled with Internet Explorer and users can download them from Microsoft's site, free of charge [Win95.Win3.Mac]. If a user does not have Verdana installed, our style sheet substitutes Arial or Helvetica (fonts that are loaded in default installations of Windows and the Mac OS). If neither Arial nor Helvetica is installed, the browser looks for the generic "sans serif" font, which is assumed to be present on every machine. Failing this, the user's default font will be displayed.

FONTS

Fonts specially designed for Web readability should be an important consideration for any site, but please do not be deceived. Again, your selection may be limited by the receiving browser. Although HTML allows you to specify a FONT-FACE attribute, the tag will be recognized only by Microsoft Internet Explorer 3.0 and Netscape Navigator 4.0 or above. Moreover, user machines must typically have the designated fonts installed on their system. Fortunately, such developments as electronic style sheets and JAVA can bring the fonts with them. Thus Microsoft's "font embedding" (for Internet Explorer) and Bitstream's "dynamic fonts" (for Netscape Navigator) allow typefaces to be downloaded with your document, much like graphics.

PULL-DOWN MENUS

Pull-down menus offer you a powerful graphical method to add depth to the navigational possibilities and extend the limits of the Miller number, or rule of seven. One can literally pack the screen with options beneath options. With this feature, your users can scan hierarchies and "grab" at the appropriate level. Your script then makes each menu item a bookmark or a link to a URL. Any good HTML editor, such as HotMetal Pro 4.0, makes such tasks relatively easy. A related solution is to use Forms to display pull-down lists or option buttons as navigation aids. In line with HTML 4.0, new products that automate the generation of code for such navigation are beginning to appear on the market. Remember, too, the borrowing option is still open and shareware sites abound.

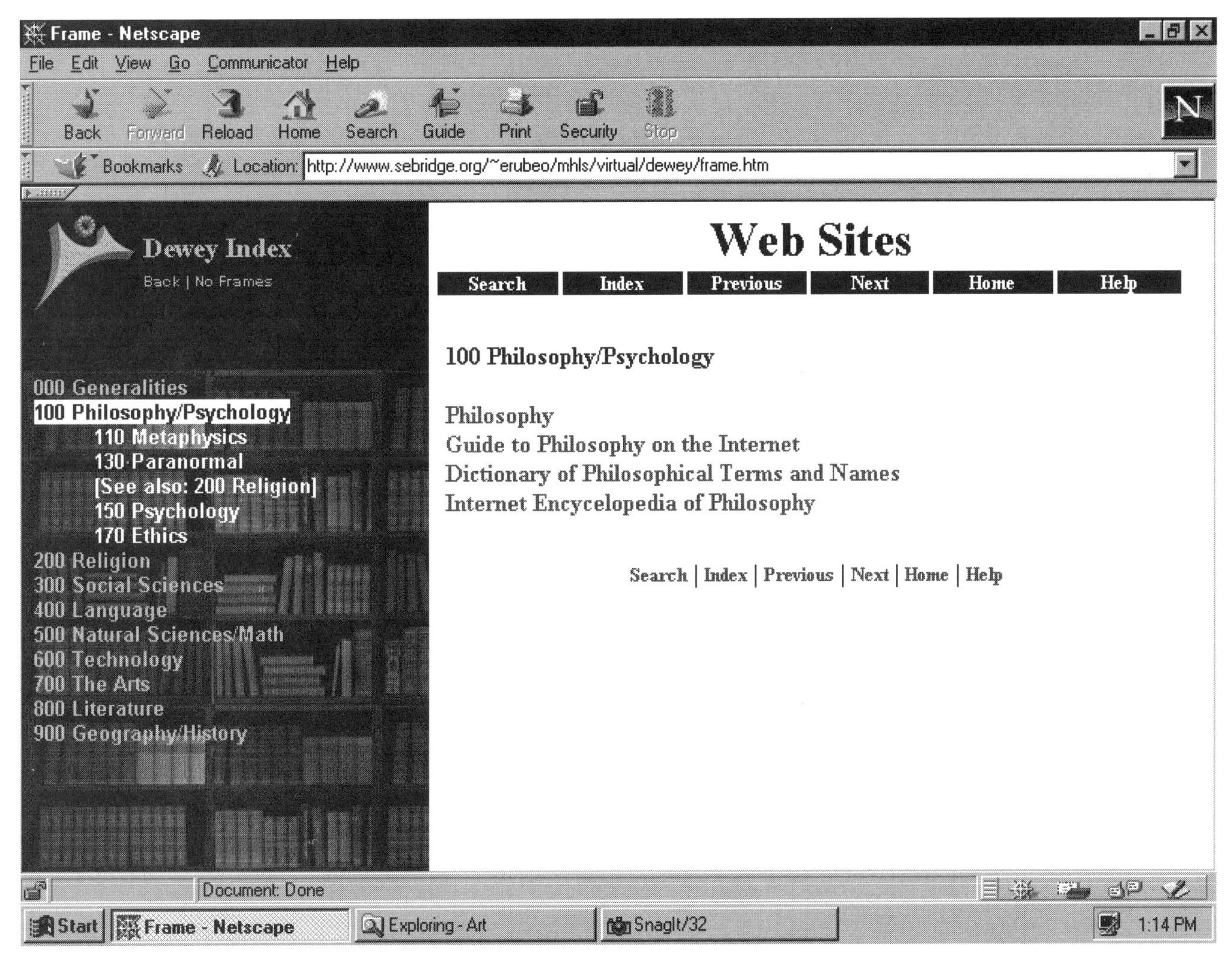

Figure 8–1: MHLS Dewey Index with Expanded Category

The pull-down feature can also be simulated with Netscape's "layers" or Microsoft's "fade" features. However, relying on those features could mean designing for two distinct browsers and having the scripts that run them peacefully coexist. Your users must also have versions 4.0 or higher of these browsers to see and operate the menus. Therefore, an alternative site or another means of navigation on the page should also be included. Should you use Forms or script-generated menus? If you require the safest code and a limited development time, we recommend forms. If you need more control over the appearance of the menu, the layers or fades option is preferable. But if your menu is very long or requires regular updates, an HTML frame is still your best bet.

SITE MONITORING

Privacy Reminder: If you collect personally identifiable information on your visitors, you should disclose this practice and any use of the information.

Use quantitative measures to help evaluate the efficiency of the site and to plan for enhancements. You must realize that evaluation may present some challenges or require some trade-offs. For instance, background instruments can command online resources and adversely affect loading time. Moreover, you encounter legal and ethical concerns whenever your efforts extend to the collection of personally identifiable information about your visitors. Available monitoring tools include counters, cookies, cookie servers, and link checkers.

"Voyeur" Services: These services monitor the various search engines across the Web and disclose traffic patterns and types of research questions asked. They are also among the most interesting and troublesome areas for the Net aficionado (see [searchenginewatch.com]).

COUNTERS

The basic management question is how many hits does the site or the different areas within it receive. Some of these data can be collected automatically as a simple byproduct of the Web or network and the newer database or dHTML software. The original trend of using visible traffic counters as billboards to announce the number of visitors is increasingly viewed as poor netiquette. Instead, hidden counters are strategically placed to monitor traffic patterns from the pilot stage on.

COOKIES

Cookies are the key tracking device for dealing with Web traffic. They are also a major area of concern with respect to the privacy issues discussed in Chapter 3. Cookies are special files that reside on your computer and are maintained by your Web browser for use by servers of sites that you visit. They can help with remote authentication and, when tied to scripts, could provide you with control over the layout produced on the user's machine. Cookies can also speed up your future contacts and are especially used to record traffic and gain information about users. While cookies start out theoretically tasteless and can contain almost any of the ingredients of the transaction, they do tend to include three basic elements:

- **Domain Name:** Normally denotes the Web server supplying the cookie.
- **Cookie Name:** An individual name supplied by the Web server so that it can retrieve the cookie quickly with return visits.
- **Expiration Date:** Indicates how long the cookie will remain on the user's machine (some last only during browsing and others remain for years). Note: You can use your browser or other "cookie cutter" software to remove cookies before the expiration date.

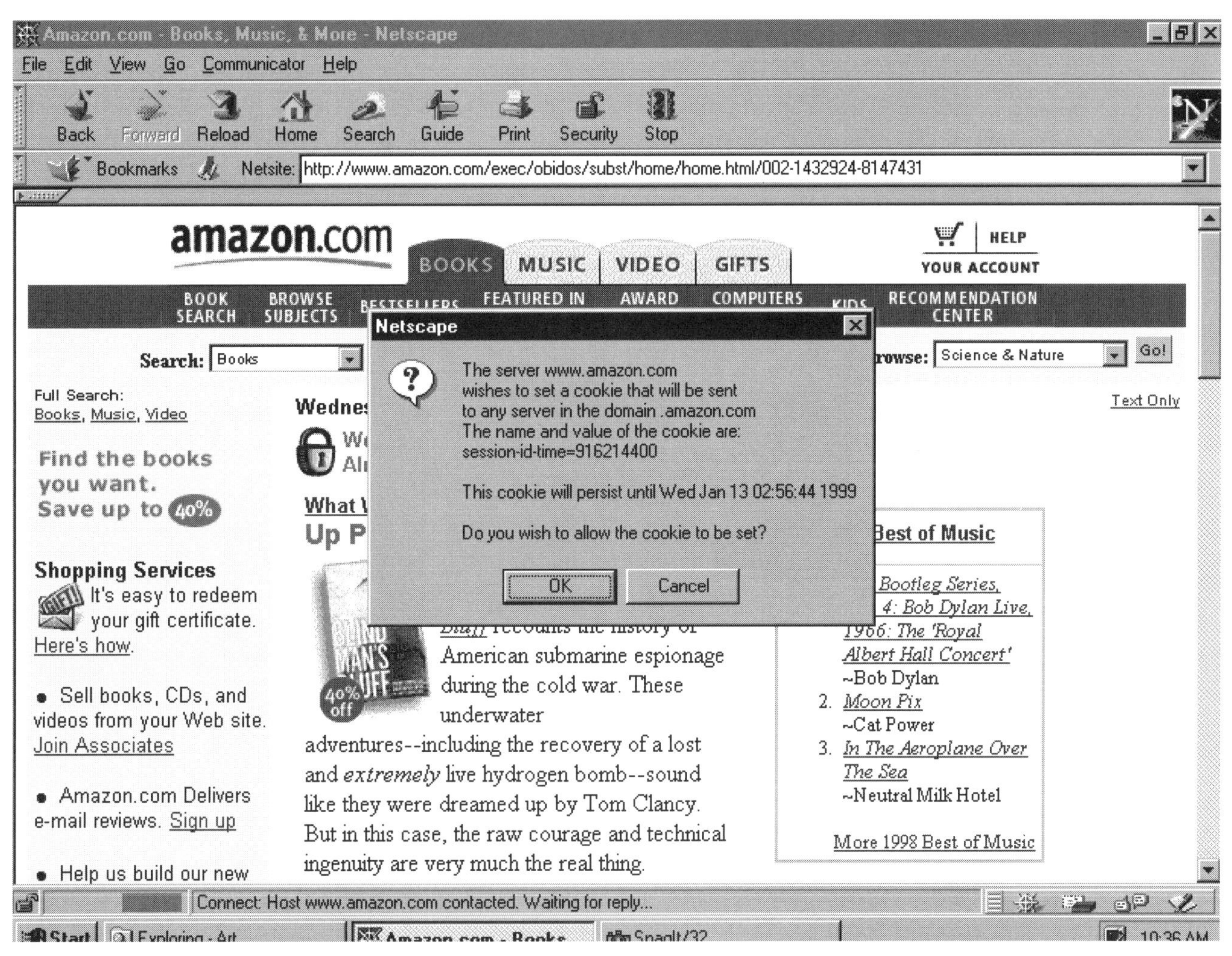

Figure 8–2: Amazon.com cookie

Mid-Hudson Note: We used Net-Trak (net-trak. stats.net/) to count a selection of pages. Generally, we opted to program only the first pages of the major sections (i.e. the home page, menu pages, and the other special sections of the virtual library, such as the Kids Room and the Teens Corner). This method helps reveal what sections of the site are frequently used and which sections are lightly used. In terms of design for browser capabilities, the results also can show the number and versions of Netscape Navigator and Microsoft Internet Explorer browsers along with Lynx, Mosaic, and even the newer Web TV hybrids.

A COOKIE SERVICE

One of the easiest ways to engage cookies for your Web site is simply to hire a service. For instance, Net-Trak services [net-trak.stats.net/] allows tracking as many pages as needed. All that is required is to slot select .gif target images into the Web page. The images provide a direct link back to the Net-Trak server. Every time one of the images is loaded onto a browser page, the counter at Net-Trak is engaged. The information gathered is quite impressive:

- normal hit counters (every single hit to the page)
- unique host counter (counts a unique host—IP address—hit once per day)
- average hits per day
- total hits for today and yesterday
- last 100 hosts/IP addresses that visited the page
- unique counts available for type of browser and operating system that visits the page

LINK CHECKERS

One of the banes of the Web is the short half-life of sites. This quality is especially common among some of the more interesting content locations that come from inventive university students, who have the annoying tendency to graduate and abandon their offspring. External links should thus be monitored at least on a monthly basis. Although staff can be assigned to such tasks, larger sites should think about using special software products. These products can be purchased, but a few free spiders and automatic checkers are also available. Examples for a Unix environment include:

- WWW Link Checker [www.ugrad.cs.ubc.ca/spider/q7f192/branch/checker.html]
- lvrfy: HTML Link Verifier [www.cs.dartmouth.edu/~crow/lvrfy.html]
- MOMspider [www.ics.uci.edu/WebSoft/MOMspider/WWW94/paper.html]

You may also wish to consider your basic file organization as another way to simplify the process (see, for example, Ron Johnson's discussions on procedures [152.20.25.1/Linkbot.html] for the Linkbot validator). Linkbot [www.linkbot.com], Tierra Highlights [www.tierra.com], and related commercial products tend to come with a free trial period. For smaller sites, you may get by with the free sampling provided by the Web Site Garage [www.websitegarage.com] and Doctor HTML [www2.image.com/RxHTML], or you can sign up for a complete subscription.

Several caveats are necessary for those using human or automated link checkers. One is to remember that sites may be only temporarily down. A single dead hit is not sufficient for removing a link from your site. Obviously, checkers require Internet access to the site, where they will not only check internal links (links between pages in the site) but also the external links that the site connects to. Since a virtual library is composed of external links, it can take the checkers a while to browse the site. Traditionally, these checker programs are resource hungry and they should be run early in the morning or late in the evening to minimize the load on the Web server.

Mid-Hudson Site Sweeper Notes: For the investment of a few hundred dollars, a product like Site-Sweeper can give relatively detailed accounting and alert you to overlooked problem areas. Its Quality Summary, for example, reveals the following type of information:

- **Broken Links:** Of the total number of links, how many were down? How many were to your pages and how many to internal or external sites?
- **Slow Pages:** Given your specified download size limit, how many pages exceeded your threshold, and what was your largest page (a size limit of 32K per page downloads at 28.8K bbs in 9 seconds)?
- **Missing ALT Attribute:** Of the inline references that should have an ALT attribute, how many are missing it?
- **Missing Width or Height:** How many of the graphical references are missing width or height attributes?
- **Distorted Images:** Of the images with width and height specified, how many are proportionally distorted.?
- **Problem Titles:** How many of the pages on the site had problem, missing, or duplicate titles?

END NOTES FROM MID-HUDSON: BUILDING AN ELECTRONIC RESOURCES LIBRARY

With some of the management issues on the table, we return to the particulars for an electronic resources library. As we discuss below, this step takes you beyond the Web. You enter into non-HTML elements along with the annoying realities and legal complications of licensing agreements.

LINKING TO FREE SITES

The public tends to focus on the free sites on the Web, which are quite simple to retrieve. Your editor will lead you to insert a target or hot link on your screen to the URL of an external site. Likewise, you can set the target designators to navigate to internally developed content on your own site. In our examples, the left-hand column of the Dewey frame or of the special resources collections connects to internal holding numbers that pop up in the right-hand column. The numbers hold the direct connections to external sites or internal data.

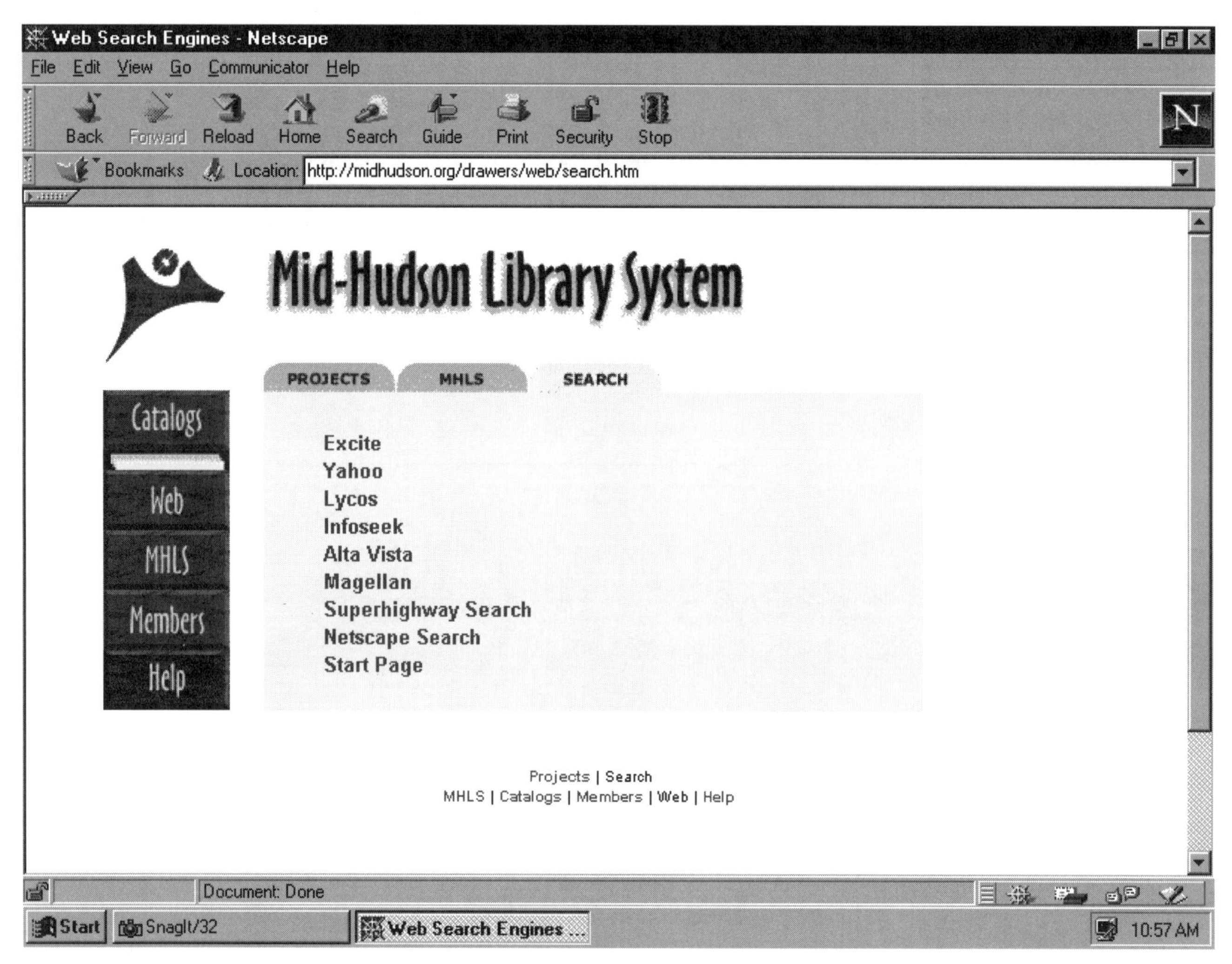

Figure 8–3: MHLS Web Search Engine Page

LINKING TO FEE-BASED SERVICES

In addition to the complimentary sites, your interface will likely provide a doorway to HTML-based magazine and other subscription data services. Even if your version of an electronic resources library relies on an intermediate Windows-based menu software, the connections may demand time, imagination, and patience. Establishing access is both a technical and contractual matter. Depending on the license, one may be limited to access within the institution. Mechanisms are available to extend across a service area, which will in the future likely feature patron card numbers and thus call forth some interesting privacy questions. Database vendors will help with your set-up while ensuring their needed controls and mechanisms for access. Typical verification methods include logins and passwords, IP address verification, and CGI scripts for verification.

Logins and passwords are the easiest methods to administer. Paid subscribers are given the legitimate login and password and those libraries can then access the database. Libraries must deal with users who log out; staff must then log in for the next user, which is inconvenient and technologically unnecessary.

Vendors seem to prefer IP address verification. For libraries that are the sole providers and any subscribers who have static IP addresses or proxy servers, IP address verification is easiest all around. The vendor's database server is configured to accept requests from specific IP addresses or ranges of such; library staff do not have to intervene. IP address verification does not operate smoothly in cases where subscribers access the Internet through a variety of ISPs, most of which assign dynamic IP addresses as sites log on. In such a situation the vendor cannot be given static IP addresses for verification. Mid-Hudson member libraries use over a dozen different ISPs, and most use dynamic IP addresses. We were unable to consider some online databases because the vendors only used IP address verification to handle subscriber access.

Another flexible authentication method uses CGI scripts, which are provided at the vendor end to authenticate subscribers. The authentication means (for example, zip codes, library card numbers) is worked out between the vendor and the subscriber. Screen prompts walk the user through the access procedure.

Finally, cookies and dHTML forms are also coming to the rescue. The information transmitted during the initial verified visit to a site can be easily captured, verified when the user next queries the site, and then automatically reproduced every time the user enters.

Hacker Warning: Although the technical reasons are beyond our present scope, you should be aware that the information gathered in cookies may not be very secure. We thus recommend encryption techniques or reliance on forms and database engines.

LINKING TO EXTERNAL LIBRARY CATALOGS AND THE COMING OF Z39.50

Users have come to expect ties to other library or archival systems, especially the Library of Congress [lcweb.loc.gov/homepage/online.html] and the National Archives [www.nara.gov], which are available with a simple URL link. One can also expect a library to have forged special borrowing and cooperative ventures with related bodies in the immediate geographic area. For example, Mid-Hudson has two partners that are also crucial to our ongoing and future information delivery plans. The neighboring Ramapo-Catskill Library System (RCLS) provides a readily available supplemental source of materials for the bulk of MHLS external interlibrary loans. RCLS is presently joining us in developing a joint Audio-Visual Bookings module for the region to sit on the Web with access through our virtual library. The Southeastern New York Library Resources Council (SENYLRC) provides the regional union serials listing, SEULS, which we retrieve through our virtual library.

In addition, our partnership with SENYLRC has led to grants for Web-based online catalogs and Z39.50-driven prospects for a region-wide shared virtual union catalog. The new standard has the potential for revolutionizing the delivery of MARC-based information services. Patrons employ a single search term and send out queries to any Z39.50-compliant library. The service is largely transparent to users, but with full (or level-3) compliance, in library parlance, the search extends to the level of current shelf status or borrowing potential of an item. Such facility is increasingly featured in the newest versions of large library automation systems (for example, DRA, Dynix, Geac, Innovative, VTLS). Of particular importance to Mid-Hudson, Z39.50 is on the drawing boards for some of the smaller stand-alone programs, like Athena and Follett. Sirs-Mandarin has already released a version for PC products and is scaling up to the bigger systems with an exceedingly affordable product.

The actual targeting of a compliant library may prove more difficult than the theory or a standard should suggest, but the end results are undeniably powerful. As we move toward electronic resource sharing we also anticipate implementation of ISO 10166 to address electronic interlibrary loan. Equally important, the staff's hard-earned HTML skills help empower us in the heretofore unthinkable tuning of OPAC interfaces, as well as the possibility for compliant online magazine services (for example, UMI's recently announced product).

NON-HTML OR LEGACY SERVICES

An electronic resources library may need to provide access to non-HTML or legacy services, which do not include graphics and may or may not provide the mouse's point-and-click potentials. Fortunately, such areas will fade as HTML or successor formats take over. For now, the planner should be aware that external inclusions come primarily through FTP (file transfer protocol) and telnet. Downloading software and files is the primary use of FTP, which also provides a major venue for uploading Web pages to a server. Telnet is the primary application for linkages within an electronic resources library and for accessing catalogs and e-mail.

Telnet

Virtual libraries interested in linking to non-Z39.50 libraries typically face making a telnet connection to the library system through the Internet. Once such a link is established, screen prompts lead the user through any login process (see Figure 8–4).

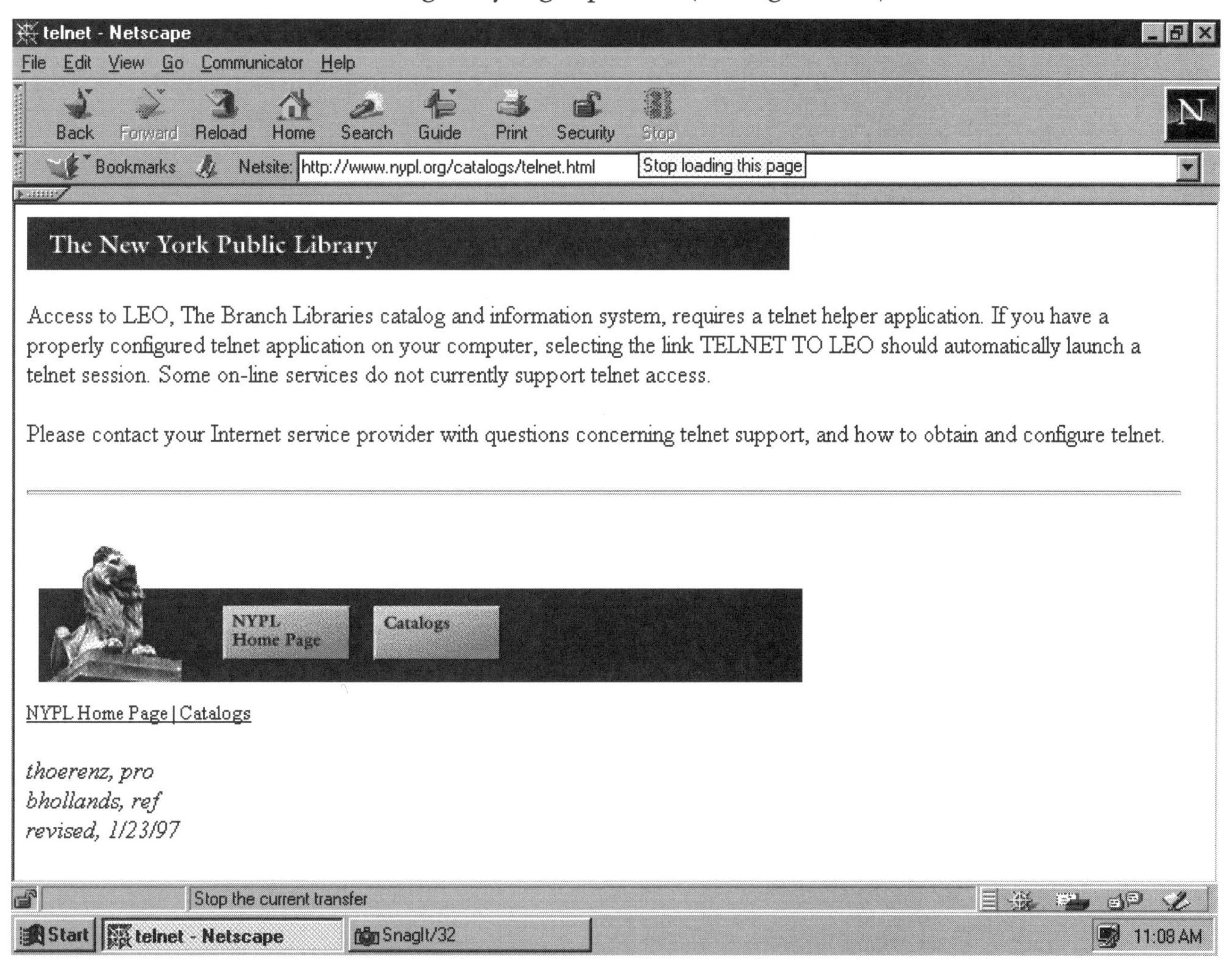

Figure 8–4: Telnet to Leo, New York Public Library

Although there are security problems to consider, an electronic resources library may need to provide telnet linkages to its own bibliographic resources. FASTCAT, the Mid-Hudson online union catalog for example, became available to member libraries via the toll-free access project called TeleCat in 1992. Access to FASTCAT broadened in 1995 via telnet on the Internet. A system to handle searching and booking of nonprint materials developed separate from FASTCAT, and dial access to this media management system became available in the mid-1980s and expanded to the Internet in 1996, again using telnet. A CD-ROM server was added to Mid-Hudson's online resources in 1994. Interest was high for graphical sources. Technically we were unable to provide these resources because of our dumb-terminal user base and speed considerations. Given the technical difficulties and the vendors' preference to provide online access rather than license titles for a wide area network, Mid-Hudson is also moving away from the CD-ROM server model.

Planning for integration to all Mid-Hudson online resources became contingent upon developing an Internet presence, creating one location that member libraries would consult to access the resources, and researching and configuring any software required to reach this goal. Once Mid-Hudson established a Web presence, development centered on the virtual library. A parallel effort was launched to locate an easy-to-use, configurable telnet application, primarily for use in accessing FASTCAT and other library catalogs. Staff turned to the Internet and TUCOWS (The Ultimate Collection of Winsock Software [http://www.tucows.com]).

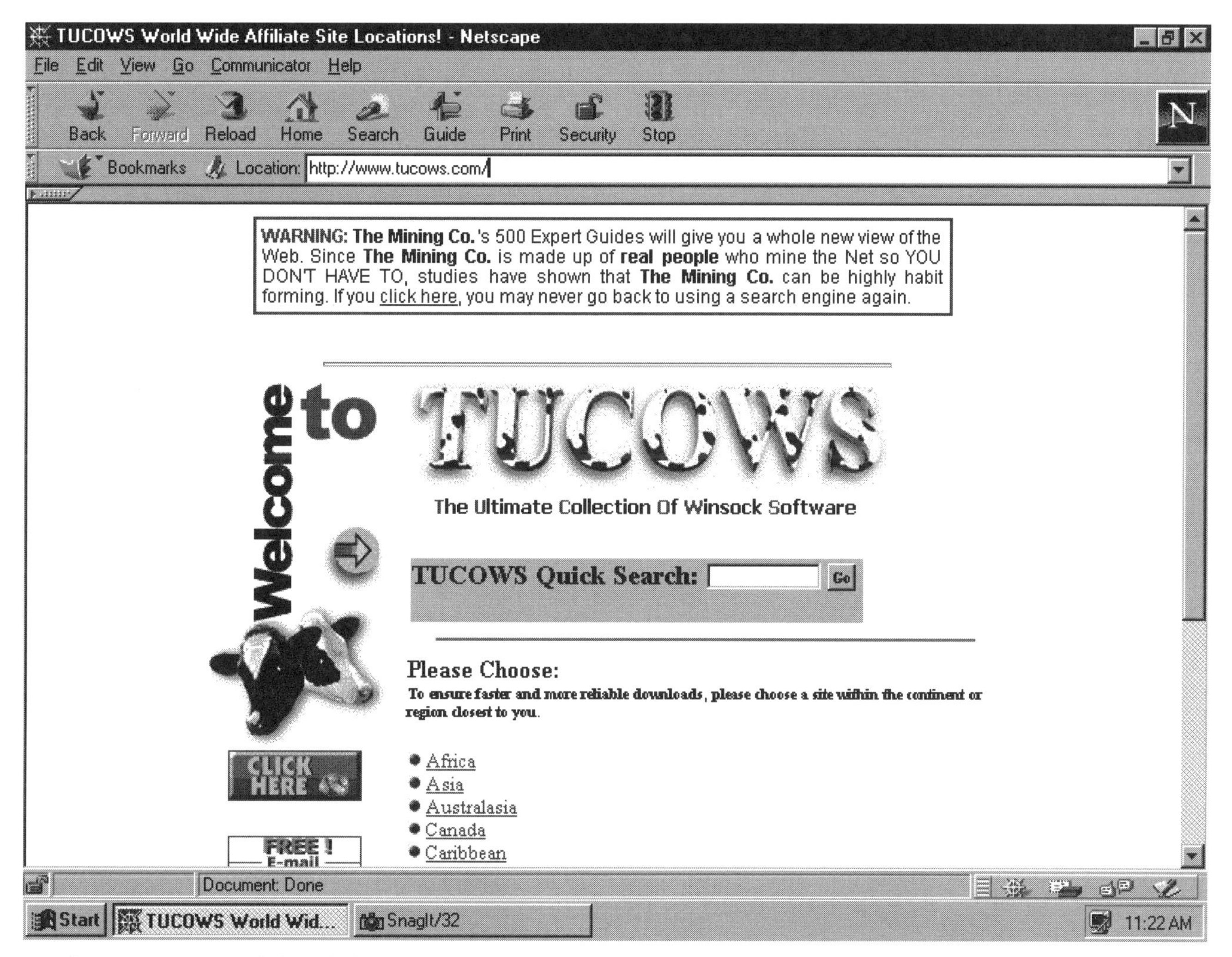

Figure 8–5: TUCOWS Software Site

NetTerm

At Mid-Hudson, telnet programs became a very controversial issue. GEAC, the company that helps to maintain the database, turned exclusively to the Web's http protocols and has not really moved beyond the dumb terminal VT100 screens for library check-ins/check-outs and data entry. As the libraries have moved to PCs, the need for a telnet program became paramount. Mid-Hudson has been recommending that the member libraries use a program called NetTerm, which would standardize the ways the libraries can telnet to the database and reduce the calls to the automation staff for support. NetTerm has many features that make it attractive, including the capability to program the function keys so that the VT100 emulation functions are still available on the PC. There is also the capability for programming scripts. This allows the library to have automatic logons for the public access computers, thus making patron access easier. The colors are customizable, and the use of sound is also an option.

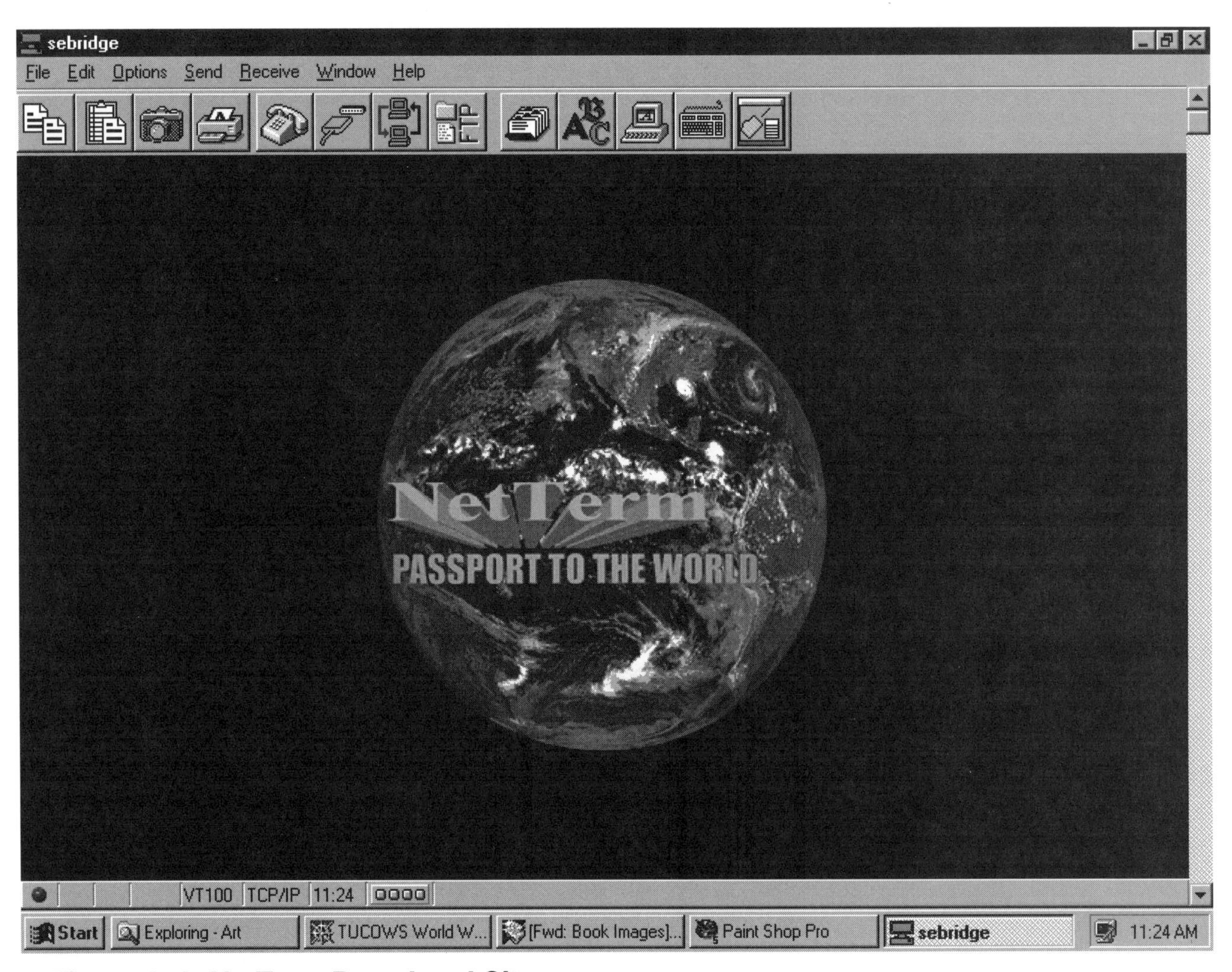

Figure 8–6: NetTerm DownLoad Site

9 ENHANCING THE VIRTUAL LIBRARY

Edward J. Rubeo, Fred Stielow, and Mohamed Toufali

Managerial Cautions: Staff enthusiasm must be balanced—especially, if they have other regular work duties. You also need to ensure a paper trail of your decisions and insist on the presence of formal policies. Also technological flourishes should not be allowed to disturb the conceptual motif, override aesthetics, or outstrip the capacity of user browsers. In sum, your common sense and the institutional mission must continue to prevail.

The previous chapters describe the construction and maintenance of a serviceable virtual library. During such adventures, the manager will likely discover that a development bug attached itself to someone on the Web team. Those bitten are ripe for assignment to the team's monitoring and enhancement duties—they are the prime audience for this chapter.

While serviceable and the norm for most Web sites, the techniques introduced to this point are limited. The following text provides the manager with a brief introduction to the limitations and challenges facing HTML—factors that must be dealt with to go beyond the basic virtual library. The essentially static approaches of the Web's first generation are being supplemented by a new array of enhancements. An intriguing list of new implementation toys and an ever-expanding list of formidable acronyms (see, for example [www.nlc-bnc.ca/ifla/ll/metadata.htm]) is entering the scene. Thus, this chapter exposes you to Web rings, GILS, and such prospects as the insertion of a search engine and emerging push and personalization techniques. The workbook pays attention to metadata and XML, along with scripting and, especially, the coming of dynamic HTML (dHTML).

WEB RINGS

Web rings employ special software to tie together sites with similar subject matter.

Web rings offer a special opportunity for collective or shared collection development and call for very little extra technical overhead. Dennis Howe originated the concept in 1994 with his EUROPa (expanding unidirectional ring of pages) chain letter. In 1995 WebRing [www.webring.com] began offering free administrative controls for starting a chain and maintaining links. Today, its RingWorld site claims over 15,000 participants in nine categories: Arts and Humanities, Business and Economy, Computers, Internet, Health, Recreation and Sports, Entertainment (by far the largest grouping), Society and Culture, and Miscellaneous (for example, the Useless Garbage Ring). The typical ring is built around one topic and has at least five members and its own ring master. The WebRing home page is shown below.

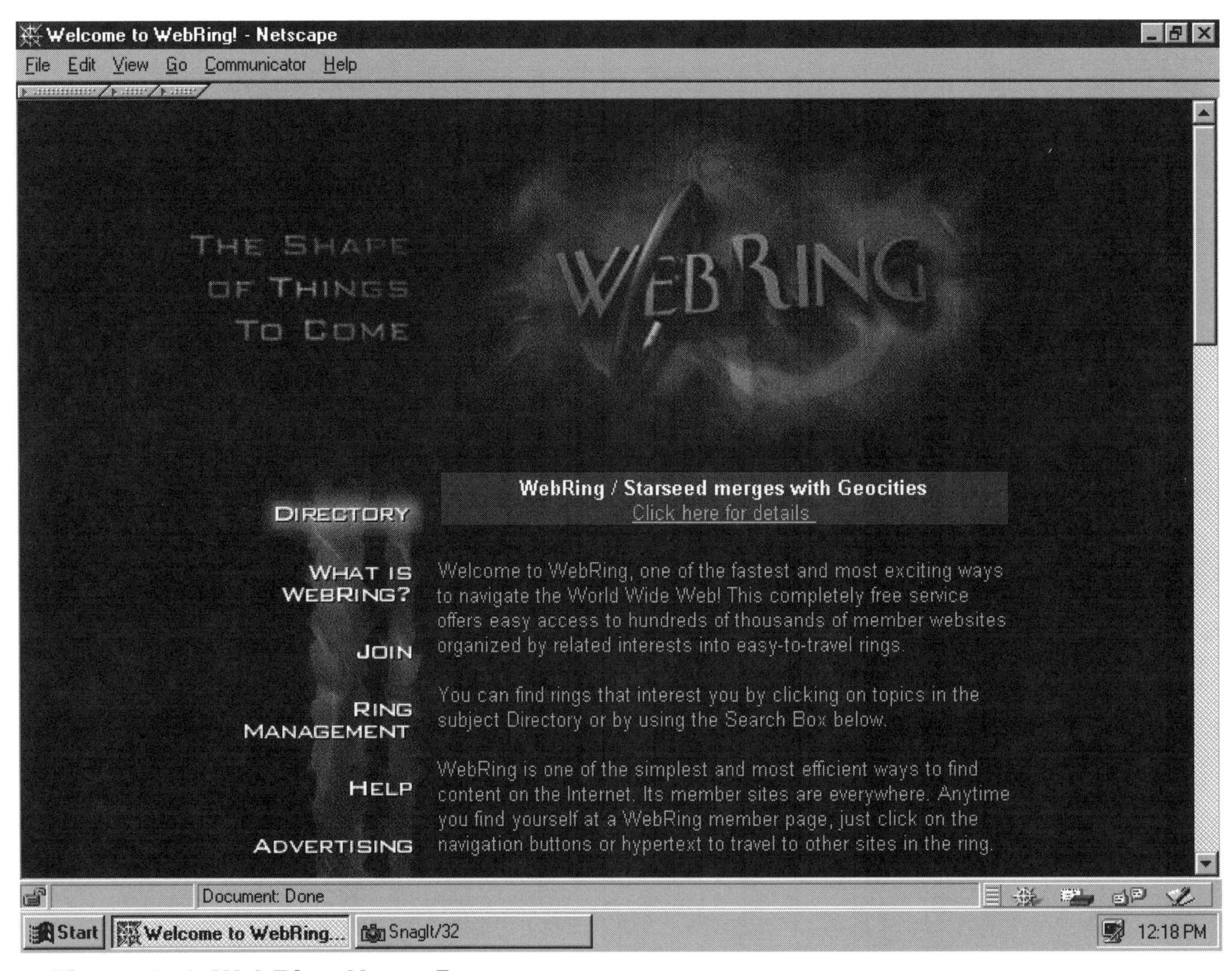

Figure 9–1: WebRing Home Page

PUSH AND PERSONALIZATION TECHNIQUES: TOWARD SMART VIRTUAL LIBRARIES

SDI is the theoretical concept of providing selected information electronically and automatically to the patron—**push** is a technology to help implement a portion of such delivery over the Web.

One of the more intriguing new areas involves push technology and personalization software. With push, users are automatically updated with news, financial reports, sports scores, or the latest magazines and books on topics of their choice. The personalization software allows for the creation of individual patron profiles and employs mathematical formulas to make logical inferences of patron interests. Commercial sites, like Amazon [amazon.com], Imagine Radio [imagineradio.com], My CDNow [cdnow.com] are actively engaging these potentials in a truly exciting fashion. In efforts to keep their customers tied to one search engine firm, portals are refining their profiling options so that users can adapt a search engine to search areas they have specified.

For libraries and archives, such developments suggest the fulfillment of the long-standing promise of selected dissemination of information (SDI). The next generation of virtual libraries will emerge as "smart." Such interactive centers learn and grow from the inquiries of patrons, who are especially empowered within their own unique virtual study carrels. With the exception of the major academic institutions, most of us face practical barriers that prevent instantaneous embrace. The barriers include the following:

- Netscape and Microsoft each use different and incompatible methods of providing "push channels." If you support one, you may need to invest in separate procedures to support the other.
- Push only works effectively on Navigator 4.0, Internet Explorer 4.0 (or more recent versions), and calls for additional hardware in the form of a proxy server.
- Z39.50 facilities are not sufficiently developed to enable full cross-platform information sharing.
- Longer-lasting privacy and policy issues immediately arise with the offering of these options.
- While Excite and other vendors are beginning to roll out the software, the costs are prohibitive and products are still not sufficiently developed for general employ.

SEARCH ENGINES

The installation of search engines is an immediately achievable goal for even the mildly adventuresome. Such applications are an expected feature for advanced sites and they are especially valuable for a virtual library environment. Although search engines can be created with HTML forms or CGI scripts, you are well advised to avoid reinventing the wheel. As the Mid-Hudson example at the end of this chapter

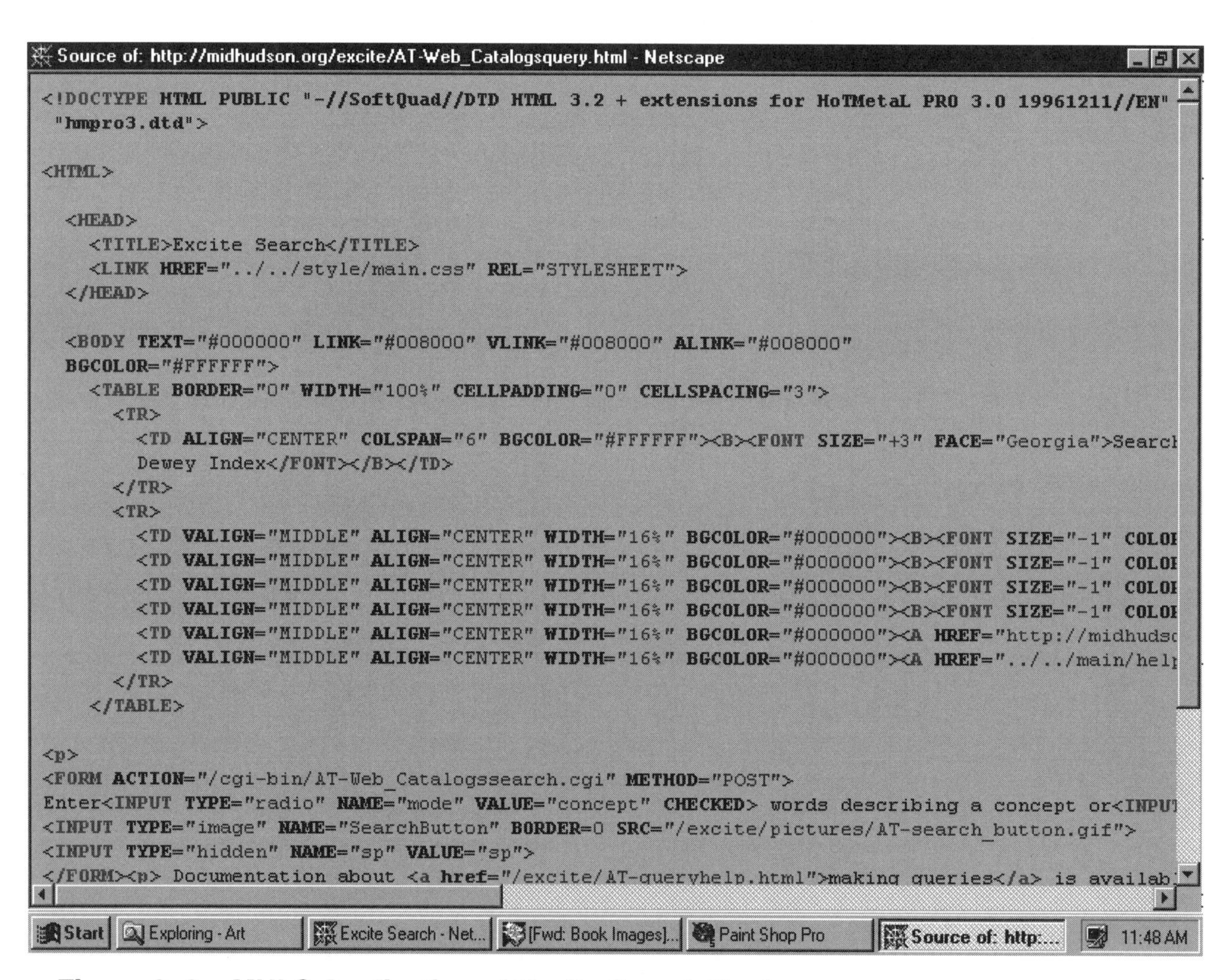


```
<!DOCTYPE HTML PUBLIC "-//SoftQuad//DTD HTML 3.2 + extensions for HoTMetaL PRO 3.0 19961211//EN"
 "hmpro3.dtd">

<HTML>

  <HEAD>
    <TITLE>Excite Search</TITLE>
    <LINK HREF="../../style/main.css" REL="STYLESHEET">
  </HEAD>

  <BODY TEXT="#000000" LINK="#008000" VLINK="#008000" ALINK="#008000"
  BGCOLOR="#FFFFFF">
    <TABLE BORDER="0" WIDTH="100%" CELLPADDING="0" CELLSPACING="3">
      <TR>
        <TD ALIGN="CENTER" COLSPAN="6" BGCOLOR="#FFFFFF"><B><FONT SIZE="+3" FACE="Georgia">Searcl
        Dewey Index</FONT></B></TD>
      </TR>
      <TR>
        <TD VALIGN="MIDDLE" ALIGN="CENTER" WIDTH="16%" BGCOLOR="#000000"><B><FONT SIZE="-1" COLOI
        <TD VALIGN="MIDDLE" ALIGN="CENTER" WIDTH="16%" BGCOLOR="#000000"><B><FONT SIZE="-1" COLOI
        <TD VALIGN="MIDDLE" ALIGN="CENTER" WIDTH="16%" BGCOLOR="#000000"><B><FONT SIZE="-1" COLOI
        <TD VALIGN="MIDDLE" ALIGN="CENTER" WIDTH="16%" BGCOLOR="#000000"><B><FONT SIZE="-1" COLOI
        <TD VALIGN="MIDDLE" ALIGN="CENTER" WIDTH="16%" BGCOLOR="#000000"><A HREF="http://midhuds
        <TD VALIGN="MIDDLE" ALIGN="CENTER" WIDTH="16%" BGCOLOR="#000000"><A HREF="../../main/hel
      </TR>
    </TABLE>

<p>
<FORM ACTION="/cgi-bin/AT-Web_Catalogssearch.cgi" METHOD="POST">
Enter<INPUT TYPE="radio" NAME="mode" VALUE="concept" CHECKED> words describing a concept or<INPU
<INPUT TYPE="image" NAME="SearchButton" BORDER=0 SRC="/excite/pictures/AT-search_button.gif">
<INPUT TYPE="hidden" NAME="sp" VALUE="sp">
</FORM><p> Documentation about <a href="/excite/AT-queryhelp.html">making queries</a> is availab
```

Figure 9–2a: MHLS Application of Excite Search Engine

attests, Excite provides a sophisticated and well-tested application with clear installation instructions. The results can reside on your in-house server and generate forms based on your own templates along with what amounts to on-the-fly CGI scripts—short queries that are automatically generated from the software in response to users' requests. The price of installation is, at the moment, up to your ethical tolerances. If you are willing to display advertisements of a commercial concern on your site, you can download a "free" copy of the search software from Excite [www.excite.com].

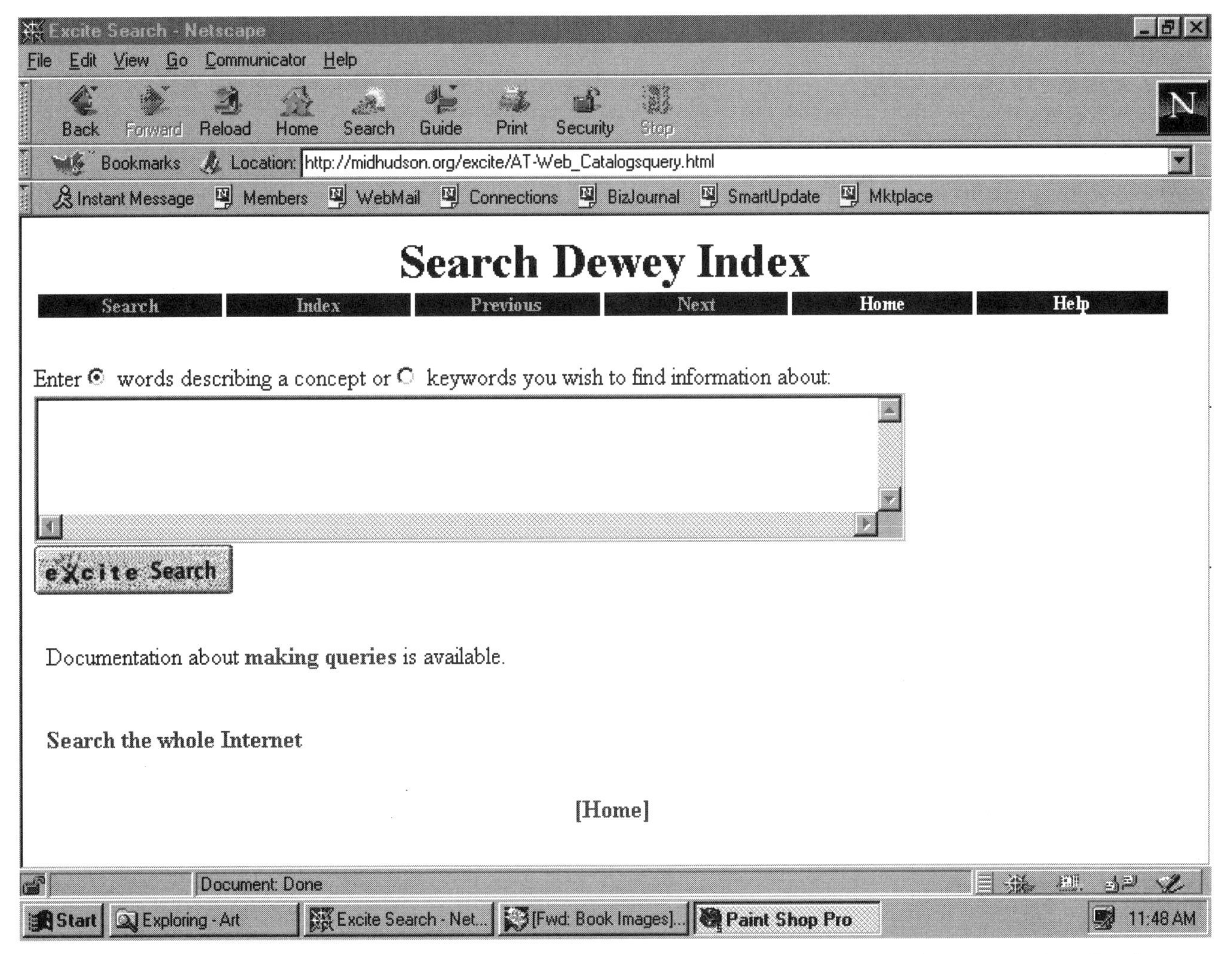

Figure 9–2b (above) shows what the user sees; Figure 9-2a (left) shows the Excite coding.

UNDERSTANDING WEB PROTOCOLS

Monitoring Web Advances: Those with burning interests in ongoing developments can monitor or even participate in standards discussions (for example, see Requests for Comments at Internic [www.internic.net].

The lure of search engines and push technology is hard to resist. Once approaching this level of sophistication, however, the manager needs to take a step back and be clear about the level of staffing and technological commitment involved. In addition, you can no longer escape the need for a technological understanding of the Web and the standards or protocols that determine it.

COMMON-SENSE GROUNDING

Let us start with a common-sense check. The Web's intuitive nature and ease of use can deceive people into thinking that it is intelligent. You should always remember that the great complexity and gloss rests on very simple structures. Indeed, effective organization for almost any automation venture begins with the most fundamental components. Computer searching for text can be reduced to the single mathematical principle of equal or not equal. In essence, we have the simple power of the computer to match characters in a string. The resulting Boolean algebra can be quite powerful, but is easily overwhelmed by the magnitude of the Web without additional organization. As you start, realize that the Web was essentially confined and produced by the confluence of only two basic standards—HTTP and HTML.

TCP/IP is a major communications standard that began in the 1960s from efforts to allow computers to talk to each other. The protocol relies on file servers.

HTTP (HyperText Transmission Protocol)

When you enter an address with *http://,* you are engaging a graphical, click-and-scroll session in a client/server environment on the World Wide Web. HTTP is a subset or "daemon" under the more encompassing TCP/IP Internet transmission protocols. It exists along with file transfer protocols (FTP) and gopher. Daemons control various aspects within their defined set of information packets (i.e., HTTP's capacity to deal with such security or performance elements as cookies, firewalls, and proxies). Don't get nervous. HTTP rarely changes—as of this writing it is only in version 1.1. More important, you only need to focus on one concept; HTTP is "stateless," that is, it doesn't reside on either server or sender machine until engaged. Basically, you are entering into a walkie-talkie type of session (half-duplex) in which each question is followed by a distinct and single response. You and the machine you are communicating with cannot both talk at the same time; moreover, you are not operating in the other machine. Instead, you ask it to transmit information for your computer to work in and you then rebundle your request and data back to the site in question.

HTML (HyperText Markup Language)

This protocol is a subset of Structured Generalized Markup Language (SGML), which was designed for a computer to typeset books. HTML is enabled through a series of elementary tagging structures. These tags cue the computer to format content by designating the structure of the site (for example, paragraph <P>, image <I>, or list <LI>) and delineating formats (for example, header size <H1> and bold face <B>). HTML also goes beyond the limits of a physical book. It allows for hypermedia with the inclusion of anchors and links to enable navigation both within the site and elsewhere on the Internet.

Unlike HTTP, HTML is constantly evolving. Within a very few years, the standard has reached its fourth generation. Such dynamism is the result of expanding market forces, which are pushing beyond the simplicity and elegance of HTML. The protocol has been challenged by new and unexpected developments along with some of its own inherent limitations:

- Theoretically, we are still automating a two-dimensional printing process rather than building from the power of modern databases.
- HTML provides the user's browser with a logical set of specifications (instead of actual physical detail) for it to interpret. For example, you can suggest a type font or the size of a table or type, but the user's browser may default to another font and adjust for a *relative* size.
- Embedded tags are a fairly inefficient type of data structure for any enhanced retrieval purposes or cross-site comparisons.
- Because HTML consists of text documents without binary information, numerical procedures and such enhancements as graphics and multimedia are still only awkwardly addressed. However, it allows for hypermedia with anchors and target links to navigate both within the site and elsewhere on the Internet. And, in a stroke of pure genius, you can go to dead or inactive links without crashing and shutting down operations.
- HTML increases the amount of formatting information within a document exponentially. It now goes well beyond bold face, indentations, italics, and headings to include hidden structural notes and meta information, which is used to enhance searching and categorize the site. As a result, the simple elegance and readability of SGML is being lost with a sea of tags.

The rest of this chapter explores three areas of current development—metatagging, scripting, and dHTML—to counter such problems. These efforts come from within and are allied to the HTML and HTTP protocols. The terms can be confusing, but understanding how they work is vital if you are to take your site beyond the static or pedestrian to the advanced and professional levels.

METATAGS: DUBLIN CORE AND OTHER POTENTIALS

Netiquette Note on Metatags: Although a site about your research may prove interesting, if you really want to learn about metatagging, go to the real experts—the commercial sex sites—to look at their descriptors. You will also find that metatagging is sometimes abused by commercial sites in an effort to lead the user to their products—regardless of the user's original searching intent. Creators of commercial sites should be aware of possible trademark infringement if they list competitors' names in their metafiles.

HTML's structural designations, such as Title and Address, can also be used by external search engines. However, such simple indicators tend to be imprecise. The very magnitude of the Web is increasingly defeating the muscle power needed for precise searching results. One HTML solution is to provide special tags to separate the information *about* the information in the form of metatags. Normally lumped together at the start of the site coding, HTML's flexible metatags (designated <META>) can contain keywords, trademarks, and other linguistic indicators about the content and nature of the site.

LIBRARIES AND METATAGGING

Library use of metatags for describing sites has primarily been stimulated by OCLC along with its academic cousin in the Research Libraries Group (RLG). OCLC even stamped the name of its home town Dublin, Ohio, on the library world's most important metatagging project to date. The Dublin Core project [purl.org/metadata/dublin_core] reflects three key ideas:

- It was intended to encourage authors and publishers to use readily searchable metatags.
- The originators wanted to stimulate market forces to produce network publishing tools with easy-to-complete templates that would facilitate its use.
- They wanted standardized metadata records to help organize the worldwide phenomenon.

The work has been extensive. Dublin Core elements are already available for HTML and have been arranged for inclusion in XML and for compatibility with Z39.50. The core project itself began with 13 repeatable subdivisions or metatags, which have now been expanded to 15.

Figure 9–3: Dublin Core Scheme

Title: The name of the resource.

Author: The person(s) primarily responsible for the intellectual content of the object.

Subject: The topic addressed by the work—typically in keywords.

Description: A narrative abstract.

Publisher: The agent or agency responsible for making the object available.

Contributor: The organization or person(s), such as editors, illustrators, and transcribers, who have made other significant intellectual contributions to the work.

Date: The date of creation of availability (use yyyy or yyyy/mm/dd).

Type: The category or genre of the resources (e.g., home page, novel, poem, dictionary, working paper).

Format: The data format to identify specific software and hardware requirements. It may also include the dimensions—the size, time, duration of the resource.

Identifier: String or number (e.g., URL, ISBN) used to identify the object uniquely.

Source: Another resource from which this object is derived. It may contain metadata about those origins, if the information would be valuable to help find the object being described.

Language: Language of the intellectual content.

Relation: Links to or ties among related resources—with terms to be taken from an authority file that is under development.

Coverage: The spatial locations and temporal durations characteristic of the object, which can be reflected by place names, geographic coordinates, scientific time periods, format in DATE element.

Rights: Links to a rights management statement or a service that provides this information.

In the course of workshops on the Dublin Core, some users became eager for more detail—thus, the Warwick Framework [www.ub2.lu.se/tk/warwick.html] emerged. Never content with simplicity, its proponents intend to wrap more descriptive information around the core scheme with extra container or packaging information. Warwick packages themselves would not be mandated, but they are available to describe the information in Figure 9–4.

Figure 9–4: Warwick Framework Package

- Dublin Core content description elements for the document
- domain-specific descriptions of the document (e.g., Geospatial, GILS)
- terms and conditions for the usage of the document
- labels and rating of the document (accommodating the PICS system)
- security information for the carrier, authenticity, signatures
- provenance of the carrier
- set of containers (as recursive structure), for compound documents and pointing to all manifestations/instances/versions of a document
- amount of the document if not entirety
- identify locus of archival responsibility

XML

The industry and some concerned information interests are interested in pushing beyond the limits of HTML's Meta function with truly "extensible" or unfixed descriptors under an XML brand of markup language (See XML Standard: www.w3.org/XML). This coming standard goes back to the parent SGML—the Standard Generalized Markup Language—for additional power and it targets data description. Instead of HTML's formatting instructions, XML allows you to build as many meta descriptors or data element definers as you wish. For instance, if you use a standard HTML command to build an undifferentiated list of terms for a community information center, you might have no easy way to categorize those items.

```
<Br><B>Any Town</B><Br>
<UL>
<LI>Town Assembly</LI>
<LI>Parks and Recreation Department</LI>
<LI>Any Town Rotary</LI>
<LI>Lions Club</LI>
<LI>Any Town Gazette</LI>
<LI>St. John's Church</LI>
<LI>Sinai Temple</LI>
</UL>
```

An XML processor acts like a simple flat file database. You add descriptive terms and create structures, which are searchable and can be transposed to other collections.

Note on XML: At the moment, you may want to resist investing a lot of time in XML (see Robin Cover's SGML/XML Web Page www.sil.org/sgml; XML www.w3.org/TR/REC.xml). The full power of such an application seems captive of the browser wars, but given the financial interests involved will undoubtedly surface to prominence.

<Community>Any Town
<Government>Town Assembly</Government>
<Recreation>Parks and Recreation Department</Recreation>
<Club>Any Town Rotary</Club>
<Club>Lions Club</Club>
<Newspaper>Any Town Gazette</Newspaper>
<Congregation>St. John's Church</Congregation>
<Congregation>Sinai Temple</Congregation>
</Community>

TEI/CIMI

Several related initiatives arose from academic confines. TEI (Text Encoding Initiative [www-tei.uic.edu/orgs/tei/apps/]), for example, dates back to 1987, and has some broad appeal in the humanities. The Consortium for the Computer Exchange of Museum Information (CIMI [www.cimi.org/]) has only been around since 1994 and is now actively pursuing Z39.50 compatibility.

EAD

In the early 1990s and just prior to the rise of the Web, the archival field began to rear its head. Archivists had never been completely happy with the 1980s movement to MARC and away from their powerful narrative finding aids and container lists. The primary electronic alternative is EAD (electronic archival descriptors). EAD is technically a DTD (document type definition) of SGML. The framework provides tags to replicate an archival finding aide—from unique provenance, collection parameters, and biographical information to its repeatable functional series and item-level descriptors. This work and related projects can be traced to a fount of many such applications at the Sunsite of the University of California at Berkeley [sunsite.berkeley.edu/FindingAids]. EAD itself is managed through the Library of Congress [lcweb.loc.gov/ead].

W3—METADATA COORDINATION

Since January 1997, the preceding and such other potentials as PICS, cascading style sheets, document object models, handicapped access, and mathematical protocols for the Web have been placed under a Metadata Coordination Group [www.w3.org/Metadata] of the World Wide Web coordinating body (W3).

GILS

Another interesting and related potential, the government information locator system (GILS) is evolving from the U.S. Government. Federal authorities are mandating GILS-compliant databases for all

Genre and Publications Prediction: The simple flat lists of sites today will eventually divide into genres. Just as with print, the latter will appear by consensus and with unforeseen flourishes. Some genres may be distinguished by subject attributes as linked through metatagging, strong navigational attributes, rings, and, especially topical search engines. Others may be distinguished for depth of content versus quick reference resources, the interactive nature of chat rooms or game sites, and formatting elements—XML, GILS, the Dublin Core, PICS, or future keys. The formatting of these features is analagous to what will eventually help to differentiate sites and equate to the extra a publisher does with the author's manuscript. Given the nature of the Web, we could also predict that such developments will call forth distinctive terminology, icons, or other labeling features.

cabinet-level agencies and several major contractors are following suit. Eliot Christian developed GILS from his efforts to open environmental information to the public. The results of these endeavors can be visited through FedWorld [www.fedworld.gov/gils] and they follow a familiar model:

> GILS acts as a card catalog that describes resources throughout agencies, and provides assistance in obtaining that information. GILS works with text search engines, but the approach can also deal with photographs, films and complex information sources—for example, chemical formulas. (*New York Times*, 3 November 1997)

COMMUNICATING WITH USERS: E-MAIL, FORMS, AND CGI LEGACIES

In our model, virtual libraries are primarily outward information channels. One important flourish on the road to your smart virtual library is the addition of mechanisms for user feedback and interactive reference services. Given the transitory nature of the Web, for instance, the more people you have helping to point out dead links or formatting problems the better. Involving your users is vital to success. If your primary audience is librarians, the advantages for content improvement are immense. The easiest method for feedback or to allow direct reference queries is to provide e-mail links (which must then be routinely answered).

Listservs and Palaces: You also have the option of implementing your own listserv, chat room, or even one of the new palace rooms (see The Palace [www.thepalace.com] for free software).

Web editors include forms controls which allow you to set up response mechanisms. This function can be difficult to engage. You must carefully ensure proper routing to a desired location and typically will engage alternate entry controls. For example, many today employ CGI (Common Gateway Interface[CGI@ncsa.uiuc.edu]) scripts to connect Web data to legacy or non-HTML electronic arenas. CGI is typically written in the Perl language and is readily adapted to building forms (for example, [www.bio.cam.ac.uk/web/form.html] and [www.q-d.com/wf.htm] are sites that assist with building CGI scripts). The results reside on your server (usually in a directory called "/cgi-bin/") and are queried through HTML "searchpart" commands, which the editor can build for you. In a virtual library environment, we normally see these commands used to direct questions to the reference staff. You may wish to contact [$mailprog = '/usr/lib/sendmail'] for one of the frequently used information request forms and encounter the following instructions:

> **Copyright Notice**
>
> Copyright 1996 Matthew M. Wright All Rights Reserved.
>
> FormMail may be used and modified free of charge by anyone so long as this copyright notice and the comments above remain intact. By using this code you agree to indemnify Matthew M. Wright from any liability that might arise from its use. Selling the code for this program without prior written consent is expressly forbidden. In other words, please ask first before you try and make money off of my program. Define Variables
>
> Detailed Information Found In README File.
>
> $mailprog defines the location of your sendmail program on your unix system.

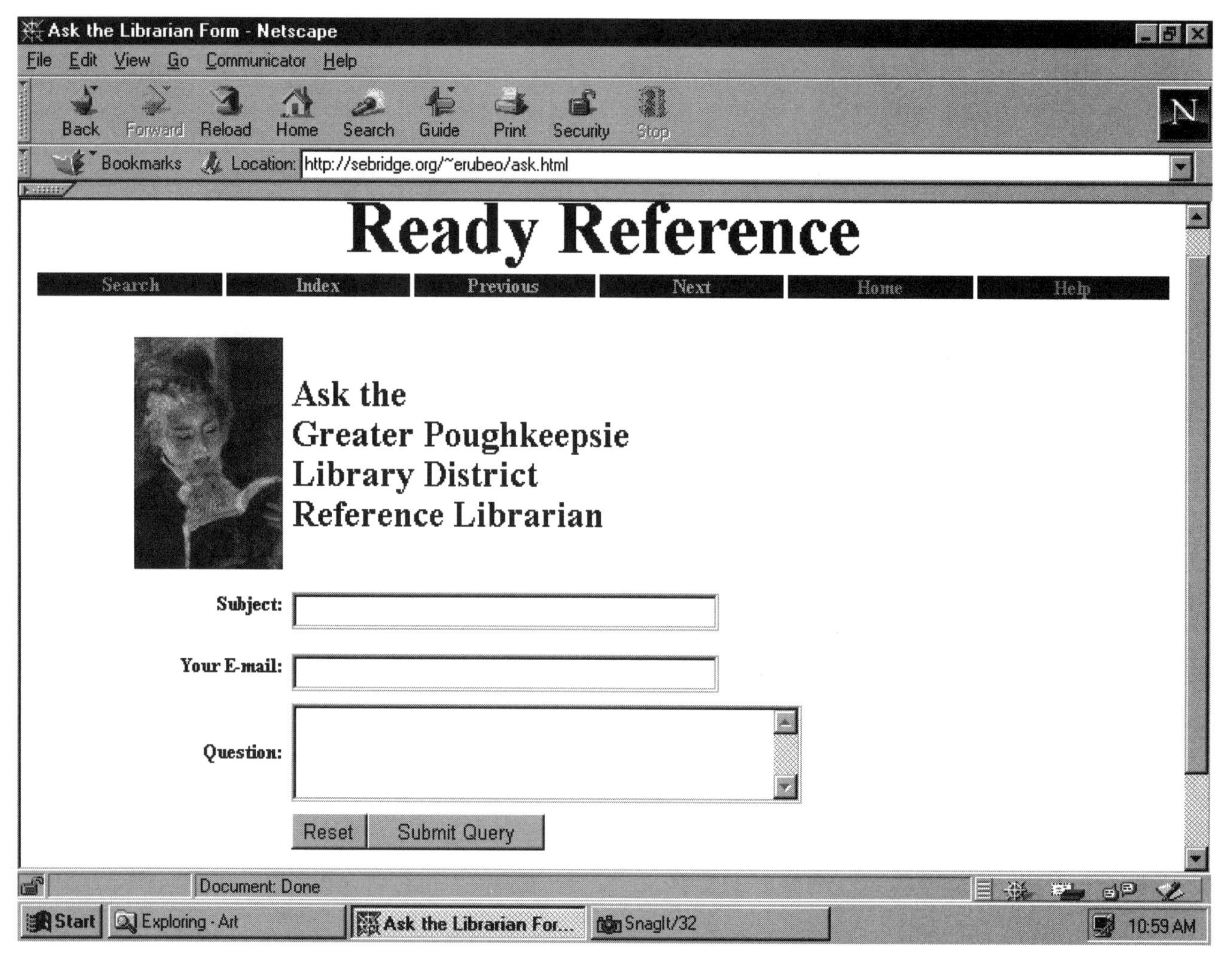

Figure 9–5: Reference Form Built from FormMail CGI Script

SCRIPTS

CGI is a form of legacy script under TCP/IP. Developers have devised other small programs or scripts that can be engaged on the user's computer through an HTML environment. Such scripts are among the most active development arenas and a primary factor in the publication of the HTML 4.0 protocols. Scripting should provide a growing avenue of development for more advanced sites.

Although scripts can be used to manipulate data and control forms or URL requests, the most common use is to enhance displays. For the first time, the designer can control the output on the viewer's screens—and truly achieve desired effects. Many good editors already allow you to program scripts, which in turn can enable users to search your site, provide feedback, and alter the interface in response to their input. Web pages can be directed to respond to the user moving his mouse over an area, moving it off an item, or clicking on it. Any number of operations can be executed, in the order you specify and in response to a single user action. You can simulate drop-down menus, highlight text, provide pop-up windows, and add many other effects using the special features of the latest browsers.

JAVA Note: Despite the great potential, you may want to wait for a bit before using JAVA. The inclusion of JAVA functions in the browsers, which was the trend when we began this book, is not as clear today. The next generations of Netscape and Explorer tout smaller application size for increased speed. Developers also seem to be frantically curtailing their use of applets and scripting in an effort to improve performance. The effectiveness of these tools can also be limited by the speed of your server, the user's Internet connection, and the system resources available at the user's end. Given such unknowns, you may want to reconsider the use of applets and scripting where another method can be effectively substituted. For example, you can substitute animated GIFs for JAVA-based animations, and post forms to MAILTO rather than use a CGI script.

JAVA

JAVA from Sun Microsystems is clearly the most exciting and revolutionary presence. The downloaded JAVA program is referred to as an applet. Many common JAVA functional commands are also being built into the newer browsers. Since this inclusion circumvents the need to include every applet, downloading time is also decreased. JAVA is already the basic engineering platform for Web developers. Sun has also announced a significant advancement for this easy-to-learn and powerful language with a new Jini application for Internet connectivity in 1999. Theoretically, JAVA could even replace our current reliance on internal operating systems.

HTML SCRIPTING

Java*Script* (for Netscape Navigator) and *Visual Basic Script* (for MS Internet Explorer) represent a related class—although they are apparently slower implementations than applets. Code is inserted between HTML's SCRIPT tags, to ensure that the script will not be displayed as text. This convention also shields the script from browsers that do not support scripting. The LANGUAGE attribute indicates the programming language used. SCRIPT tags themselves are usually placed in the HEAD of an HTML document, to ensure that they are loaded first. Yet, if the user clicks on the browser's Stop button while a script is loading, the danger exists that the complete code may not be transferred to his machine. The scripting language is simply ignored by browsers that do not support it. (Note: provided that you place its code within a "comment" tag.)

Such scripts can define specific functions and functional elements (such as *Button, Form, Input, Label, Select, Textarea*). They also let you easily control on-screen events with equally understandable syntax. For example, *onmouseover* engages a screen terrain for possible action as the mouse moves over it; *onsubmit* indicates the submission of a form.

IMPLEMENTATION QUESTIONS

Perhaps the best advice we can offer beginners, not too far removed from ourselves, is to try adapting the sample scripts included with most HTML editors. These examples tend to be heavily tested and debugged and they are therefore less likely to cause trouble. To respond to user input, you can also import some of the many free JAVA and CGI scripts (in Perl, C++, and the like) available on the Web. (Just be sure to give proper credit to the author.) The adept beginners may even start programming on their own. We did find JavaScript easy to learn (see the tutorial at [www.builder.com]) and eminently copiable should you encounter an interesting procedure. Finally, compatibility, as always, remains an issue. You must be aware that Microsoft had chosen to alter the original Sun JAVA coding for its own environment.

DBMS AND dHTML PROSPECTS

Scripts work well in enhancing the design attributes within what may be the most exciting set of Web site advances—dynamic HTML (dHTML). The technical problems with the stateless transfer of operations under HTTP are supplemented by the operations of relational database management software within the contact site. This trend is one of the most active Web commercial arenas and reflects a far more robust data structure than tagging alone. The differences here are similar to a comparison between the searching power available from your word processor (which is like HTML), to that from a database engine (like Access, dBase, FileMaker Pro, FoxPro, or Paradox). The latter uses the enhanced computational power of relational rows and columns along with the benefits that derive from strict data element dictionary controls. These tabular forms can also be readily linked into associations with other tables and interrelated network structures.

On the Web, a relational database replaces the repetitive need for inserting flat HTML coding with a dynamic engine to generate code on the fly. Instead of having repeatedly to redo your pages and recopy HTML code, you create a standard format file with placeholders on the Web page for the appropriate data elements. The static page is now powered with a database engine to inject your updates and the coding automatically. Thus you can concentrate on designing templates for the items in your database in a far more efficient and reliable method than with HTML's FORM command. Since the operations are totally controlled within your environment, the resulting arrangements are transparent to the user and can eliminate much of the browser design problem. In addition, updates can be instantaneous, security is enhanced, the need for cookies is eliminated, the staff is free to concentrate on content, and new potentials are easily enabled.

The first organizations using this technology had sophisticated

DBMS (Database Management Software) programs on their servers. Their applications were usually UNIX based and required experienced programmers to install and maintain. The good news is that new database software is reaching the market at an ever-increasing rate, and a number of vendors are starting to open reasonably priced remote services.

Alternatively, you can invest a little money in FileMaker Pro or Access (and soon most of the available DBMSs) and do the work on your own site. Although becoming more "discoverable," such software still requires you to work with an editor and is not for the novice. However, we do note that the major HTML editors appear to be working on integrated dHTML solutions from their end, which should be far easier to implement.

END NOTES FROM MID-HUDSON

Mid-Hudson's journeys beyond the static began with some practical extensions out of the metatagging swamp—efforts with added significance for learning to think and implement in hypermedia. HTML lets you use metatags to tweak the performance of search engines to suit your needs. META "keyword" tags add information to a page that can be read by search engines while remaining invisible to the user. Similarly, META "description" tags attach a brief synopsis to a page, which is shown as a summary in query results.

Mid-Hudson is attempting to marry metatagging and database concepts directly from our use of library classification systems. The same tables that allow traditional libraries to organize their bibliographic resources can act as a data element dictionary or tag list. The results form powerful retrieval frameworks based on objective subject categories. Moreover, the classified schemes come replete with standardized terminology and numerical codes. They can also facilitate the development of special resource collections in-house and heighten the future prospects of integrating Web resources with library materials on our members' shelves.

With such an environment, therefore, we can begin to look forward to a single search engine to unite access across all media. The end goal of a truly information-driven electronic resources library becomes a very real prospect. For the moment, we set our sights somewhat lower. Unlike some of our wealthier academic and scientific relatives, Mid-Hudson could only afford to scratch the surface of possible applications. Excite, which was already available, was impressive and proved simple to apply.

SEARCH ENGINE ADDITION

Two key factors help determine how well an in-house search engine performs: the structure of the data on the server and the descriptive information supplied within a document.

For us, the potential of library classification systems was reaffirmed. To facilitate quicker and more accurate queries, you only need divide global Web library data into separate pages by Dewey class. Since search engines list results by title, you name each page by its Dewey code number and include the narrative terms or definitions. For example, the TITLE tag for the list of links to online dictionaries is "403 Dictionaries," which provides a number and a term for the engine. In keeping with filenaming conventions explained in Chapter 8, such pages can be in a directory named "/webcat" on your server. Excite is then configured to index only this directory, which incidentally also eliminates the possibility of false hits from the Dewey and alphabetical index terms.

With the proper setup, the Excite engine defaults into a quasi-"fuzzy logic" search and returns documents that match the concept of the words you enter. Optionally, you can choose to limit the search to only those documents that *contain* those words. For example, if you conducted a "keyword search" for the term "book" in the Web Catalog, Excite would search the pages in our "/webcat" directory and display the titles of all documents containing the word "book." It might include entries such as:

010 Books & Bibliography (summary)
384 Communications, Telecommunications & Phone Books (summary)

On the other hand, if you accepted the default parameters, the search would yield all pages containing the word "book" *plus* those that relate to the *concept* of books. This would result in a longer list, such as the following:

010 Books & Bibliography (summary)
384 Communications, Telecommunications & Phone Books (summary)
808 Electronic Printed Text/General Literature (summary)
403 Dictionaries (summary)
020 Library & Information Sciences (summary)

The user can choose to display the results ranked by Subject Confidence, after the search is completed. ("Confidence" is Excite's term for how closely the results match the entered text. It is determined by how often the text, and words related to it, appear in a document.) Since Excite for Web Servers allows Web site designers to customize the appearance of query and results pages, you can place your header, menu, and other links on both pages. This design helps to integrate the search engine with the look of the site.

This coding example illustrates how Excite works. The "497 Native Americans" page might contain links to Native American literature. Therefore, Excite would include "497 Native Americans" in its result for a fuzzy logic (or "concept") query on the term "book." However, that page would not appear in the results for a similar query on the phrase "New York." If one of the sites on the page "497 Native Americans" contained references to the Iroquois (a tribe native to New York) and the words "New York" did not appear on it, we could force this document to be included in the search results with the following code:

```
<HEAD><META NAME="keywords" CONTENT="New York"></HEAD>
```

The results for a fuzzy logic search on "New York" would then include:

497 Native Americans (summary)

If no META "description" tag is provided, clicking on the word "summary" in a results list would display the first few words of the document. On our site, this would include the document title, the menu bar text, and a portion of the first link:

Web Catalog Search Index Previous Next Home Help 497 Native Americans Native American Resources

We can add a proper (and more readable) summary using the following code:

```
<HEAD><META NAME="description" CONTENT="Local Native American Tribes, their history, art and contributions to our culture."><META NAME="keywords" CONTENT="New York"></HEAD>
```

Which would appear as:

Local Native American Tribes, their history, art and contributions to our culture.

dHTML IN PROCESS

Mid-Hudson's adventures with dHTML are only beginning. For us, this step is a logical extension from our original database disciplines and library model. Instead of relying on special data entry skills to rebuild the static HTML pages, selectors are being empowered to make direct entries and update our mirror site on the fly. In the future, we hope to engage the new facility for enhanced inquiries from users and such flourishes as "virtual shopping carts." For the moment, we can report on a little trial and tribulation—plus a little luck we had with our initial conversions.

ACCESS

MHLS is currently converting to Microsoft's Office Suite, which includes the Access database management system. As the fates would have it, a graduate computer student from nearby Marist College has agreed to an internship with us. He piloted the use of Access as part of an integrated solution to our overall information management. Unfortunately, we did not progress very far with this. We found that Access demanded extra time and expertise with Visual Basic programming that was somewhat prohibitive. We needed to turn to FileMaker Pro to enable the direct entry of data and automatic inclusion of operable Web links. We have not given up on an integrated solution. We have found some potential help with Drumbeat software, which promises to reduce the skills needed to work with Access to a more manageable and sustainable level for us.

FILEMAKER PRO

This product was the only fully enabled and readily usable option for dHTML at our level of technical expertise at the time of this writing. The product helped to recreate much of the MHLS site. Although the management decisions on the software and dHTML were made with a little trepidation and reliance on a single part-time employee, we must acknowledge another bit of serendipity. After watching a bit of our frustration on the listserv, Jesse Feiler (one of Mid-Hudson's Board members) graciously stepped forward. He provided us with a workshop and a prepublication copy of his *FileMaker Pro and the World Wide Web* (Boston: Academic Press, 1998), which had been in the works unbeknownst to us. We are delighted to recommend it to you.

DATABASE FEATURES

Staff found FileMaker Pro's approach to instant and custom Web publishing better suited to our needs. With FileMaker Pro, staff can solve Web design problems without having to learn additional skills. The FileMaker Pro Web Companion module allows individual or FileMaker Pro databases to be shared via the Web. With a few keystrokes, authorized users can access the database through their favorite browser. The MHLS Web designer used this feature to display an interface page to list available databases for updates and data entry (see example below).

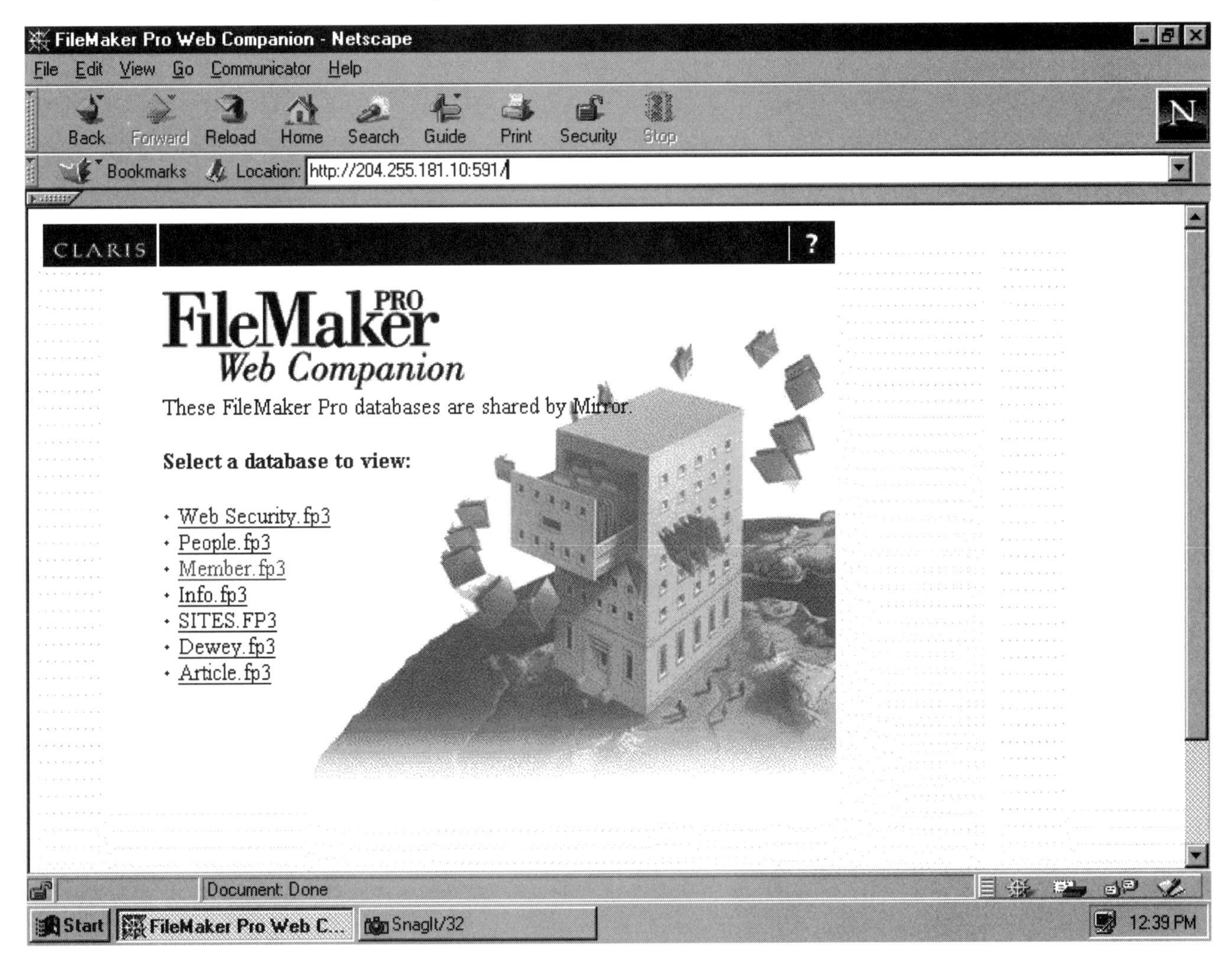

Figure 9–6: MHLS FileMaker Pro Database File, Original

Updates can now be made by accessing the data from specially assigned files within the FileMaker Pro database. Data can be pulled from a master file and put in a working file in two ways:

- **Lookup** copies fields from the master file and inserts them in the working file. After the data are copied, they become part of the working file. This establishes a relationship between the working file and the master file.
- **Relational database** allows data from a file to be displayed, edited, and manipulated in the working file, without copying. Data displayed in the working file change as the values in the other file change.

To use data from another file (through lookup or a relational database), you must define a relationship between the master file and the related file. A relationship is an expression that includes the name of the match field in the master file, the related file name, and the name of the match field in the related file.

Those general procedures can be tied to FileMaker Pro's security procedures to foster project control and management. At the top level, only the Web Master has the option of opening a new database or special resources collection area. We also control for the addition of Dewey numbers, which must be approved by a staff librarian. Access for creating new numbers in the virtual stacks is limited by password control to our computer operators. Then, appropriate selectors are assigned their own passwords to enter appropriate titles and URLs in a special resources collection file, which automatically updates the entry into the virtual stacks. In a final check, such data are being entered into our mirror site, which is available for proofreading and debugging before it comes online.

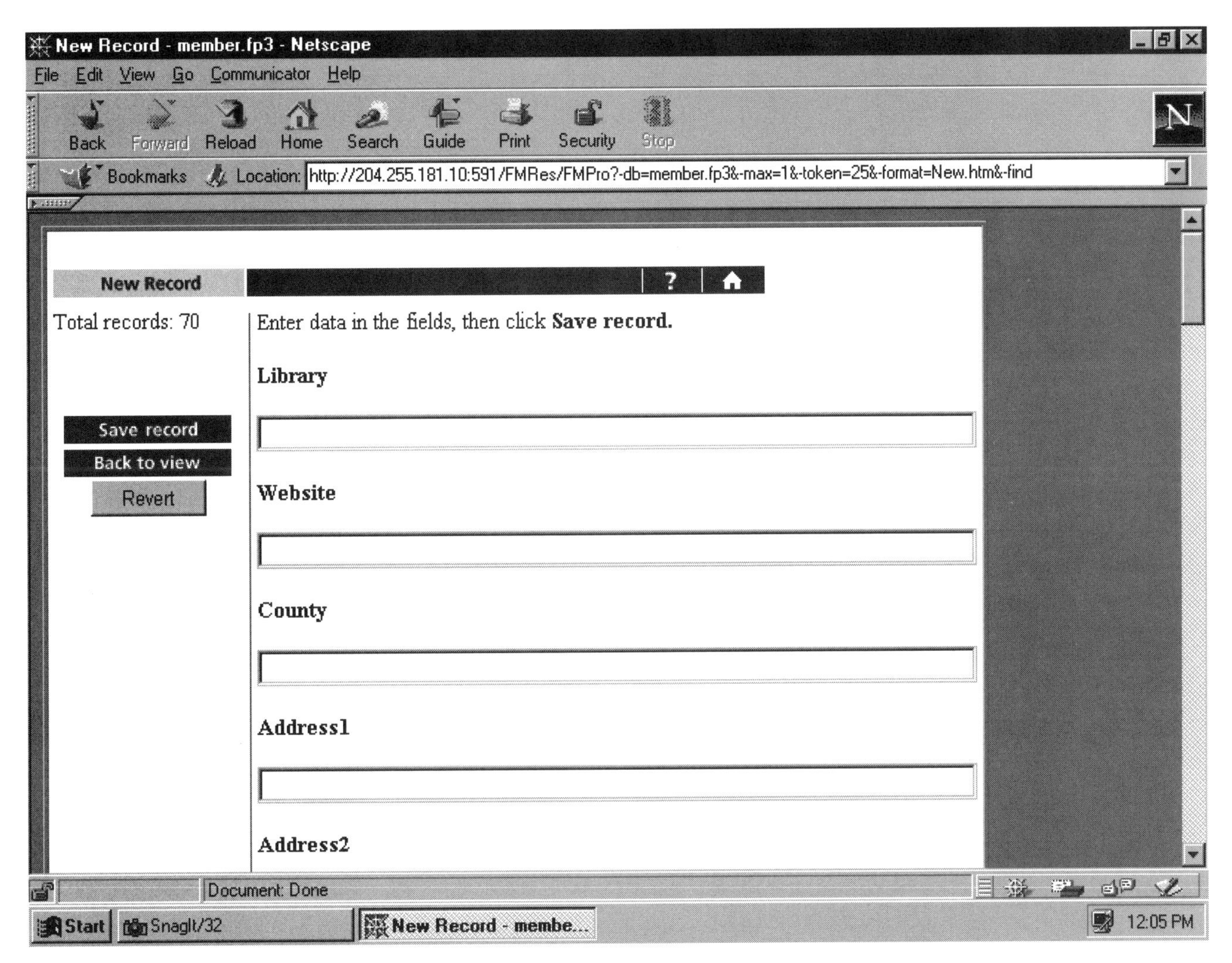

Figure 9–7: MHLS Data Entry Screen for Members

OUTSOURCING QUESTION

Finally, after all of our explorations and even with a regular staff and computer facilities, Mid-Hudson is starting to question its commitment to onsite facilities. The rapid spread of the Internet and the growth of sizeable ISPs present what may prove a viable alternative to the traditional model. We may be able to save money and expand our service hours by divesting ourselves of our own ISP equipment and co-locating some of our file servers in a host site or by purchasing computer and Internet services directly from an external vendor.

RESOURCE NOTE

For additional materials, the reader may wish to look back at Chapters 7 and 8 and at the Resource Notes section in Chapter 1. Following appropriate training, check out some of the higher level engineering sites, such as Internet Engineering Task Force [www.ietf.cnri. reston.va.us/home.html]; Information Sources on the Internet [www.rpi.edu/Internet/Guides/decemj/internet-cmc.html]; MIT WWW Consortium [www.w3.org]. Advanced readers interested in dHTML may want to begin by exploring the nuances between using the "searchpart" for visible coding strings (e.g., .../cgi-bin/?...) and the more private "forms" to detail action, as well as between the text default of the "Get Method" and the more expansive "Post Method," which allows for MIME encoding and graphics. For overall coverage and trends see the following:

- dHTML in Netscape Communicator [developer.netscape.com/library/documentation/communicator/dynhtml/index.htm]
- dHTML Index [www.all-links.com/dynamic]
- Dynamic HTML Lab [webreference.com/dhtml]
- Microsoft dHTML Gallery [www.microsoft.com/gallery/files/dhtml]

WEBLIOGRAPHY

Following is a comprehensive list of the various Web addresses or URLs cited in the text. These mentions in no way imply an endorsement of the sites. However, the information in these sites augments the figures and samples in the book. These addresses are accurate as of the writing of this book.

A

Aboriginal Virtual Library [www.ciolek.com/WWWVL-Aboriginal.html]
Alertbox: Current Issues in Web Useability [www.useit.com/alertbox]
Alexa [www.alexa.com]
Amazon.com [www.amazon.com/exec/obidos/subst/editors/editors.html/]
American Association of School Librarians KidsConnect [AskKC@iconnect.syr.edu]
American Library Association [www.ala.org]
ARL Digital Library Definition [sunsite.berkeley.edu/ARL/definition.htm]
Apache Web server program [www.apache.org]
Apple Web Design [applenet.apple.com/hi/web/intro.html]
Argus Clearing House for Subject-Oriented Internet Resource Guides [www.clearinghouse.net/]
Association of Research Libraries [sunsite.berkeley.edu/ARL/definition.html].
Australia [www.nla.gov.au]

B

Background Sampler [home.netscape.com/home/bg/]
Beginner's Guide to HTML [www.ncsa.uiuc.edu/General/Internet/WWW/HTMLPrimer.html]
Book Stacks [www.books.com/]
Bowker's Library Services and Supplier [www.bowker.com/ald/index.html]
Brazil [www.sup.br/sigi/sibi.html]
British Museum Portico [portico.bl.uk/gabriel]
BrowserWatch [www.ski.mskcc.org/browserwatch/]
Building forms [www.bio.cam.ac.uk/web/form.html] and [www.q-d.com/wf.htm]

C

C/Net Central [cnet.com]
Canada [www.nlc-bnc.ca]
Career Path [Careerpath.com]

Caywood's Guiding Children through Cyberspace [ww6.pilot.infi.net/^carolyn/guide.html]
CETH (Center for Electronic Texts in the Humanities) [www.ceth.rutgers.edu]
CGI introduction [CGI@ncsa.uiuc.edu]
CIMI (Consortium for the Computer Exchange of Museum Information) [www.cimi.org/]
Coalition for Networked Information [www.cni.org]
Content Standards for Geospatial Metadata [www.mews.org/nsdi/revis497.pdf]
CORC (Cooperative Online Resource Catalog) [www.oclc.org/oclc/research/projects/corc/]
Cyber Patrol [www.microsys.com/cyber/cp_info.html/]
Cyberspace Laws [www.cyberspacelaws.com]

D
D-Lib Magazine [www.dil.org/dlib/]
dHTML Index [www.all-links.com/dynamic]
dHTML in Netscape Communicator [developer.netscape.com/library/documentation/communicator/dynhtml/index.htm]
Digital Libraries Initiative [dli.grainger.uiuc.edu/national.htm] and [dli.granger.uiuc.edu/pubsnatsynch.htm]
Digital Library Foundation [www.loc.gov/loc/ndlf/ndlfhome.html]
Digital Scriptorum [odyssey.lib.duke.edu/scriptorium]
Doctor HTML [www2.image.com/RxHTML]
Dublin Core Home Page [purl.oclc.org/dc]
Dublin Protocols [purl.org/metadata/dublin_core]
Digital Scriptorium [odyssey.lib.duke.edu/scriptorium/]
Dynamic HTML Lab [webreference.com/dhtml]

E
EAD (encoded archival description) [lcweb.loc.gov/ead]
EAD Sunsite [sunsite.berkeley.edu/FindingAids]
Environmental Planning and Geographic Information Systems [elib.cs.berkeley.edu/]
EPIC (Electronic Privacy Information Center) [www2.epic.org]
Excite [www.excite.com]

F
Federating Repositories of Scientific Information [dli.grainger.uiuc.edu]
FedWorld [www.fedworld.gov/gils]
FortuneCity [www.fortunecity.com]
Foundations Project [bridges.state.mn.us]

G

GILS (Government Indicator Locator System) [www.fedworld.gov/gils]

Gutenberg's Bible [www.osl.state.or.us/bible/page4bw.GIF]

H

How to Announce Your New Web Site [ep.com/faq/webannounce.html]

How to Select an Internet Service Provider [web.cnam.fr/Network/Internet-access/how_to_select.html]

HTML Quick Reference [www.cc.ukans.edu/~acs/docs/HTML_quick.html]

Human and Computer Interface VL [usableweb.com/hcivl]

Hyployt Trace Route [hyployt.obspm.fr/cgi.bin/nph-traceroute]

I

Icons for Web Pages [www.jsc.nasa.gov/~mccoy/Icons/index.html]

Imagine Radio [imagineradio.com]

Information Provider's Guide to Web Servers [www.vuw.ac.nz/who/Nathan.Torkington/ideas/www-servers.html]

Information Source on the Internet [www.rpi.edu/Internet/Guides/decemj/internet-cmc.html]

Informedia Digital Video Library [www.informedia.cs.cmu.edu]

Infomine [lib-www.vcr.edu/Main.html]

Intelligent Agents for Information Location [www.si.umich.edu/UMDL/]

Internet Advocate for librarians and educators [WW1/monroe.lib.in.us/^lchampel/netadv.html]

Internet Engineering Task Force [www.ietf.cnri.reston.va.us/home.html]

Internet for Librarians [www.itcompany.com/inforetriever/acq_revw.htm]

Internet Public Library [www.ipl.org/ref/]

Interoperation Mechanisms among Heterogeneous Services [diglib.stanford.edu/]

ISP Checker [www.ispcheck.com]

J

Japan [www.nacis.ac.jp/nacsis.f-index.html]

JavaScript tutorial [www.builder.com]

Job Hunter [www.rvp.com/jh/search.shtml]

K

KidsClick! [sunsite.berkeley.edu/KidsClick!/]

Kirsanov's Top Ten Tips [www.design.ru/ttt/]

L

Librarian's Guide to Cyberspace for Parents and Kids [www.ala.org/parentspage/greatsites]
Librarian's Index to the Internet [sunsite.berkely.edu/InternetIndex]
Library Corporation's cataloguer reference shelf [www.tlcdelivers.com/tlc/crs/crs0000.htm]
Library of Congress [www.loc.gov]
Library of Congress, EAD Site [lcweb.loc.gov/ead]
Libweb [www.lib.washington.edu/^tdowling/libweb.html]
Linkbot Comments [152.20.25.1/Linkbot.html]
Linkbot validator [www.linkbot.com]

M

MARCit module [www.marcit.com]
Metadata Coordination Group [www.w3.org/Metadata]
Metadata Terms [www.nlc-bnc.ca/ifla/ll/metadata.htm]
Microsoft [www.microsoft.com]
Microsoft dHTML Gallery [www.microsoft.com/gallery/files/dhtml]
Mid-Hudson Library System, NY [midhudson.org]
Minnesota Metadata Guidelines [bridges.state.mn.us/metadata.html]
Mirage's Reader Advisory page [www.prairienet.org/mirage/ra.html]
MOMspider [www.ics.uci.edu/WebSoft/MOMspider/WWW94/paper.html]
Morton Grove, IL, Dewey Library [www.nslsilus.org/mgkhome/orrs/webrary.html]
Multnomah Library Kids Page [www.multnomah.lib.or.us/lib/kids]
My CDNow [cdnow.com]

N

National Archives [www.nara.gov]
National Science Foundation Publications [www.nsf.gov/pubs/]
Net aficionado [See: searchenginewatch.com]
Netscape [www.netscape.com]
NetTrak services [net-trak.stats.net/]
New York Public Library's A Safety Net for the Internet [www.nypl.org/branch/safety.html]
News search [www.prnewswire.com]
Northern Light [www.northernlight.com]
NSF/DARPA/NASA Digital Libraries Initiative Projects [www.cise.nsf.gov/iris/DLHome.html]

O

OCLC CORC Project [www.oclc.org/oclc/research/projects/corc]

OCLC Internet Cataloging Project [www.oclc.org/oclc/man/catproj/catcall.htm]

P

The Palace [www.thepalace.com]
Parental Control [www.worldvillage.com/wv/school/html/control.com]
Peacefire [www.peacefire.org]
Pennsylvania's Delaware County libraries Kids Rules for Online Safety [www.libertynet.org/^delcolib/pweb.html]
Physics Virtual Library [www.fisk.edu/vl/Physics/Overview.html]
PICS (Platform for Internet Content Services) [www.w3.org/PICS/]
Privacy screen [www.mmm.com]
Project Bartleby [www.cc.columbia.edu/acis/bartleby]
Project Gutenberg [www.promo.net/pg/]
Project Gutenberg's digitized books [www.promo.net/pg/]
PubLib List [sunsite.Berkeley.EDU/PubLib/]
Public Library Policies [www.ciloswego.or.us/library/poli.htm]
Public Library Server Page [sjcpl.lib.in.us/homepage/PublicLibraries / PublicLibraryServers.html]

R

Ramapo-Catskill Library System DeskRef [ansernet.rcls.org/deskref/]
Recessed desks [www.novadesk.com]
Recreational Software Advisory Council's RASCi codings [www.rsac.org/homepage.asp]
Ringworld [www.webring.com]
Robin Cover's SGML/XML Web Page [www.sil.org/sgml/]

S

Sandra's Clip Art [www.cs.yale.edu/homes/sjl/clipart.html]
School Library Policies [www.enet.edu/tenet-info/accept.html]
Search.Com [www.search.com/]
Search Engine [search.com]
Seattle Times [www.seattletimes.com]
SIRS Corporation [www.sirs.com]
Spacially Referenced Map Information [alexandria.sdc.ucsb.edu/]
Stanford's Fair Use [fairuse.stanford.edu]
Sun Style Guide [www.Sun.COM/styleguide/]
Sunsite of the University of California at Berkeley [sunsite.berkeley.edu/FindingAids]

T

TEI (Text Encoding Initiative) [www-tei.uic.edu/orgs/tei/apps/]
Texas's Intellectual Property [www.utsystem.edu/ogc/IntellectualProperty/cprtindx.htm]
Tierra Highlights [www.tierra.com]
Trace route [www.online.com/cgi.bin/ntetesting]
TUCOWS (The Ultimate Collection of Winsock Software) [http://www.tucows.com]

U

UK Office for Library and Information Networking [www.ukoln.ac.uk]
UNIX-based technology C/net central [cnet.com]
US Copyright Office [lcweb.loc.gov/copyright/]

V

lvrfy: HTML Link Verifier [www.cs.dartmouth.edu/~crow/lvrfy.html]
Virtual Library [virtualmaster@test.com]
Virtual Physics Library [www.fisk.edu/vl/Physics/Overview.html]

W

Warwick Framework [www.ub2.lu.se/tk/warwick.html]
Web Consortium [validator.w3.org]
Web Design for Librarians [scc01.rutgers.edu/SCCHome/web.htm#/WebDesignResources]
Web Developers Virtual Library [www.stars.com]
Web Library [/gen_web/]
Web Page Design [ds.dial.pipex.com/pixelp/wpdesign/wpdintro.htm]
Web Pages That Suck [www.webpagesthatsuck.com]
Web Review [www.webreview.com]
Web Site Garage [www.websitegarage.com]
Webmaster T's World of Design [www.globalserve.net/~iwb/world]
Webring [www.webring.com]
World Wide Web Consortium [www.w3.org]
World Wide Web Virtual Library [vlib.stanford.edu/Overview.html]
WWW Link Checker [www.ugrad.cs.ubc.ca/spider/q7f192/branch/checker.html]
WWW Virtual Library [www.w3.org/hypertext/DataSources/bySubject/LibraryOfCongress.htm]
WWW Web Server Software [www.w3.org/pub/WWW/Servers.html]

X

XML [www.w3.org/TR/REC.xml]

Y

Yale Style Manual [info.med.yale.edu/caim/StyleManual_Top.html]

Z

Z39.50 [www.loc.gov/Z39.50/agency]

Zoonet Virtual Library [www.mindspring.com/~zoonet/www_virtual_lib/zoos.html]

INDEX

D

E

F

G

H

I

J

K

L

M

X

Z